KT-914-761

DICTIONARY OF
LIBRARY
AND
INFORMATION
MANAGEMENT

Janet Stevenson

University of Loughborough

PՔP

PETER COLLIN PUBLISHING

First published in Great Britain 1997

Published by Peter Collin Publishing Ltd
1 Cambridge Road, Teddington, Middlesex, TW11 8DT

© Janet Stevenson & Peter Collin Publishing Ltd 1997

All rights reserved. No part of this publication may
be reproduced in any form or by any means without the
permission of the publishers.

British Library Cataloguing in Publication Data
A catalogue record for this book is available from the British Library

ISBN 0-948549-68-8

Text set by PCP
Printed and bound in Finland by WSOY
Cover design by Gary Weston

MACCLESFIELD COLLEGE
OF FURTHER EDUCATION
LIBRARY

12 OCT 1998

LD

T

T
4000430595   R 020.3

PREFACE

This dictionary provides the information worker with the vocabulary as it is used in the field. It covers the basic words, with grammatical definitions, used in library organisation and management, and the language of classification and cataloguing, as well as the language of the electronic world of information management and communication. Words that are used in special ways are illustrated by examples of use.

The supplement covers different types of information necessary to a librarian, including lists of book prizes and awards.

Aa

A3 European standard size paper, twice the size of A4: 297 x 420mm (11.69 x 16.54 inches)

A4 European standard size paper, 210 x 297mm (8.27 x 11.69 inches)

A5 European standard size paper, half the size of A4: 148 x 210mm (5.83 x 8.27 inches)

AACR 2 Rev Anglo-American cataloguing rules, revised second version

abbreviate [ə'briːvieɪt] *verb* to make shorter by leaving out some letters or by using only the first few letters of each word

abbreviated entry [ə'briːvieɪtɪd 'entri] *noun* shortened form of a bibliographic entry usually giving author, title and date only

abbreviation [əbriːvɪ'eɪʃn] *noun* short form of a word

ability [ə'bɪlɪti] *noun* quality or skill which makes it possible to do something

-ability [ə'bɪlɪti] *suffix* added to adjectives to form nouns referring to a quality or state such as readability

abort [ə'bɔːt] *verb* to stop a process or plan before it is finished

abridge [ə'brɪdʒ] *verb* to make something shorter

abridged document [ə'brɪdʒd 'dɒkjuːmənt] *noun* written document which has been made shorter while keeping the main points

abridged edition [ə'brɪdʒd ɪ'dɪʃn] *noun* shortened text but keeping the main points or story

abstract 1 ['æbstrækt] *noun* summary of the contents of a document **2** [əb'strækt] *verb* to summarize the main points of a document

abstracting journal [əb'stræktɪŋ 'dʒɜːnəl] *noun* journal containing summaries of documents or articles in a given field

academic [ækə'demɪk] **1** *adjective* related to studying; **academic library** = library associated with institutes of higher and further education; *the library in a university is an academic library;* **academic point** = only theoretical, not practical; *it was an academic point because there was no money to buy any software to do the work* **2** *noun* person who teaches or does research usually in higher education

accent ['æksənt] *noun* mark put above or below a letter in writing or printing to show the type of sound when it is spoken; **acute accent** = mark usually over the letter e (é) to show how it should be pronounced; **grave accent** = mark placed over a vowel (è) to show how it should be pronounced

acceptance [ək'septəns] *noun* (a) act of receiving something (b) recognizing that you cannot change a situation

access ['ækses] **1** *noun* opportunity or right to use something; *they were given access to all relevant information;* closed access = system of organizing a collection so that items must be fetched for users by the staff; **open access** = system of organizing a collection where the users can find what they want for themselves; *people have open access to the books in a public library;* **access code** = code used for information retrieval to show where something can be found; **access time** = amount of time taken to get into a computer program **2** *verb* to obtain, examine or be able to reach something; *to access information is to find it either in a library or a computer*

accessibility [əksesɪ'bɪlɪti] *noun* quality of being able to be found and used

accessible [ək'sesɪbl] *adjective* easy to find and use

accession [ək'seʃn] *noun* new addition to a library or collection; **accession list** = list of new purchases or additions to a library; **accession number** = consecutive number used to identify new additions to a library/collection in an inventory system; **accession register** = physical record of new purchases or additions to a library/collection

accessory [ək'sesəri] *noun* extra part added to something to enable it to perform other functions; *a printer is an accessory to a computer*

accompany [ə'kʌmpni] *verb* (a) to be used with something else; *several pictures will accompany the text* (b) to go with someone especially on a journey (c) to play a musical instrument to provide a second part for a piece of music

account [ə'kaunt] *verb* **to take account of something** *or* **take something into account**

= to consider something when you are thinking about a situation

accountant [ə'kauntənt] *noun* person whose job is to keep the financial accounts for a business

accounting [ə'kauntɪŋ] *noun* process of keeping financial records for a company or organization; **accounting year** = any period of twelve months which an organization uses to control its money; *many universities have an accounting year from August to August*

accounts [ə'kaunts] *plural noun* detailed records of money received and spent by a business or person

accumulate [ə'kju:mjuleɪt] *verb* to collect things over a period of time; *we have accumulated a large collection of reference materials*

accumulation [əkju:mju'leɪʃn] *noun* collection of items gained over a period of time

acetate ['æsɪteɪt] *noun* transparent plastic used for writing or drawing on, for use with an overhead projector

achieve [ə'tʃi:v] *verb* to succeed in what you are trying to do

achievement [ə'tʃi:vmənt] *noun* something which someone has succeeded in doing, often after considerable effort

acknowledge [ək'nɒlɪdʒ] *verb* to inform the sender that a message or object has been received

acknowledgements [ək'nɒlɪdʒmənts] *noun* text printed at the beginning of a written document thanking people who have helped in its production

acoustic hood [ə'ku:stɪk 'hud] *noun* soundproof covering placed over such things as public telephones or computer printers, to cut out noise

acquiescence [ækwɪ'esəns] *noun* agreement with what someone wants to do

acquire [ə'kwaɪə] *verb* (a) to obtain or learn something; *you can acquire a book* (b) to acquire a skill

acquisition [ækwɪ'zɪʃn] *noun* (a) object or item which is obtained, purchased or received as a donation to a library; **acquisition policy** = plan for what types of stock will be bought by a library; **acquisition register** = list of all books and materials obtained by a library (b) learning of a skill; *the acquisition of a new language is a long process*

acronym ['ækrənɪm] *noun* word made from the initial letters of other words such as DIANE Direct Information Access Network Europe

Act of Parliament ['ækt əv 'pɑːləmənt] *noun* decision which has been approved by Parliament and so becomes law; (NOTE: US equivalent is **Act of Congress**)

action ['ækʃn] *noun* something that is done for a particular purpose; **action shot** = still photograph showing an action still taking place such as a person running, jumping or throwing something; **to be out of action** = not working or unable to be used normally; **to put into action** = to begin to use a policy or an idea, plan or budget

activate ['æktɪveɪt] *verb* to cause something to start working

active ['æktɪv] *adjective* busy, being used, working

activity [æk'tɪvɪti] *noun* job or task you spend time doing; **activity log** = written account of things that are done in a given period of time; *she kept an activity log of her daily tasks for one week*

actual ['æktjʊəl] *adjective* real, not imagined

ad hoc [æd 'hɒk] *adjective* unplanned or only organized to meet a particular short-term unexpected situation

adapt [ə'dæpt] *verb* to change a person or thing in order to make it suitable for a specific purpose; *has the play been adapted for the cinema?; she adapted the story for TV*

adaptation [ædæp'teɪʃn] *noun* film or play based on a story or novel

adapter [ə'dæptə] *noun* someone who adapts a literary work to another format such as a novel to a play

added entry ['ædɪd 'entri] *noun* secondary entry in an index or catalogue

addendum [ə'dendəm] *noun* added section at the end of a document giving extra information; (NOTE: plural is **addenda**)

addition [ə'dɪʃn] *noun* something extra to what is already there; **in addition to something** = added; *in addition to what has already been said I wish to say ...*

address [ə'dres] **1** *noun* (a) details of where you live or where your business premises are; **e-mail address** = details of how you can be contacted by an electronic mailing system (b) label, number or name which locates where information is stored **2** *verb* to deal with something; *he addressed the problem*

addressee [ædre'siː] *noun* person to whom a letter, package or communication is addressed

adequate ['ædɪkwət] *adjective* large or good enough for the purpose

adherent [əd'hiːrənt] *noun* someone who holds a particular belief or view or supports a particular group

adhesive [əd'hiːzɪv] *noun* substance used to make things stick together

adjacent [ə'dʒeisənt] *adjective* next to or near to something

adjust [ə'dʒʌst] *verb* to change something to fit so that it works better

adjustable shelving [ə'dʒʌstəbl 'ʃelvɪŋ] *noun* shelves which can be raised or lowered to meet the requirements of different sized books

administer [əd'mɪnɪstə] *verb* to be responsible for managing a company or institution or organization

administration [ədmɪnɪ'streɪʃn] *noun* (a) group of people who are responsible for the management of a company or institution or country (b) range of activities connected with management

adopt [ə'dɒpt] *verb* to accept ideas or plans or attitudes so that you are willing to carry them out

adult ['ædʌlt or ə'dʌlt] *noun* mature person who is legally responsible for his/her actions; **adult education** = courses designed especially for adults outside the formal system of schooling; **adult literacy** = level of reading and writing ability in the adult population of a community

advance [əd'vɑːns] *adjective* happening or arriving before the expected time; **advance copy** = copy of a book sent to certain people before the official publication date; **advance order** = order for goods or services to be supplied at a later date

advanced [əd'vɑːnst] *adjective* (a) modern and developed from earlier versions (b) at a high level of study or achievement, difficult to learn

advantage [əd'vɑːntɪdʒ] *noun* something which puts you in a stronger position than another person; **to take advantage of** = to use something for your own benefit, sometimes unfairly; **to your advantage** = something which you can use for your benefit

advertisement file [əd'vɜːtɪsmənt 'faɪl] *noun* file of advertisements arranged by the name of the product or firm

advertising ['ædvətaɪzɪŋ] *noun* act of telling people about products or events in order to make them want to buy them or take part

aerial ['eəriəl] *noun* device which enables a radio or television to receive signals

affect [ə'fekt] *verb* to influence or change something

affiliate [ə'fɪlieɪt] *verb* to form a close official link with an organization

affirmative [ə'fɜːmətɪv] *adjective* meaning 'yes' or agreement or approval

afford [ə'fɔːd] *verb* (a) to be able to allow something to happen; *we cannot afford another argument* (b) to have enough money to pay for something

AFNOR = ASSOCIATION FRANÇAISE DE NORMALISATION

After Dark ['ɑːftə 'dɑːk] non-prime time database service of BRS allowing access to the database at cheaper rates at night

age of information ['eɪdʒ əv ɪnfə'meɪʃn] *phrase* description of the period in history during the second half of the twentieth century when computers made information easily accessible to large numbers of people

agenda [ə'dʒendə] *noun* list of items to be discussed at a meeting

agent ['eɪdʒənt] *noun* someone who arranges work or business for other people for a fee

aggregate ['ægrɪgət] *noun* total of several figures added together

agree [ə'griː] *verb* to have the same opinion as someone

agreement [ə'griːmənt] *noun* formal document stating what two or more people have decided together

Agricultural System for the Storage and Subsequent Selection of Information (ASSASSIN) software package of particular use to workers in agricultural information

aim [eɪm] *noun* what an action or plan is intended to achieve

aim for ['eɪm 'fɔː] *verb* to plan or hope to achieve something

airmail ['eəmeɪl] *noun* system of transporting letters and packages by air

ALA ['eɪ 'el 'eɪ] **(a)** = ASSOCIATE OF THE LIBRARY ASSOCIATION (UK) **(b)** = AMERICAN LIBRARY ASSOCIATION

alarm [ə'lɑːm] *noun* automatic device which warns you of danger

alias ['eɪliəs] *noun* **(a)** name used instead of a real name **(b)** copy of a computer application

align [ə'laɪn] *verb* to place two objects side by side in a line

all over style [ɔːl 'əʊvə 'staɪl] *phrase* style of cover decoration which uses the whole cover instead of just the front

all published ['ɔːl 'pʌblɪʃt] *adjectival phrase* catalogue entry to show that a series or periodical run has not been completed

all rights reserved ['ɔːl 'raɪts rɪ'zɜːvd] *phrase* printed on books and documents to show that they are subject to copyright

allocate ['æləkeɪt] *verb* to give a certain amount of money or goods or tasks to someone for a particular purpose

allocation [ælə'keɪʃn] *noun* specified amount of something allowed for a particular purpose; *all the staff had an allocation of time for extra study;* allocation of funds = certain amount of money given to a person or department for a specific purpose

allonym ['ælɒnɪm] *noun* false name often used by authors; *see also* ALIAS, PSEUDONYM

allow [ə'laʊ] *verb* to give permission

allowance [ə'laʊəns] *noun* amount of something given for a specific purpose; *they were given an allowance of money to buy children's books*

allusion book [ə'luːʒn 'bʊk] *noun* collection of allusions to a writer from other works

almanac ['ɔːlmənæk] *noun* book of information, often in tables, about events on certain days of the year such as tides, new moons, times of sunset, festivals, etc.

alphabet ['ælfəbet] *noun* set of letters or symbols in a fixed order used for writing the words of a language

alphabetical order [ælfə'betɪkl 'ɔːdə] *noun* arrangement according to the normal order of letters in an alphabet

alphabetize ['ælfəbetaɪz] *verb* to sort into alphabetical order

alphanumeric(al) [ælfənjuː'merɪkl] *adjective* combination of symbols made up of Roman letters and Arabic numerals including punctuation marks; **alphanumeric indexing** = system which uses both numbers and letters such as 940SPA

alter ['ɒltə] *verb* to change

alternate 1 [ɔːl'tɜːnət] *adjective* occurring regularly at one time and then missing a time but occurring again the next time; *the library van comes on alternate Tuesdays (every other Tuesday)* **2** ['ɔːltəneɪt] *verb* to cause things to happen alternately

alternative [ɔːl'tɜːnətɪv] *noun* something which you can do instead of another;

alternative title = other title information, also used to describe a subtitle

alumni list [ə'lʌmnaɪ] 'lɪst] *noun* list of past members of an educational institution

ambient ['æmbiənt] *adjective* normal background conditions; *ambient temperature*

ambiguity [æmbɪ'gjuːɪti] *noun* confusion arising from double meanings to words or writing

ambiguous [æm'bɪgjuəs] *adjective* which can be understood in more than one way; having double meaning

ambitious [æm'bɪʃəs] *adjective* **(a)** planned on a large scale and needing a lot of work to be successful **(b)** (person) wanting to be successful

amend [ə'mend] *verb* to change something written or said

amendment [ə'mendmənt] *noun* something that is added to a written or verbal statement in order to change it

amenities [ə'miːnɪtɪz] *noun* facilities provided for people's convenience or enjoyment; *a library is an amenity*

American Library Association (ALA) oldest and largest library association in the world for the support of qualified librarians and information workers

American National Standards Institute (ANSI) organization for issuing guidelines for production and distribution of goods and services in the USA

American Society for Information Science (ASIS)professional support group for information workers in the USA

American Standard Code for Information Interchange (ASCII) computer code which represents alphanumeric characters as binary code

ampersand ['æmpəsænd] *noun* abbreviated sign for 'and': &

amplifier ['æmplɪfaɪə] *noun* electronic device for making signals sound louder

analects ['ænəlekts] *plural noun* collection of miscellaneous writings

analogue ['ænəlɒg] *adjective* describes data in physical rather than numerical form

analogy [ə'nælədʒi] *noun* way of describing similarities between two different things; **indexing by analogy** = using terms already in the system

analyse ['ænəlaɪz] *verb* to examine a situation in detail in order to understand it better

analysis [ə'nælɪsɪs] *noun* process of examining something in detail

analyst ['ænəlɪst] *noun* person who analyses data

analytical entry [ænə'lɪtɪkl 'entri] *noun* entry for a part of a book or periodical which refers to the work containing it

anchor ['æŋkə] *verb* to hold firmly to a solid base; **anchor man** = person in a radio or television broadcast who remains in the studio to act as a link between broadcasters outside and different parts of the programme

ancillary [æn'sɪləri] *adjective* supporting the main structure; **ancillary worker** = person in an institution or company whose work supports the main aims

animate ['ænɪmeɪt] *verb* to draw pictures for films which make cartoon characters appear to move

animation [ænɪ'meɪʃn] *noun* technique of drawing or photographing successive pictures to create the idea of movement

animator ['ænɪmeɪtə] *noun* person who draws or photographs the pictures to make cartoons

annotate ['ænəteɪt] *verb* to add notes to something written in order to explain it more fully; **annotated catalogue** = alphabetical list of items with additional notes of explanation

annotation [ænə'teɪʃn] *noun* note written to explain items in a text

annual ['ænjuəl] **1** *adjective* **(a)** happening once a year; **annual review** = inspection which takes place once a year **(b)** (serial publication) coming out once a year, such as a yearbook, directory, etc.; **annual publication** = book, journal or document that is published once a year **2** *noun* book which is published and updated once a year

anon [ə'nɒn] = ANONYMOUS

anonymous [ə'nɒnɪməs] *adjective* of unknown name or authorship

Anonymous FTP File Transfer Protocol on a computer which gives access to public domain software

ANSI = AMERICAN NATIONAL STANDARDS INSTITUTE

answerphone *or* **answer machine** ['ɑːnsəfəʊn *or* 'ɑːnsə mə'ʃiːn] *noun* cassette recorder attached to a telephone which relays a pre-recorded message to callers and records messages

anti- ['ænti] *prefix* against

anticipate [æn'tɪsɪpeɪt] *verb* to realize in advance that something is going to happen and to prepare for it

Antiope French videotex system also known as Teletel

antonym ['æntənɪm] *noun* word which has the opposite meaning to another word

apocryphal [ə'pɒkrɪfl] *adjective* of unknown authorship

apostil [ə'pɒstɪl] *noun* margin note or annotation

apostrophe [ə'pɒstrəfi] *noun* punctuation mark which indicates (i) that a letter or letters have been left out, such as don't; or (ii) that the word following belongs to the preceding word, such as the book's cover , the books' covers

apparent [ə'pærənt] *adjective* **(a)** clear or obvious; *it is apparent that he is good at his job* **(b)** seems to be so but is uncertain; *the apparent success of the business is still unproved*

appeal [ə'piːl] *noun* **(a)** request for something to be reconsidered **(b)** request for financial contributions

appendix [ə'pendɪks] *noun* section at the end of a document giving extra information (plural) appendices; (NOTE: plural is **appendices** [ə'pendɪsiːz]

applicant ['æplɪkənt] *noun* person who formally asks to be considered for a job

application [æplɪ'keɪʃn] *noun* **(a)** written request for something; *job application;* **application form** = standardized form to be filled in when applying for something **(b)** use of a rule or piece of equipment in a particular situation; *computer applications are electronic packages which allow particular tasks to be performed*

apply for [ə'plaɪ 'fɔː] *verb* to make a formal, usually written, request for something

appoint [ə'pɔɪnt] *verb* to choose someone to do a job

appreciate [ə'priːʃɪeɪt] *verb* **(a)** to understand and know what a situation involves **(b)** to like something because you recognize its good qualities **(c)** to increase in value

approach [ə'prəʊtʃ] *noun* way of thinking about or handling a situation or problem

appropriate [ə'prəupriət] *adjective* suitable or acceptable for a particular situation

approve [ə'pru:v] *verb* to agree to; *to approve the terms of a contract;* **to approve of** = to think something is good; *they approved of the new signs for the library*

approximate [ə'prɒksɪmət] *adjective* not exact, almost correct

ARCHIE ['ɑːtʃi] retrieval software which gives access to Internet databases

architecture ['ɑːkɪtektʃə] *noun* planning and design of buildings or systems

archival management ['ɑːkaɪvəl 'mænɪdʒmənt] *noun* control of archives

archive ['ɑːkaɪvz] *noun* **(a)** public record, document or photograph, etc. of historical interest kept in an official repository **(b)** collection of documents and records relating to the history of an organization; **archive library** *see* LIBRARY

archivist ['ɑːkɪvɪst] *noun* person who organizes archives

areas ['eərɪəz] *noun* spaces in a building such as a library, designated for particular purposes such as reference areas

argue ['ɑːgjuː] *verb* to disagree with someone often angrily

argument ['ɑːgjumənt] *noun* **(a)** disagreement between two or more people **(b)** set of reasons used to try to convince people

arrange [ə'reɪndʒ] *verb* to put things into a correct or desired order

arrangement [ə'reɪndʒmənt] *noun* something that has been planned, agreed or put into order

arrears [ə'rɪəz] *plural noun* money that is owing from the past and should have been already paid

article ['ɑːtɪkl] *noun* **(a)** piece of writing in a newspaper or magazine **(b)** one message sent to an electronic newsgroup; if you want to say something that any other user can read, you would 'post' an article to the newsgroup

articulated indexing [ɑː'tɪkjuleɪtɪd 'ɪndeksɪŋ] *noun* method of producing computer generated subject indexes

artificial [ɑːtɪ'fɪʃl] *adjective* made by humans often as a copy of something natural; **artificial indexing language** = signs and symbols used as a controlled language in inverted order for subject indexing; **artificial intelligence** = computers which imitate some human characteristics; **artificial language** = man-made language for use in communicating with computers

artistic map [ɑː'tɪstɪk 'mæp] *noun* made by an artist rather than a map maker

artwork ['ɑːtwɜːk] *noun* drawings, photographs and text prepared for inclusion in a book or advertisement

ascend [ə'send] *verb* to move upwards

ascending order [ə'sendɪŋ 'ɔːdə] *noun* organization of things so that each item is bigger than the one before it or comes later in the system; *the list was arranged in ascending order from A-Z*

ASCII ['æskiː] = AMERICAN STANDARD CODE FOR INFORMATION INTERCHANGE

ASI = AUSTRALIAN SOCIETY OF INDEXERS

ASIS = AMERICAN SOCIETY FOR INFORMATION SCIENCE

ASLIB ['æzlɪb] = ASSOCIATION OF INFORMATION MANAGEMENT

ASSASSIN = AGRICULTURAL SYSTEM FOR THE STORAGE AND SUBSEQUENT SELECTION OF INFORMATION

assemble [ə'sembl] *verb* **(a)** to bring the parts of a collection together **(b)** to fit the parts of something together to make it whole

assertion [ə'sɜːʃn] *noun* firm statement of belief

assess [ə'ses] *verb* to judge the importance or value of something

assessed work [ə'sest 'wɜːk] *noun* assignments that have been judged as part of a course of training

assign [ə'saɪn] *verb* to allocate a task to a person or send someone to work in a particular place

assignment [ə'saɪnmənt] *noun* task often given as part of a programme of study

assimilate [ə'sɪmɪleɪt] *verb* to learn and make use of something

assimilation [əsɪmɪ'leɪʃn] *noun* absorption of ideas or people; *the assimilation of immigrants by the host culture is a long process*

assist [ə'sɪst] *verb* to help someone, for example by giving them information

assistant [ə'sɪstənt] *noun* someone who is employed to help another in their work; **assistant librarian** = someone who is qualified as a librarian and usually works with a more senior person

associate 1 [ə'səʊsiət] *noun* someone you work with **2** [ə'səʊsieɪt] *verb* to connect something with another having a similar background

Association Française de Normalisation (AFNOR) French official body responsible for issuing standards

Association of Information Management (ASLIB) gives advice and guidelines on the management of information within companies, and publishes

ASLIB Information, ASLIB Proceedings and Journal of Documentation

assume [ə'sjuːm] *verb* to accept the truth of something or to take something on; *he assumed responsibility for the information service*

asterisk ['æstərɪsk] *noun* symbol in the form of a star used to mark things to be noted: *

asynchronous [eɪ'sɪŋkrənəs] *adjective* not needing to be synchronized

asyndetic [æsɪn'detɪk] *adjective* without cross references

at a time ['æt ə 'taɪm] *adverb* using only one thing each time

at frequent intervals [æt 'friːkwənt 'ɪntəvəlz] *adverb* very often and regularly

at least [ət 'liːst] *adverb* minimum number; *at least two*

at low cost [ət 'ləʊ 'kɒst] *adverb* cheaply

at the outset ['æt ðə 'aʊtset] *adverb* at the beginning

at the same rate ['æt ðə 'seɪm 'reɪt] *adverb* at the same speed

at the same time ['æt ðə 'seɪm 'taɪm] *adverb* simultaneously

atlas ['ætləs] *noun* book of maps

attach [ə'tætʃ] *verb* to fasten on to; *he asked them to attach the documents for his information;* **to be attached to** = working with a company or person for a short time

attachment [ə'tætʃmənt] *noun* computer file that is transferred together with an electronic mail message

attempt [ə'tempt] **1** *noun* effort to do something often unsuccessful **2** *verb* to try to achieve something

attend [ə'tend] *verb* to go to; *to attend a meeting;* **to attend to** = to deal with something, such as to find a solution to a problem

attendance [ə'tendəns] *noun* number of people at a meeting

attitude ['ætɪtjuːd] *noun* way someone thinks or feels about something

attractive [ə'træktɪv] *adjective* interesting because it brings you advantage; *the job offered an attractive salary*

attribute [ə'trɪbjuːt] *verb* to say that someone did something; *to attribute a piece of writing to a particular person*

attributed author [ə'trɪbjuːtɪd 'ɔːθə] *noun* name of a possible author when there is doubt about authenticity

audience ['ɔːdiəns] *noun* group of people gathered together to watch or listen to something

audio ['ɔːdɪəʊ] *adjective* which can be heard; **audio conference** = meeting that is held with the use of several linked telephones to connect the people who want to talk together; **audio media** = communication tools which use sound only such as radio; **audio tape** *see* TAPE

audio-visual [ɔːdɪəʊ'vɪzjʊəl] *adjective* can be both heard and seen; **audio-visual aids** = things which help learning through listening and seeing such as pictures, tape cassettes, television; **audio-visual materials** = materials which can be listened to or looked at such as slides or tapes

audit ['ɔːdɪt] *verb* to examine something officially to make sure it is correct

Audit Commission ['ɔːdɪt kə'mɪʃn] *noun* government body which ensures that financial affairs are conducted according to approved standards, and examines the accounts of government departments, local government organizations, etc.

aural ['ɔːrəl] *adjective* can be listened to; **aural materials** = materials which can be listened to such as tapes; **aural tests** = tests of an individual's ability to listen and understand

Australian Society of Indexers (ASI) professional support group for professional indexers in Australasia

authentic [ɔː'θentɪk] *adjective* known to be real and not a copy

authenticity [ɔːθen'tɪsɪti] *noun* quality of being authentic

author ['ɔːθə] *noun* someone who writes books or articles; **author catalogue** *or* **author index** = catalogue which is organized according to an alphabetical list of writers' surnames; **author entry** = catalogue entry under the name of the person or organization responsible for writing or compiling a work

authoring software ['ɔːθərɪŋ 'sɒftweə] *noun* software which allows the user to add their own text and to link text, pictures and sound within a given framework

authoritative [ɔː'θɒrɪtətɪv] *adjective* reliable, official

authority [ɔː'θɒrɪti] *noun* expert in the field; **authority control** = list of headings used in a retrieval system; **authority file** = list of authoritative forms such as names, subject headings to be used in bibliographic records

authorize ['ɔːθəraɪz] *verb* to give official permission for something to be done

Authorized Version ['ɔːθəraɪzd 'vɜːʃn] English translation of the Bible made in England in 1611 A.D. also known as the King James Bible

autobiography [ɔːtəbaɪ'ɒɡrəfi] *noun* person's life written by him or herself

auto-encode ['ɔːtəʊɪŋ'kəʊd] *noun* to select keywords automatically by computer

autograph ['ɔːtəgrɑːf] *noun* signature of someone famous

automate ['ɔːtəmeɪt] *verb* to use machines to do work previously done by people

automatic [ɔːtə'mætɪk] *adjective* which works by itself; **automatic indexing** = process of using a computer to select and generate keywords as indexing entries

automation [ɔːtə'meɪʃn] *noun* use of machines to do work with very little supervision

autonomy [ɔː'tɒnəmi] *noun* opportunity to make your own decisions without being told what to do by someone else

auxiliary [ɔːg'zɪliəri] *adjective* used to describe a person or a machine which helps a more important worker; **auxiliary number** = additional number placed after the class number to allow materials to be further grouped into subgroups

available [ə'veɪləbl] *adjective* ready to be used; *available time or information*

availability [əveɪlə'bɪliti] *noun* being able to be obtained, used or seen; *the new books were given limited availability of one week per person, so that more people could read them*

average ['ævərɪdʒ] *adjective* standard or normal, neither very good nor very bad

avoid [ə'vɔɪd] *verb* to take action to prevent something from happening

award [ə'wɔːd] **1** *noun* **(a)** prize given for doing something well **(b)** sum of money given for a specific purpose; *an award to help you to study* **2** *verb* to give a prize or monetary grant

awarding body [ə'wɔːdɪŋ 'bɒdi] *noun* organization which gives a prize or scholarship

awareness [ə'weənəs] *noun* knowing about things; **current awareness** = keeping up to date; **current awareness service** = service which provides users with up-to-date information on specific topics

axis ['æksɪs] *noun* fixed line against which other positions can be measured, such as the vertical and horizontal axes on a graph; (NOTE: plural is **axes**)

Bb

backdate [bæk'deɪt] *verb* to make effective from an earlier date than the current one; **backdated** = with the date written earlier than the current day's date

background ['bækgraʊnd] *noun* (a) context of a situation, which helps to explain it (b) scenery behind the main people and objects in a picture or photograph

backing ['bækɪŋ] *noun* money or support given to a person or an organization for a particular project

backlog ['bæklɒg] *noun* work waiting to be done and causing delays

back number *or* **back issue** ['bæk 'nʌmbə *or* 'bæk 'ɪʃuː] *noun* edition of a magazine, newspaper or other document which is not the most recent edition

back order ['bæk 'ɔːdə] *noun* uncompleted order which is held back for delivery when stock becomes available

backslash ['bækslæʃ] *noun* punctuation mark; \these words are between backslashes\

back title ['bæk 'taɪtl] *noun* title on the spine or back of a book

backup ['bækʌp] **1** *adjective* assistance; *we offer an after sales backup service* **2** *noun* duplicate copy of a file on a computer

balance ['bæləns] **1** *verb* financial term meaning to keep expenditure equal to income **2** *noun* (a) placing of text and graphics on a page in an attractive way (b) **in the balance** = not yet decided; **on balance** = phrase used to show that you are giving a considered opinion

bank [bæŋk] **1** *noun* somewhere to store things ready for use; **bank sort code** = set of numbers printed on cheques which identifies a particular bank; *see also* DATA BANK **2** *verb* **to bank on** = to rely on something happening

bankrupt ['bæŋkrʌpt] *adjective* not having enough money to pay one's debts

banned [bænd] *adjective* prohibited from use by authorities

banner ['bænə] *noun* heading or title across the width of a page; **banner headline** = extra large newspaper headline

BAPLA = BRITISH ASSOCIATION OF PICTURE LIBRARIES AND AGENCIES

bar [bɑː] **1** *noun* thick band of colour **2** *verb* to prevent someone from doing something or going somewhere

barcode ['bɑː 'kəʊd] *noun* line of printed stripes of different thickness representing a numeric code which can be read electronically; **barcode reader** *or* **barcode**

scanner = electronic device used to read bar codes

bar chart ['bɑː 'tʃɑːt] *noun* graph in which the data is represented by horizontal or vertical bars

barrier ['bæriə] *noun* something which makes it difficult or impossible to achieve your aims

base [beɪs] **1** *noun* foundations of something **2** *verb* **to base on** = to develop an idea from the foundations of a previous idea

BASIC = BEGINNER'S ALL-PURPOSE SYMBOLIC INSTRUCTION CODE computer programming language

basic stock ['beɪsɪk 'stɒk] *noun* standard titles which are considered necessary to form the core of an authoritative book stock

basis ['beɪsɪs] *noun* foundation or reason for something

batch [bætʃ] *noun* group of things which are made or dealt with all at one time; **batch control** = system for organizing groups of products; **batch file** = combination of files which are treated as one unit; **batch number** = number used to identify a particular group; **batch system** = way of dealing with tasks in groups

battery ['bætəri] *noun* **(a)** large number of things or people **(b)** portable source of electric power

bay [beɪ] *noun* space or area used for a particular purpose; *a book bay in a library*

BBC ['biː biː 'siː] = BRITISH BROADCASTING CORPORATION

BBIP = BRITISH BOOKS IN PRINT

bcc = BLIND CARBON COPY

Beginner's All-Purpose Symbolic Instruction Code *see* BASIC

beginning [bɪ'gɪnɪŋ] *noun* first part

BEI = BRITISH EDUCATION INDEX

benchmark ['bentʃmɑːk] *noun* something of accepted quality which is used to provide a standard for comparison

beneficial [benɪ'fɪʃl] *adjective* providing advantage or benefit

benefit ['benɪfɪt] *noun* advantage to a person or organization; **to give someone benefit of the doubt** = to assume innocence rather than guilt

best seller [best'selə] *noun* popular book of which a very large number of copies are sold

BHI = BRITISH HUMANITIES INDEX

bi-annually [baɪ'ænjuəli] *adverb* issued every two years

bias ['baɪəs] *noun* unfair judgement influenced by opinions rather than facts

bias phrase ['baɪəs 'freɪz] *noun* in classification, the name of a specific group for whom a work is intended, such as bankers

biased ['baɪəst] *adjective* holding views based on opinions rather than facts

biblio ['bɪblɪəʊ] *noun* bibliographic details printed on the back of the title page

bibliographic [bɪblɪə'græfɪk] *adjective* related to bibliographies; **bibliographic control** = creation and management of bibliographic records and the system which enables users to access them; **bibliographic database** = database containing bibliographic information, designed to locate specific items; **bibliographic details** = information about a publication, often printed on the back of the title page, which enables it to be identified, such as date of publication, ISBN, etc.; **bibliographic entry** = details of written material, set out in a list for reference

bibliography [bɪblɪ'ɒgrəfi] *noun* **(a)** list of books and/or other materials on one particular subject **(b)** list of books or articles referred to in another book or article

bibliomania [ˌbɪblɪəʊˈmeɪnɪə] *noun* obsession with collecting books

bibliophile [ˈbɪblɪəfaɪl] *noun* lover of books who can distinguish good and bad editions

bifurcate classification [ˈbaɪfəkeɪt klæsɪfɪˈkeɪʃn] *noun* system of classification based on branching positive and negative pairs

bilingual dictionary [baɪˈlɪŋgwəl ˈdɪkʃənri] *noun* dictionary in two languages; *see also* MONOLINGUAL, MULTILINGUAL

billion [ˈbɪljən] *noun* **(a)** *GB* a million million **(b)** *USA* a thousand million (NOTE: the US usage is now becoming common in GB; also used generally to mean a very large amount)

bimonthly [baɪˈmʌnθli] *adjective* issued or published every two months

binary [ˈbaɪnəri] *adjective* numerical system using only the digits 0 and 1, used especially in computing; **binary search** = system of searching by repeatedly rejecting one of a pair until the required item is found

bind [baɪnd] *verb* to join the pages of a book together and enclose them in a cover (NOTE: binding-bound)

binder [ˈbaɪndə] *noun* person or company which specializes in binding books

bindery [ˈbaɪndəri] *noun* factory where books are bound

binding [ˈbaɪndɪŋ] **1** *noun* **(a)** cover of a book **(b)** action of putting a cover on a book; **binding record** = record of all books sent to the binder **2** *adjective* demanding an obligation; *the contract was binding in law*

biographical details [baɪəˈgræfɪkl ˈdiːteɪlz] *plural noun* information about the main events in someone's life

biography [baɪˈɒgrəfi] *noun* account of someone's life and work written by someone else

BIS = BUSINESS INFORMATION SERVICE

BIT binary digit 0 or 1

BITNET *acronym* network of IBM mainframe computers which can be accessed through gateways, such as @MITMVMA.mit.edu or @CUNYVM.cuny.edu

BL = BRITISH LIBRARY

black [blæk] *adjective* darkest possible colour; **black economy** = money that is earned without paying government taxes; **black market** = illegal trading; **to be in the black** = to have money in the bank

black list [ˈblæk ˈlɪst] **1** *noun* list of people or organizations not to be trusted or used **2** *verb* to make a list of untrustworthy people or organizations

BLAISE [ˈbleɪz] = BRITISH LIBRARY AUTOMATED INFORMATION SERVICE **BLAISE Records** = online machine readable records from the MARC database for use on automated catalogues

blank [blæŋk] **1** *noun* empty space in a form **2** *adjective* empty or with nothing on it; *a blank tape; a blank piece of paper*

blank cheque [ˈblæŋk ˈtʃek] *noun* **(a)** bank cheque with the amount of money to be filled in by the recipient **(b)** authority to do whatever you consider to be right

blanket agreement [ˈblæŋkɪt əˈgriːmənt] *noun* agreement which covers many items

blanket order [ˈblæŋkɪt ˈɔːdə] *noun* order with several different items

blast freeze [ˈblɑːst ˈfriːz] *verb* to reduce the temperature to below freezing using very cold air; sometimes used as a method for conserving wet paper

blind carbon copy (bcc) ['blaɪnd 'kɑːbən 'kɒpi] *noun* feature of many electronic mail programs that allows a user to send one message to several users at a time (a carbon copy) but does not display this list to the recipients *see also* CC

blind reference ['blaɪnd 'refrəns] *noun* reference in a catalogue or index to a heading which has no entry

blip coding ['blɪp 'kəʊdɪŋ] *noun* process of coding tapes with warning bleeps

BLDSC = BRITISH LIBRARY DOCUMENT SUPPLY CENTRE

block capital ['blɒk 'kæpɪtəlz] *noun* upper case letter such as A, B, C, as opposed to lower case a, b, c

block letter style ['blɒk 'letə staɪl] *noun* style of writing using only capital letters

blow up ['bləʊ 'ʌp] *verb* to enlarge a photograph

blowup ['bləʊʌp] *noun* photograph or illustration greatly enlarged for exhibition purposes

BLR&DD = BRITISH LIBRARY RESEARCH & DEVELOPMENT DEPARTMENT

blueprint ['bluːprɪnt] *noun* **(a)** photographic copy of construction plans usually printed in white on blue paper **(b)** detailed plan of something

blurred [blɜːd] *adjective* unclear because there is no distinct outline

BNB ['biː en 'biː] = BRITISH NATIONAL BIBLIOGRAPHY

Bodleian Library ['bɒdliən 'laɪbrəri] main library serving the University of Oxford (UK)

board [bɔːd] *noun* controlling group of people in a company or organization also known as the board of directors; **board meeting** = meeting of the directors to discuss company business; **board room** = room where the board meetings are held; **editorial board** = group of people with the power to make decisions about the contents of documents; **across the board** = decision or action which affects everyone in a particular group

body ['bɒdi] *noun* **(a)** official group of people **(b)** main part of the text in a document or electronic mail message

bold type *or* **bold face** ['bəʊld 'taɪp *or* 'bəʊld 'feɪs] *noun* thicker and darker form of typeface used for emphasis

book [bʊk] *noun* collection of pages containing text and/or pictures, bound together inside a cover **book bay** = area in a library surrounded by book shelves; **book bus** = bus converted to act as a mobile library usually in residential areas; **book club** = system of buying and selling books often by post; the books are usually on specialist subjects or literary genre; **book club edition** = edition of a book specially printed and bound for a book club for sale to its members; **book council** *see* NATIONAL BOOK COUNCIL **book cover** *or* **bookjacket** *see* DUST COVER **book distribution** = system of delivering books to institutions or people; **book donation** = book given to an organization as a gift; **book export** = book produced in one country and sold in another; **book fair** = trade exhibition with the object of publicizing, selling and exchanging books; a particularly well known one is held each year at Frankfurt, Germany; **book list** = list of books on a specific subject or by a particular author; **book market** = number of potential buyers for books; **book plate** = decorated piece of paper stuck in the front of the book with the name of the owner written or printed on it; **book review** = critical comments on a book especially when it is first published; **book token** = card bought to give as a gift which can only be used to buy books; **book trade** = business of buying and selling books

Book Aid International started in 1954 by the Earl and Countess of Ranfurly and formerly known as Ranfurly Library Service; a service which collects unwanted books from individuals and institutions and sends them abroad to help fight illiteracy; now also encourages local publishing

bookcase ['bʊkkeɪs] *noun* piece of furniture with shelves for books

bookend ['bʊkend] *noun* one of a pair of supports used to keep a row of books upright

bookings ['bʊkɪŋz] *noun* arrangement to reserve something; *the bookings were low for the theatre performance*

bookkeeping ['bʊkkiːpɪŋ] *noun* keeping records of the income and expenditure of an organization or company

booklet ['bʊklət] *noun* small book with a paper cover often used for information

bookmark ['bʊkmɑːk] *noun* **(a)** narrow strip of material or paper used to mark the place where the reader has stopped reading temporarily **(b)** code used by a multimedia title or wordprocessor or Web browser that allows the user to move straight back to this point at a later date. The software keeps a list of all the bookmarks you have inserted together with the relevant page number

bookseller ['bʊkselə] *noun* person or company that sells books

Bookseller, The [ðə 'bʊkselə] journal providing information especially interesting to booksellers and publishers

bookshelf ['bʊkʃelf] *noun* horizontal piece of wood or metal used to store books; (NOTE: plural is **bookshelves)**

bookshop ['bʊkʃɒp] *noun* shop which specializes in selling books

bookstall *or* **bookstand** ['bʊkstɔːl or 'bʊkstænd] *noun* table in a market or fair where books are sold

bookstore ['bʊkstɔː] *noun* **(a)** space in a library devoted to storage of books and documents not frequently used **(b)** *(especially in USA)* bookshop

Books in Print (BBIP) ['bʊkz ɪn 'prɪnt] *see* BRITISH BOOKS IN PRINT

Book Trust ['bʊk 'trʌst] independent body, formerly known as the National Book League, which promotes books and reading and also offers an information service

bookwork ['bʊkwɜːk] *noun* keeping of financial records

bookworm ['bʊkwɜːm] *noun* person who is very fond of reading

Boolean logic ['buːliən 'lɒdʒɪk] *noun* rules set down to simplify logical functions in searching; **Boolean operators** = 'and', 'or', 'not', frequently used in online searching

boost [buːst] *verb* to increase something; *to boost the market for books*

bootleg ['buːtleg] *adjective* something which is imported or sold illegally

border ['bɔːdə] *noun* strip, line or band around the edge of something

borderline ['bɔːdəlaɪn] *adjective* only just acceptable; *he was a borderline case in the examination, but they allowed him to pass*

borrow ['bɒrəʊ] *verb* to take away temporarily with the intention of returning it

borrower ['bɒrəwə] *noun* person who borrows something; *borrowers who return items late will be fined;* **borrower card** *or* **borrower ticket** = card issued to a member of a library so that items borrowed can be recorded in his or her name

borrowing systems ['bɒrəʊɪŋ 'sɪstəmz] *noun* systems for organizing items which are taken away temporarily and need to be returned

bottom line ['bɒtəm 'laɪn] *noun* most important consideration in a discussion

bottom price ['bɒtəm 'praɪs] *noun* lowest possible price

bounce [baʊns] **1** *noun* electronic mail that is returned to the sender because the address is incorrect or the user is not known at the mail server **2** *verb (of a message)* not to be delivered; *if you send e-mail to a bad address it bounces back to your mailbox*

bound journal ['baʊnd 'dʒɜːnəl] *noun* set of regular journal issues collected in date order and put inside a stiff cover

bounds [baʊndz] *noun* limits of what can be done

bowdlerize ['baʊdləraɪz] *verb* to change the text by omitting anything which may be thought to be offensive; so called after Thomas Bowdler who in 1818 'cleaned up' an edition of Shakespeare's plays

box [bɒks] *verb* to pack into boxes for transport or sale

box number ['bɒks 'nʌmbə] *noun* number used as an address often in reply to an advertisement in a newspaper or magazine

bracket ['brækɪt] **1** *noun* **age bracket** = range of ages; *these books are suitable for the younger age bracket;* **price bracket** = limited range of prices; *the goods were in the cheaper price bracket* **2** *verb* to **bracket together** = to put two or more things together because they are thought to be similar

brackets ['brækɪts] *plural noun* **(a)** punctuation marks put round words to show that they contain additional information; *(these words are inside brackets)* **(b)** pieces of metal or wood fastened to a wall to support something

Braille [breɪl] *noun* system of printing that enables blind people to read by feeling with

their fingers letters which are printed as groups of raised dots

brainstorm ['breɪnstɔːm] *verb* to gather together the random thoughts on a given subject, of all the people at a meeting or seminar

branch [brɑːntʃ] *noun* local sub section of a business, or organization; **branch library** = small library which is managed from a central authority; **branch manager** = person who runs a local branch

branching classification ['brɑːntʃɪŋ klæsɪfɪ'keɪʃn] *noun* system of classification with two or more main divisions which can be further subdivided as often as necessary

brand name ['brænd 'neɪm] *noun* version of a product recognized by a name or design

breach [briːtʃ] **1** *verb* to break an agreement or contract **2** *noun* **breach of contract** = failure to carry out the terms of an agreement

break [breɪk] *verb* to destroy a system or promise or object so that it can no longer be used; **break down** = to separate something into smaller parts so that it is easier to deal with; **break even** = to make enough money to cover your expenses but making neither a profit nor a loss; **break into** = to use a computer system without permission

bridge [brɪdʒ] *verb* to overcome differences between people; **to bridge an information gap** = to provide relevant information

brief [briːf] *noun* set of instructions needed to perform a task; often used for legal instructions

briefing ['briːfɪŋ] *noun* meeting at which people are given instructions and information

British Association of Picture Libraries and Agencies (BAPLA)

support group providing information guidelines and standards for special picture libraries

British Books in Print (BBIP)

publication containing bibliographical details of all published books in the UK

British Broadcasting Corporation (BBC)

controlling body for most radio and some TV in Britain

British Council government funded body to promote the United Kingdom abroad by means of information offices, cultural relations, educational aid schemes and agencies for low priced book schemes

British Education Index (BEI) index to articles about education from over 250 periodicals with online access through DIALOG

British Humanities Index (BHI)

quarterly index to articles in periodicals about the humanities published by the Library Association

British Library (BL) national library of the UK which contains a copy of every publication in Britain through the copyright deposit system

British Library Automated Information Service (BLAISE)

now divided into BLAISE-LINE standard bibliographic database and BLAISE-LINK online database host

British Library Document Supply Centre (BLDSC)

closed collection kept for use by inter-library loan

British Library Research & Development Department (BLR&DD)

part of the British Library devoted to research into all aspects of library and information work

British National Bibliography (BNB)

organization which issues a weekly list in printed form and on CD-ROM of all the books published in Great Britain and produces monthly and annual cumulative indexes

British Society of Indexers (BSI)

support association for professional indexers

British Standards Institution (BSI)

approved British body for the preparation and publication of national standards for the production of goods and services

British Talking Book Service for the Blind organization which arranges for written materials to be recorded onto audio tape so that blind people can listen to them

British Telecom (BT) main company running the telephone communications system in the UK

broadcast ['brɔːdkɑːst] **1** *noun* programme made for transmission on radio or television **2** *verb* **(a)** to send out words, music or signals by radio waves **(b)** to make widely known

broadsheet ['brɔːdʃiːt] *noun* anything printed on large sheets of paper, but especially the more serious newspapers

broad term ['brɔːd 'tɜːm] *noun* indexing term heading a string of narrower terms

brochure ['brəʊʃə] *noun* magazine or booklet with pictures giving information about a product or service

broken order ['brəʊkən 'ɔːdə] *noun* system which is not in the expected or normal order, used deliberately in certain circumstances to facilitate use

broker ['brəʊkə] *noun* someone who does the business of buying and selling for someone else

brokerage ['brəʊkərɪdʒ] *noun* **(a)** business of buying and selling goods and services for other people **(b)** fee charged by a broker

Brown issuing system system of recording loans from a library which uses individual book cards, which are kept in small cardboard members' tickets until the book is returned

browse [braʊz] *verb* to look through a book, magazine, database or shop in a casual way without definite intentions

browser *or* **web browser** ['braʊzə] *noun* software program that is used to navigate through WWW pages stored on the internet; a browser program asks the internet server to send it a page of information, this page is stored in the HTML layout language that is decoded by the browser and displayed on screen

BSI ['biː es 'aɪ] **(a)** = BRITISH STANDARDS INSTITUTION **(b)** = BRITISH SOCIETY OF INDEXERS

BT ['biː 'tiː] = BRITISH TELECOM

BTEC ['biːtek] work-related technical qualification usually at school-leaving level

BUBL = BULLETIN BOARDS FOR LIBRARIES electronic discussion list subscribed to by librarians worldwide

budget ['bʌdʒɪt] **1** *noun* financial plan showing how much money is available and how it is proposed to spend it **2** *verb* to allow certain amounts of money for specific purposes

bug [bʌg] *noun* **(a)** problem or mistake in a computer program **(b)** tracking or surveillance device

built-in ['bɪltɪn] *adjective* included as part of the original structure or plan; *see also* OBSOLESCENCE

bulk [bʌlk] *noun* large quantity; **bulk purchase** = buying of a large quantity of something to obtain a cheaper price; **bulk storage** = storing large amounts of information on a database; **the bulk of something** = most of it; **to buy in bulk** = to buy large quantities

bulletin ['bʊlɪtɪn] *noun* short report on the latest situation; **bulletin board** = electronic discussion network and information database; electronic version of a noticeboard; **Bulletin Boards for Libraries** *see* BUBL

bundled service ['bʌndld 'sɜːvɪs] *noun* collection of several different services sold as a package

bureau ['bjʊərəʊ] *noun* office organization or government department that collects and distributes information

business ['bɪznəs] *noun* organization which produces and sells goods or provides a service; **business card** = small card giving the name and business details of a person; **business letter** *see* LETTER **business plan** = usually presented to a bank or other institution when asking for a loan; **business relationship** = way people in business work together; **business school** = college which teaches people how to manage a business or other organization; **business system** = way of organizing business following a fixed set of rules

Business Information Service (BIS) service to promote awareness of the British Libraries' holdings on business information, based at the Science Reference and Information Service

businesslike ['bɪznəslaɪk] *adjective* working in an efficient and timesaving way

BUSLIB electronic bulletin board for business libraries

busy ['bɪzi] *adjective* fully occupied doing something

button ['bʌtn] *noun* picture on a computer screen which can be used with a mouse to perform specific functions

buy into ['baɪ 'ɪntʊ] *phrasal verb* to buy part of a business or organization in order to gain some control

buy out ['baɪ 'aʊt] *phrasal verb* to buy someone's share of a business that you previously owned together

buzzer ['bʌzə] *noun* electronic device making a loud hum often used as an alarm

by hand *see* HAND

byline ['baɪlaɪn] *noun* line giving the name of the author of a newspaper or magazine article

by-product ['baɪprɒdʌkt] *noun* **(a)** something which is an unexpected or unplanned outcome of a situation **(b)** something which is produced during the manufacture of something else

byte [baɪt] *noun* single unit of data in a computer that is made up of eight binary bits and can normally contain one character

Cc

© symbol denoting copyright placed by law before the name of the owner of the copyright and the year of first publication

ca. = CIRCA

cabinet ['kæbɪnət] *noun* piece of furniture with doors and drawers used for storing things; *see also* FILING CABINET

cable ['keɪbl] **1** *noun* flexible wire link for electrical equipment **2** *verb* **to cable someone** = to send a telegram or message by telegraph

cable television *or* **cable TV** ['keɪbl 'tiː 'viː] *noun* system whereby signals are relayed to viewers homes by fibre optic cables often underground

CAD = COMPUTER AIDED DESIGN

CAL = COMPUTER AIDED LEARNING

calculate ['kælkjʊleɪt] *verb* **(a)** to consider the effects of an action; *he calculated the effects carefully before making a decision* **(b)** to work out a solution using numbers

calculated ['kælkjʊleɪtɪd] *adjective* planned to have a particular effect

calculator ['kælkjʊleɪtə] *noun* electronic device for working out the answers to numerical problems

calendar ['kælendə] *noun* printed table or chart which shows the days, weeks and months of the year; **calendar month** = period of time, usually 30 or 31 days, measured according to an established western calendar rather than natural changes of the moon; **calendar year** = period of time, usually 12 months, measured according to an established western calendar rather than natural changes of the moon

calfskin ['kɑːfskɪn] *noun* soft leather used in bookbinding

call number ['kɔːl 'nʌmbə] *noun* number used to identify and locate a book; *see also* SPINE NUMBER

calligraphy [kə'lɪgrəfi] *noun* artistic use of handwriting

camcorder ['kæmkɔːdə] *noun* small video recorder which can be held in the hand

camera ['kæmərə] *noun* device for taking photographs on light sensitive film; **camera-ready copy (CRC)** = typescript which is ready to be photographed as part of book production

campus ['kæmpəs] *noun* area of land containing the main buildings of a college or university

cancel ['kænsl] *verb* to cause something to be no longer valid, such as a cheque or reservation; **cancel out** = to combine two things having opposite effects so as to produce no effect

cancellation [kænsə'leɪʃn] *noun* instruction to say that something is no longer needed

candidate ['kændɪdət] *noun* (a) person who is being considered for a job, or who is standing for election (b) someone who is taking an examination (c) person who or company which is considered suitable for a particular purpose; *small libraries are likely candidates for closure*

capability [keɪpə'bɪlɪti] *noun* ability to do something; *the capability to understand computers*

capable ['keɪpəbl] *adjective* able to do things well

capacity [kə'pæsɪti] *noun* (a) amount that something can hold (b) *(in industry)* the amount that can be produced or work done; **capacity planning** = planning work so that the best use is made of the abilities and equipment available (c) ability to do things; *he has the capacity to perform well as division head*

capital ['kæpɪtl] *noun* (a) money which is used to set up a business or invested to make more money; **capital expenditure** = money spent on equipment or buildings (b) main city in a country, usually where the government meets (c) **capital letter** = upper case form of a letter used at the beginning of sentences and names, such as A, B, C as opposed to a, b, c; *see also* BLOCK CAPITAL

caption ['kæpʃn] *noun* note or heading to a picture or illustration

capture ['kæptʃə] *verb* to obtain control over something; *to capture the market;* **capture data** = to put data into a computer

carbon copy (cc.) ['kɑːbən 'kɒpi] *noun* (a) used at the ends of letters, memos, reports, etc., to indicate that an identical copy

has been sent to named people; these days more likely to be a photocopy (b) feature of electronic mail software that allows you to send a copy of a message to another user *see also* BLIND CARBON COPY

carbon paper ['kɑːbən 'peɪpə] *noun* thin paper with one side covered in a dark substance so that it can be used between two sheets of ordinary paper to produce a second copy; **carbonless** *or* **self carboning paper** = paper which will produce a copy of anything written on it on paper placed underneath it, without the need for carbon paper

card [kɑːd] *noun* piece of thick and stiff paper; **card catalogue** = list of contents written on index cards and arranged according to a system which aids retrieval; **card index** = series of cards usually standard size 12.5 x 7.5 cm (5 x 3 inches) used to record holdings and kept in specially designed drawers or boxes; **file cards** = cards with information written on them which can be stored in a given order to aid retrieval of the information

care ['keə] *noun* attention to detail in order to avoid mistakes

careful ['keəful] *adjective* doing something well and with a lot of attention

careless ['keələs] *adjective* doing something in a casual way, unworried and without attention

career [kə'rɪə] *noun* job or profession which is followed for a long time with the expectation of progression; **career ladder** = steps by which a person gains promotion in their chosen career; **career path planning** = planning a route through a career in order to gain maximum opportunities for promotion; **career stage** = level of progress made in promotion

caret mark *or* **caret sign** ['kærɪt 'mɑːk *or* 'saɪn] *noun* proof reading symbol to indicate that something should be inserted into the text

Carnegie library [kɑːˈniːgi ˈlaɪbrəri] *noun* public library system that was developed nationally from money donated by Andrew Carnegie, a Scottish born American who gave money to public education and libraries (1835-1919)

carrel [ˈkærəl] *noun* enclosed area for private study within a larger space like a classroom or a library

carry [ˈkæri] *verb* **(a)** to transport something from one place to another **(b)** to contain or broadcast; *a newspaper or radio carries an article or a report;* **carry on** = to continue to do something; **carry out** = to perform a task; **carry over** = in accounts to take a total from the bottom of one page to the top of the next; **carry through** = to continue an action until it is finished

cartel [kɑːˈtel] *noun* group of similar companies which agree to control prices to prevent competition

cartography [kɑːˈtɒgrəfi] *noun* art of drawing maps

cartographer [kɑːˈtɒgrəfə] *noun* person who draws maps

cartographic [kɑːtəˈgræfik] *adjective* of maps; *the library had a large cartographic collection*

cartoon [kɑːˈtuːn] *noun* **(a)** first draft drawing done on paper which can be transferred to larger paintings **(b)** comic or satirical drawing **(c)** animated film made by photographing a series of drawings

cartridge paper [ˈkɑːtrɪdʒ ˈpeɪpə] *noun* strong, thick, usually white paper used for drawing

casebound *or* **cased** [ˈkeɪsbaʊnd or keɪst] *adjective* enclosed in a hard cover; *the book was available in both casebound and paperback versions*

cash [kæʃ] **1** *noun* money in the form of notes and coins rather than cheques; **cash book** = book in which a record is kept of income and expenditure; **cash desk** = place where you go in a large shop to pay for your purchases; **cash flow** = movement of money in and out of a business; **cash on delivery (c.o.d)** = means that goods must be paid for as soon as they are received; **cash register** = machine which is used to record sales and to add up the amount of money to be paid; **cash value** = amount of money which anyone will pay for a something **2** *verb* **to cash in** = to exchange something for what it is worth in cash; **to cash in on** = use a situation to gain advantage for yourself

cassette [kəˈset] *noun* small rectangular plastic container for magnetic tape which can be used for recording and playing back speech or music

catalogue *US* **catalog** [ˈkætəlɒg] **1** *noun* list of contents arranged according to a system which aids retrieval; **catalogue card** = small card used for writing catalogue entries and stored in boxes or drawers in a manual catalogue **2** *verb* to make a detailed list of items; *to catalogue the holdings in a library*

catch letter [ˈkætʃ ˈletə] *noun* group of letters, usually three, which appears at the top of the page in reference books such as dictionaries or directories, to indicate the first or last word on that page or column

catchword index [ˈkætʃwɜːd ˈɪndeks] *noun* system which uses a keyword from a title or text to index an item

categorize [ˈkætɪgəraɪz] *verb* to put into a category

category [ˈkætɪgəri] *noun* division or class in a system used to group items according to their type

cater for [ˈkeɪtə] *verb* to provide what people need

CBT (a) = COMPUTER BASED TRAINING **(b)** = COMPUTER BASED TUTORIAL

cc. = CARBON COPY

CCTV = CLOSED CIRCUIT TELEVISION

CD-ROM ['siː 'diː rɒm] = COMPACT DISC - READ ONLY MEMORY

CD-I = COMPACT DISC INTERACTIVE

cease [siːs] *verb* to finish or stop doing something; **ceased publication** = no longer published, often used to describe serials

cedilla [sɪ'dɪlə] *noun* small mark, used in some languages under the letter c (ç), to soften it when pronounced

CEEFAX ['siːfæks] viewdata system used by the BBC for broadcasting textual information

censor ['sɛnsə] **1** *noun* person who decides what may be published, shown or distributed to the general public **2** *verb* to edit published material or films with regard to what is considered decent for selling, showing or distributing to the general public

censorship ['sɛnsəʃɪp] *noun* prohibition of the production, distribution or sale of items considered to be objectionable on political, religious or moral grounds

census ['sɛnsəs] *noun* official survey to count and analyse the population of a country

centimetre *US* **centimeter**
['sɛntɪmiːtə] *noun* one hundredth part of a metre

Central Statistical Office (CSO)
government department which produces national statistical publications in the UK

centralized ['sɛntrəlaɪzd] *adjective* placed in the middle; often as the most important or controlling feature; **centralized copying** = service for all users located in a central position; **centralized purchasing** = method of buying everything needed for an organization through a central purchasing office; **centralized records storage** = system used by organizations by which records are stored in a central unit but can be accessed by all members of the organization

century ['sɛntʃəri] *noun* period of one hundred years

ceremony ['sɛrɪməni] *noun* established order of formal ritual used to mark special occasions

certificate [sɜː'tɪfɪkət] *noun* official document given to confirm certain facts; *birth certificate; health certificate; degree certificate*

chain indexing ['tʃeɪn 'ɪndɛksɪŋ] *noun* alphabetical system of indexing using subject headings and hierarchical sub-headings

change [tʃeɪndʒ] **1** *noun* **(a)** coins or money given when a purchase is paid for with more money than is necessary **(b)** becoming different; **change agent** = catalyst which causes something to change **2** *verb* **(a)** to cause to become different **(b)** to become different

channel ['tʃænl] *noun* **(a)** spoken, written, or electronic means by which something is passed on **(b)** major interest area on the Internet that is easily accessible; *see also* INFORMATION CHANNEL **(c)** *(in graphics)* one layer of an image that can be worked on separately or which can be used to create special effects

chanop ['tʃænɒp] *noun* channel operator, person who controls the messages within a channel on the Internet

chapter ['tʃæptə] *noun* one of the divisions of a book or document

characteristic [kærəktə'rɪstɪk] *noun* typical feature of a person, place or thing

charge [tʃɑːdʒ] *verb* to ask people to pay for goods or services; **to charge out** = to make a record of a loan; **charging system** = any method of recording loans from a library

charter ['tʃɑːtə] *noun* official document giving certain rights to a person, organization or community

chartered librarian ['tʃɑːtəd laɪ'breərɪən] *noun* librarian who has successfully undertaken training and completed specific tasks, including a professional development report, according to the criteria set by the Library Association

charts [tʃɑːts] *noun* visual representation of information

check [tʃek] **1** *noun* inspection of something to make sure it is correct **2** *verb* **(a)** to look at something closely to make sure there are no mistakes; **check digit** = number added to a numeric code to enable a computer program to detect any errors in the code **(b)** **check in** = to record the receipt of something; **check out** = to record the loan of something

checklist ['tʃeklɪst] *noun* **(a)** list which acts as a reminder of things to be done or accounted for **(b)** list used to identify items from a minimum amount of information

cheque *US* **check** [tʃek] *noun* method of paying money from a bank account, by filling in a standard form and without using coins or notes

chief [tʃiːf] *adjective* most important person or part of something; *chief librarian*

Chief Information Officer (CIO)

person who has responsibility for the organization and control of information flow in a company or organization

children's book group ['tʃɪldrənz 'bʊk gruːp] *noun* unofficial group of interested people concerned to encourage the promotion of books to children

children's librarian ['tʃɪldrənz laɪ'breərɪən] *noun* librarian who specializes in the provision of library services to children

chip [tʃɪp] *noun* small piece of plastic containing a set of electronic instructions to work computers and other machines

chronological sequence [krɒnə'lɒdʒɪkl 'siːkwəns] *noun* arrangement by the order of the time at which events happened

CIO = CHIEF INFORMATION OFFICER

cipher ['saɪfə] *noun* system of writing secrets in code

circa (ca.) ['sɜːkə] about or approximately; used to show uncertainty especially about numbers or dates; *no-one is sure when the book was written, but it is circa 1760*

circular ['sɜːkjʊlə] *noun* letter or advertisement sent to a large number of people at the same time

circulation [sɜːkjʊ'leɪʃn] *noun* **(a)** number of copies of a newspaper or magazine sold each time it is produced **(b)** distribution of journals, books, etc., to people who may be interested in them; **circulation desk** = area of a library where the staff record the loans and returns of books; **circulation list** *see* DISTRIBUTION LIST **out of circulation** = not available for issue or reference

circumflex accent ['sɜːkəmfleks 'æksənt] *noun* small mark used in certain languages usually over the letter a (â), to show pronunciation

cite [saɪt] *verb* to quote or mention something especially as proof of your point

citation [saɪ'teɪʃn] *noun* formal word for quotation or reference; **citation index** = list of articles which quote a specific article; **citation order** = order of component parts when constructing a classification string

claim [kleɪm] *noun* **(a)** demand for something to which you think you have a right **(b)** statement which may be untrue but cannot be proved to be so

class [klɑːs] *noun* division of a classification scheme; **class entry** = entry in a catalogue under the class rather than the specific subject; **class list** = list of the items in a particular class, specially used in archival management

classify ['klæsɪfaɪ] *verb* **(a)** to place into a sequence according to a classification scheme **(b)** to restrict the distribution of a document for reasons of security

classification [klæsɪfɪ'keɪʃn] *noun* **(a)** division or category within a system according to their degrees of similarity **(b)** process of putting things into groups according to similarities or relationships; **classification number** *or* **classification mark** = number given to a classification heading in an information retrieval system; **classification system** *or* **classification scheme** = system of organizing things by dividing them into groups based on their similarities; *in libraries books are often arranged according to the Dewey decimal classification system;* **classification string** = sequence working from broad to narrow terms

classified ['klæsɪfaɪd] *adjective* **(a)** listed in a catalogue and given an identification; **classified catalogue** = list of contents arranged according to the classification system used to control them; **classified index** = list of holdings organized under general headings rather than one alphabetical sequence; *in a classified index, publishers would appear under the general heading 'Publishers' and not in the normal alphabetical order of their names* **(b)** having access restricted to certain named people; *the document was classified so only members of the government could read it*

clerical error ['klerɪkl 'erə] *noun* mistake made by an office worker

click [klɪk] *verb* to do the action needed to activate a computer mouse; *you must click three times to highlight the text*

client ['klaɪənt] *noun* **(a)** person using the services of a professional organization **(b)** computer that is connected to a network or the internet, or a computer that is using the resources of another computer; if you are connected to the internet, your computer is the client and runs client software *see also* GOPHER

clipboard ['klɪpbɔːd] *noun* small board with a clip at the top to hold paper, so that it can carried around and written on

closed [kləuzd] *adjective* not open; **closed access** *see* ACCESS **closed circuit television (CCTV)** = internal video system often used for security purposes or for relaying conferences, etc.; **closed question** = question which can only be answered by Yes or No; **closed shop** = business or factory in which all the workers are required to be members of a named trade union

closure ['kləuʒə] *noun* act of closing something down; *they are fighting against library closures*

clothbound ['klɒθbaund] *adjective* used to describe books which are covered in a specific type of material made originally from natural fibres, now often synthetic

cluster ['klʌstə] *noun* small group of similar things; **cluster sample** = method of sampling in statistical analysis, which compares small groups

C.O.D = CASH ON DELIVERY

code [kəud] *noun* group of numbers or letters used to identify something; *see also* BARCODE **code index** = any system which directs the user to information by use of a code number; **code of practice** = set of written rules describing how people in a particular job or profession are expected to behave; **dialling code** = numbers used in the telephone system to identify towns or countries or individual phone lines and so enable connection by phone or fax; **postcode** = system of letters and numbers used by the post office to identify towns and roads to aid the delivery of letters; (NOTE: in the USA known as zipcode)

coden ['kəʊdən] *noun* system of classification which combines numbers and letters

coffee table book ['kɒfi 'teɪbl 'bʊk] *noun* glossy book with many colour illustrations designed to be browsed through rather than read

coherent [kəʊ'hɪərənt] *adjective* clear and easy to understand

cohesion [kəʊ'hiːʒn] *noun* situation when all parts of an organization work together to form a united whole

coin [kɔɪn] **1** *noun* small, flat piece of metal made and stamped by a government to be used as money **2** *verb* **(a)** to make coins from metal **(b)** to invent words or phrases

collaborator [kə'læbəreɪtə] *noun* person who works with another to produce a literary or artistic work

collate [kə'leɪt] *verb* **(a)** to gather pieces of information together **(b)** to organize materials into a specific order and to check that they are complete

collected works [kə'ketɪd 'wɜːks] *noun* all the writings of one author collected and published in one volume

collection [kə'lekʃən] *noun* group of similar or related things; *the stock of a special library is called a collection*

collective [kə'lektɪv] *noun* group, such as audience, class, library

collective cataloguing [kə'lektɪv 'kætəlɒgɪŋ] *noun* system used to collect small items together and catalogue them under a heading or collective title which is given a class number for retrieval

colon ['kəʊlən] *noun* punctuation mark used to introduce lists; *the titles were: Rumplestiltskin, Cinderella and Little Red Riding Hood*

colour coding ['kʌlə 'kəʊdɪŋ] *noun* system of organizing items by labelling similar contents with the same colour; *all the pages on finance were colour coded by printing them on blue paper*

colour copying ['kʌlə 'kɒpiɪŋ] *noun* production of coloured copies of documents

colour supplement ['kʌlə 'sʌplɪmənt] *noun* **(a)** magazine which comes with the weekend newspapers **(b)** section of coloured illustrations in the centre of a book or magazine, often removable

column ['kɒləm] *noun* **(a)** vertical section of writing in a book, newspaper or magazine **(b)** regular section or article contributed to a newspaper or magazine by the same writer

combination [kɒmbɪ'neɪʃn] *noun* mixture of things which can be used together; **combination lock** = lock which can be opened using a pre-set order of numbers; **combination ordering** = system whereby several departments join together to order items; **combination storage** = system whereby several departments use communal storage facilities

come into force ['kʌm ɪntʊ 'fɔːs] *verb (of a law)* to become active and so must be obeyed

comic ['kɒmɪk] **1** *noun* **(a)** magazine for children, telling stories written with captions on strips of pictures **(b)** person who makes others laugh **2** *adjective* causing laughter

comma ['kɒmə] *noun* punctuation mark (,) used to show the natural breaks in written sentences

command [kə'mɑːnd] *verb* to order someone to do something

command papers [kə'mɑːnd 'peɪpəz] *noun* government publications containing the proceedings and proposals of government committees

comment ['kɒment] *noun* statement which expresses an opinion

commercial [kə'mɜːʃl] *adjective* related to buying and selling things; **commercial information supplier** = business which buys and sells information; **commercial gateway package** = electronic code which can be bought for a subscription and which allows access to online databases; **commercial records centre** = organization which keeps records of a business's financial dealings

commitment [kə'mɪtmənt] *noun* task which you undertake to do

communicate [kə'mjuːnɪkeɪt] *verb* to give information

communications [kəmjuːnɪ'keɪʃnz] *plural noun* systems by which information is transmitted; **communications audit** = survey of the methods used to send information around an organization; **communication channel** = method used to communicate with other people; *a communication channel can be written, spoken or electronic;* **communication skill** = ability to give information clearly and appropriately to other people

community [kə'mjuːnɪti] *noun* group of people who live in a particular area; *the residents of 15 European countries are members of a political and economic community called the European Union;* **community analysis** = survey of the different types of people who live in a community; **community information** = local information relating to a small geographical area; **community profiling** = drawing a picture of the needs of a particular community

compact disc (CD) ['kɒmpækt 'dɪsk] *noun* plastic disc coated so that it can record large amounts of data which can be read by laser; **compact disc player** = electronic device which uses lasers to read signals on a disc to produce very high quality reproduction; **compact disc interactive (CD-I)** = compact disc with electronic information which can be changed by the user; **compact disc - read only memory (CD-ROM)** = electronic method of storing large quantities of information which can be read by laser

company ['kʌmpəni] *noun* business which makes money by making or buying and selling goods, or providing a service; **company file** = file containing and collating information specific to a company

compatible [kəm'pætəbl] *adjective* working well together

competition [kɒmpə'tɪʃn] *noun* **(a)** situation where two or more companies with similar products try to persuade people to buy theirs **(b)** informal test of skill or ability; *the children's library ran a competition to see who read the most books during the school holiday*

competitive [kəm'petɪtɪv] *adjective* **(a)** liking to take part in competitions **(b)** offered at the same low or cheaper price than similar goods

competitor [kəm'petɪtə] *noun* **(a)** person who takes part in competitions **(b)** person or company that sells similar types of goods or services which can reduce the market for others

compile [kəm'paɪl] *verb* to put together different pieces of information in order to make them into one document

compilation [kɒmpɪ'leɪʃn] *noun* work produced by combining material from other books or documents

compiler [kəm'paɪlə] *noun* person who collects and edits material taken from various sources for publication as a new work

complementary [kɒmplɪ'mentəri] *adjective* fitting well together to make a harmonious whole

complete [kəm'pliːt] **1** *adjective* containing all the parts that are needed to make it whole **2** *verb* to finish doing or making something

completion date [kəm'pliːʃn 'deɪt] *noun* date by which something must be finished

compliance tests [kəm'plaɪəns 'tests] *noun* tests to ensure that something conforms to the regulations; **compliance certificate** = official statement that something has passed all the necessary tests for the regulations

complicated ['kɒmplɪkeɪtɪd] *adjective* difficult to understand

complimentary copy [kɒmplɪ'mentəri 'kɒpi] *noun* copy of a book or tickets, etc., given free as a favour, reward or mark of respect

component [kəm'pəʊnənt] *noun* part of something, used together with other parts to create a whole

compose [kəm'pəʊz] *verb* **(a)** to create a musical or literary work **(b)** to create something using concentration and skill; *he composed a letter of apology*

composer [kəm'pəʊzə] *noun* person who composes especially one who writes music; **composer entry** = entry usually for a musical composition in a catalogue under the name of the composer

composite subject ['kɒmpəzɪt 'sʌbdʒəkt] *noun* classification subject which consists of more than one element

composition [kɒmpə'zɪʃn] *noun* way the parts of something are put together

compound ['kɒmpaʊnd] *adjective* mixture of several components; **compound interest** = money that is paid as interest both on the original capital and also on the interest earned; **compound name** = name which has two or more parts joined by a hyphen, such as 'Mrs. Brownley-Smith'; **compound subject heading** = heading which consists of words which are always associated together, such as Treaty of Rome

comprehensive [kɒmprɪ'hensɪv] *adjective* covering all the possible aspects of a subject

compression of data ['kɒmpreʃn əv 'deɪtə] *noun* making blocks of data in a computer system smaller by removing spaces or reducing the memory space needed; compressed filenames end with .ZIP, .TAR, or .ARC

comprise [kəm'praɪz] *verb* to be made up of different parts; *overseas students comprise 10% of the college population*

CompuServe ['kɒmpjʊsɜːv] very large commercial online information service

computer [kəm'pjuːtə] *noun* electronic machine that processes data very quickly using a stored program; **computer-aided design (CAD)** = using a computer and a graphics terminal to work out designs; **computer-aided learning (CAL)** = form of self-study which can be done with the aid of specially written computer programs; **computer-assisted retrieval system** = automated method of finding information; **computer-based training (CBT)** = method of teaching which uses computers as the main teaching tool; **computer-based tutorials (CBT)** = software packages which teach the user how to use a program; **computer conferencing** = ways of communicating with groups of other people by means of electronic networks; **computer graphics** = visual display of information on a computer screen or printout, such as graphs and charts; **computer indexing** = automated methods of producing indexes; **computer language** = language made up of numbers and characters used to give instructions to a computer; **computer literate** = able to understand and use computers efficiently; **computer-readable** = (data) which can be read by a computer

computer services [kəm'pjuːtə 'sɜːvɪsɪz] *plural noun* **(a)** support services for computer users **(b)** work done on a computer for clients by experts

computerized [kəm'pjuːtəraɪzd] *adjective* changed from a manual system to an automated system

computing facilities [kəm'pjuːtɪŋ fə'sɪlɪtɪz] *plural noun* computers and the services which help the staff of an organization to use them

conceal [kən'siːl] *verb* to hide or keep secret

concentrate *verb* ['kɒnsəntreɪt] **(a)** to **concentrate on something** = to give something all your attention **(b)** to direct all the strength of something into one place

concept ['kɒnsept] *noun* idea or principle

concern [kən'sɜːn] *noun* **(a)** worry; *it is a cause for concern* **(b)** company or business used in the phrase 'a going concern'

concerned [kən'sɜːnd] *adjective* **to be concerned about** = to worry about and give attention to something which is important to you

conclusion [kən'kluːʒn] *noun* something drawn from what has gone before

concordance [kən'kɔːdəns] *noun* alphabetical index of all the words in a document; *a bible concordance*

concurrent [kən'kʌrənt] *adjective* happening at the same time

condition [kən'dɪʃn] *noun* something that must happen before something else is possible

conference ['kɒnfərəns] *noun* meeting often lasting several days where people discuss a common subject or shared interest

confidential [kɒnfɪ'denʃl] *adjective* spoken or written in secret and intended to be kept secret; *as this information is confidential you must not give it to anyone else*

configure [kən'fɪɡə] *verb* to plan computer hardware and software so that they will work together

confirm [kən'fɜːm] *verb* to state that something is definite or true; **to confirm in writing** = to write a letter to say that an agreement is definite

confiscate ['kɒnfɪskeɪt] *verb* to remove private property as a punishment; *the police are allowed to confiscate pornographic material*

conform [kən'fɔːm] *verb* **(a)** to behave according to accepted standards **(b)** to be in accordance with laws or regulations

congestion [kən'dʒestʃn] *noun* state where there is too much data for the capacity of the system

connect [kə'nekt] *verb* to join two things together

consecutive [kən'sekjʊtɪv] *adjective* happening one after the other without interruption

consequence ['kɒnsɪkwəns] *noun* result or effect of something happening

conservation [kɒnsə'veɪʃn] *noun* process of ensuring the survival of materials, such as library books, through repair and controlled storage conditions; **conservation unit** *or* **department** = group of people who take responsibility for the conservation of the stock

conservator ['kɒnsəveɪtə] *noun* person who works to conserve things

consider [kən'sɪdə] *verb* (a) to think carefully about something (b) to pay attention to someone's thoughts or feelings

considerably [kən'sɪdrəbli] *adverb* to a large amount or degree; *his work had improved considerably*

consignment [kən'saɪnmənt] *noun* delivery of goods

consist of [kən'sɪst ɒv] *phrasal verb* to be made up of; *the committee consists of librarians and information scientists*

consonant ['kɒnsənənt] *noun* all the letters of the roman alphabet except the five vowels (a,e,i,o,u)

consortium [kən'sɔːtiəm] *noun* group of companies or organizations working together for a common purpose

construct [kən'strʌkt] **1** *noun* complex idea, built up from various elements **2** *verb* to build or create something

consult [kən'sʌlt] *verb* to ask for advice or an opinion

consultant [kən'sʌltənt] *noun* expert who gives advice in a professional field

consultation [kɒnsʌl'teɪʃn] *noun* meeting where expert advice is sought and given; **consultation document** = document with proposals on which people's opinion is requested

consultative leadership style [kɒn'sʌltətɪv] *noun* way of leading a group by asking them for their opinions

consumables [kən'sjuːməblz] *noun* items necessary for work which get used up and need to be replaced, such as stationery

consumer [kən'sjuːmə] *noun* person who buys goods or uses services; **consumer characteristics** = specific features which distinguish one consumer group from another; **consumer demands** = what the consumer is asking for; **consumer group** = people in certain age or income or geographic groups for example, who would have a particular interest in specific good or services; **consumer needs** = services which consumers think are essential; **consumer targeting** = aiming the advertising of goods or services at specific groups of consumers

consumption [kən'sʌmpʃn] *noun* act of buying and using up goods, food, etc.

contact name ['kɒntækt 'neɪm] *noun* name of the person within particular department or service who may be contacted for information

contain [kən'teɪn] *verb* to hold or control things or feelings

contemporary [kən'temprəri] *adjective* happening or existing at the same time as something else

contents ['kɒntents] *noun* list of items that are contained within something else; **contents page** = page at the beginning of a document listing the things in it

context ['kɒntekst] *noun* background situation to an event which helps it to be understood; **out of context** = seen as an individual item not related to its background

contingency fund [kən'tɪndʒənsi 'fʌnd] *noun* sum of money put aside in case it is needed for an unexpected event; *see also* PLAN

continuation list [kəntɪnjʊ'eɪʃn 'lɪst] *noun* method of recording books and documents which are issued in parts and for which there are standing orders

continuous assessment [kən'tɪnjʊəs ə'sesmənt] *noun* system of assessing the progress of a student by coursework rather than by an examination at the end

contract ['kɒntrækt] *noun* written legal agreement

contrast ['kɒntrɑːst] *noun* big difference between two things which is clear when they are compared

contribute [kən'trɪbjuːt] *verb* to provide part of a whole; *to contribute an article to a magazine; to contribute money to help pay for something*

control [kən'trəʊl] **1** *noun* power or authority to make decisions about how something is managed **2** *verb* to organize something so that it works the way you want it to; **document control** = way documents are organized to provide easy retrieval

controlled term list [kən'trəʊld 'tɜːm lɪst] *noun* list of terms with fixed meanings to be used in cataloguing

controlled language [kən'trəʊld 'læŋgwɪdʒ] *noun* limited vocabulary used for compiling indexes or writing instructions, etc.

controversial [kɒntrə'vɜːʃl] *adjective* causing argument and disagreement

convenient [kən'viːnjənt] *adjective* easy to use and saving time or effort

convention [kən'venʃn] *noun* large meeting of an organization or political group

conventional [kən'venʃənəl] *adjective* conforming to what most people consider to be normal

convey [kən'veɪ] *verb* to make information or ideas known and understood

convince [kən'vɪns] *verb* to persuade other people to do or believe in something; **convincing argument** = set of ideas that has qualities that make people believe it

co-ordinate 1 [kəʊ'ɔːdɪnət] *noun* value from an axis on a graph used to locate a specific point **2** [kəʊ'ɔːdɪneɪt] *verb* to combine different items so that they work well together

co-ordinator [kəʊ'ɔːdɪneɪtə] *noun* person who ensures that people and activities work well together

copier ['kɒpjə] *see* PHOTOCOPIER

coping pattern *or* **coping strategy** ['kəʊpɪŋ] *noun* method of managing to deal with problems successfully

copy ['kɒpi] **1** *noun* **(a)** something that is made to look exactly the same as the original; **fair copy** = final version of work which has no mistakes; **hard copy** = printed version of work done on a computer; **master copy** = original document from which photocopies are made **(b)** text of a MS or advertising material; **copy editor** = person whose job is to check material ready for printing for accuracy and consistency of typeface, punctuation, etc.; *see also* TYPIST **2** *verb* to make something look exactly the same as the original

copyright ['kɒpɪraɪt] *noun* legal right, which the creator of an original work has, to only allow copying of the work with permission and sometimes on payment of royalties or copyright fee; **copyright fee** = money paid to the holder of a copyright for permission to use their work; **copyright infringement** = act of illegally copying or using a work which is covered by copyright law; **copyright law** = law which protects the rights to copyright; **copyright licence** = official permission to produce, copy and sell works which are protected by copyright law

corner ['kɔːnə] *verb* to gain control of a particular market

corporate ['kɔːpərət] *adjective* **(a)** owned by one or more large businesses **(b)** shared by all the members of an organization; **corporate author** = body such as a society, institution or government body which publishes documents, and whose name is used as the catalogue heading; **corporate body** *see* CORPORATION **corporate database** = source of electronic information shared by all members of the organization; **corporate headquarters** = head office of a corporation or large business

corporation [kɔːpəˈreɪʃn] *noun* large company or business

corpus of knowledge [ˈkɔːpəs əv ˈnɒlɪdʒ] *noun* large collection of the major works about a specific field of knowledge

correct [kəˈrekt] **1** *adjective* accurate and without mistakes **2** *verb* to mark mistakes so that they can be put right

correlation [kɒrəˈleɪʃn] *noun* close connections which influence each other

correspondence [kɒrɪˈspɒndəns] *noun* letters sent and received

correspondent [kɒrɪˈspɒndənt] *noun* **(a)** someone who writes or receives letters **(b)** television or newspaper reporter on specialist subjects

corrupt [kəˈrʌpt] *adjective* **(a)** dishonest or illegal person or regime **(b)** containing errors; *corrupt computer data*

cost [kɒst] *noun* amount of money needed to buy, do or make something; **cost benefits** = level of advantage gained for a given level of expenditure; **cost-benefit analysis** = investigation of the level of benefit gained to decide whether it is worth the expenditure

cost-effective [ˈkɒstɪˈfektɪv] *adjective* saving money in comparison with the amount of time or money spent

costly [ˈkɒstli] *adjective* very expensive in time, effort or money

count [kaunt] *verb* to add up the items in a group to see how many there are; **to keep count** = to keep a record of how many or how often things are done

counter [ˈkauntə] *see* CIRCULATION DESK

country code [ˈkʌntri ˈkaud] *noun* last part of an e-mail address which indicates the country of origin

coursework [ˈkɔːswɜːk] *noun* assignments which are done as part of a course

cover [ˈkʌvə] *noun* something which is put over an object to protect it; *the cover of a book is the outside paper or board;* **cover date** = date which appears on the cover of a publication such as a pamphlet

coverage [ˈkʌvrɪdʒ] *noun* amount of time or space given to a topic by the media

crash [kræʃ] *verb* **(a)** to come to a sudden stop as a result of an accident **(b)** *(of computer systems)* to stop working

CRC [ˈsiː ɑː ˈsiː] = CAMERA READY COPY

create [krɪˈeɪt] *verb* to make something new; **create a file** = in computing, to open a new file

credit [ˈkredɪt] **1** *noun* **(a)** system of paying for goods some time after you have bought them; **credit card** = plastic card issued by banks to their customers which allows them to buy goods on credit or to borrow money; **credit limit** = amount of money which is the maximum you can borrow at one time; **credit note** = issued by a company stating that you can replace faulty goods with goods to the same value; **in credit** = to have money in the bank; **on credit** = to buy goods and pay for them later **(b)** acknowledgement of something positive; *she gave them credit for their good work* **2** *verb* to acknowledge something positive

creditworthy [ˈkredɪtwɜːði] *adjective* person or organization which has a good record of paying their bills

crime [kraɪm] *noun* behaviour which breaks the law

crime fiction ['kraɪm 'fɪkʃn] *noun* type of writing about imaginary crimes and detectives

Crime Writers Association

organization in the UK which is responsible for the administration of several annual literary awards

critic ['krɪtɪk] *noun* person who writes reviews or gives opinions about books, films, music and art

critical ['krɪtɪkəl] *adjective* **(a)** expressing severe opinions about someone or something **(b)** very serious or dangerous

critical factor ['krɪtɪkəl 'fæktə] *noun* factor in a situation which must be considered very carefully because it can have serious effects

criticism ['krɪtɪsɪzm] *noun* serious judgement or an expression of disapproval of something

CRLIS = CURRENT RESEARCH IN LIBRARY AND INFORMATION SCIENCE

crosscheck ['krɒstʃek] *verb* to evaluate the results of an investigation by checking it by an alternative method

cross-reference [krɒs'refərəns] *noun* footnote in a document which tells you that there is other relevant information in another part of the document

cross-section ['krɒssekʃən] *noun* representative sample of a group of people or things

crucial ['kruːʃl] *adjective* extremely important or essential

culture ['kʌltʃə] *noun* ideas, customs and artistic productions of any society; **organizational culture** = expectations and conventions in the management of an organization

cumulative index ['kjuːmjʊlətɪv 'ɪndeks] *noun* index which is built up by additions to all the previously published entries, at specified times, such as monthly or annually

curator [kjʊ'reɪtə] *noun* person responsible for managing a museum or art gallery, etc.

current ['kʌrənt] *adjective* happening at the present time; **current awareness** = knowing what is the most up-to-date information on specific subjects; **current awareness service** = organization or individual who notifies customers of the most up-to-date information in their field; **current journal** *or* **serial** = latest edition of a regular publication

Current Research in Library and Information Science (CRLIS)

quarterly journal with abstracts of current research

curriculum [kə'rɪkjʊləm] *noun* all the courses that are taught in a school or college; **core curriculum** = courses in a school or college which are compulsory for all students

curriculum vitae (CV) [kə'rɪkjʊləm 'viːtaɪ] brief summary of your personal details, education and career

cursor ['kɜːsə] *noun* mark on a computer screen which shows where the next character you type will appear; the cursor can be moved around with a mouse or arrow keys on a keyboard

customer ['kʌstəmə] *noun* anyone who buys a product or service; **customer account** = system whereby a customer can buy things and pay for them at set times, such as a bill for on-line searches which is paid monthly; **customer details** = record of the transactions with any one particular customer; *see also* FILE

customize ['kʌstəmaɪz] *verb* to adapt something to a particular persons requirements; **customized interface** = computer system which has been adapted to a particular user's needs

cut and paste ['kʌt nd 'peɪst] *phrase* to select a section of text or an image, cut it from the original document and then paste it into a new document; normally you cut by selecting the Edit/Cut menu option and paste by selecting the Edit/Paste menu option

cutting ['kʌtɪŋ] *noun* item cut from a newspaper or periodical; (NOTE: US equivalent is **clipping**)

CV [si: 'vi:] = CURRICULUM VITAE

cybernetics [saɪbə'netɪks] *noun* study of how machines can be made to imitate human actions

cyberspace ['saɪbəspeɪs] *noun* world in which computers and people interact, normally via the internet; *we met by writing to each other on the world wide web in cyberspace*

cycle ['saɪkl] *noun* series of events that is repeated again and again always in the same order

Dd

dagger (†) ['dægə] *noun* **(a)** second reference mark for footnotes **(b)** when placed before an English name it signifies 'dead'

daily ['deɪli] **1** *adjective* happening every day **2** *noun* newspaper published every weekday

daisy wheel printer ['deɪzi wiːl 'prɪntə] *noun* device for printing work from a computer, which uses a wheel-shaped printing head with the characters at the ends of spokes

damages ['dæmɪdʒɪz] *noun* money that is paid by court order to someone to compensate for harm done to them or their reputation

darkroom ['dɑːkruːm] *noun* room protected from daylight and using infrared light only, where films can be developed and printed

dash [dæʃ] *noun* punctuation mark (-) that is a short horizontal line used to mark off a section of a sentence

data ['deɪtə] *noun* information usually in the form of facts or statistics which can be analysed; **data acquisition** *or* **collection** = gathering data about a particular subject; **data analysis** = drawing conclusions from data; **data bank** = (i) large amount of data stored in a structured way; (ii) personal records stored on a computer; **data disk** = computer disk used for storing information; **data entry** = method of putting data into a computer; **data file** = computer file storing data rather than program instructions; **data management** *or* **data administration** = maintenance and updating of a database; **data network** = system which allows transmission of data to a number of linked computers; **data preparation** *or* **handling** = conversion of data into machine readable format; **data protection** = methods of making sure that data is kept secret and confidential; **Data Protection Act (1984)** = government Act in the UK which gives protection to people whose personal details are stored on a computer; any organization collecting personal data on mechanized files is required to register with the ;Data Protection Registry **data retrieval** = process of searching, selecting and reading data from a stored file; **data security** *see* DATA PROTECTION **data services** = public services, such as telephones, which allow data to be transmitted

database ['deɪtəbeɪs] *noun* **(a)** software which enables the user to organize data for easy retrieval **(b)** collection of data stored in a computer which can be easily and quickly retrieved; **database administrator** = person who undertakes responsibility for the control of a database; **database management system (DBMS)** = series of computer programs which allows the user to create and maintain databases

DATASTAR Swiss-based online database host

date [deɪt] **1** *noun* particular day in the calendar; *1st January is a date well known as the start of a new year* **2** *verb* to date a document is to record on it the date when it is written or received; **backdated** = with the date written earlier than the current day's date

date label ['deɪt 'leɪbl] *noun* label pasted in a library book so that the date for return can be stamped on it

day [deɪ] *noun* one 24-hour period of time; **day off** = day when you do not have to go to work; **day release** = system of training by which workers are allowed a regular day each week to attend college

DBMS = DATABASE MANAGEMENT SYSTEM

deadline ['dedlaɪn] *noun* stated time or date by which work must be finished

deadlock ['dedlɒk] *noun* position in an argument when neither side is willing to give in, so no agreement can be reached

deal [diːl] *noun* arrangement or agreement in business

dealer ['diːlə] *noun* person whose business is buying or selling things

debate [dɪ'beɪt] **1** *noun* meeting about a question in which at least two opinions are expressed **2** *verb* to discuss something, considering arguments for and against it

decade ['dekeɪd] *noun* period of ten years especially one that begins with a year ending in 0, such as the 1990s

decay [dɪ'keɪ] *verb* to become old, rotten, weak or corrupt

decentralize [diː'sentrəlaɪz] *verb* to move departments away from the main administrative area and to give more power to local branches

decide [dɪ'saɪd] *verb* to choose to follow a certain course of action

decimal ['desɪml] *adjective* counting in base ten; **decimal classification system** = system of organizing items using a numerical order in base ten

decipher [dɪ'saɪfə] *verb* to work out what something means, even if it is difficult to read or understand

decision [dɪ'sɪʒn] *noun* choice about a course of action

declassify [diː'klæsɪfaɪ] *verb* to state that information or documents no longer have security classification and are not secret or confidential

decode [diː'kəud] *verb* to change information which has been written in code into ordinary language

decrease **1** ['diːkriːs] *noun* reduction in the size or quantity of something **2** [diː'kriːs] *verb* to make something smaller

dedicated ['dedɪkeɪtɪd] *adjective* reserved for a particular use; **dedicated channel** = communications channel reserved for a particular use or user

dedication [dedɪ'keɪʃn] *noun* words used to offer a book, work or performance to honour someone

deduct [dɪ'dʌkt] *verb* to remove something from a total

deduction [dɪ'dʌkʃn] *noun* amount removed from a total sum

de facto [diː'fæktəu] *adjective* accepted as fact by reason of usage; *he was the de facto ruler although he had no legal right to the position*

default [dɪ'fɒlt] *noun* failure to carry out a contract; **default setting** = setting which a computer or printer will use if no other instructions are given

defect ['di:fekt] *noun* fault in a machine or a person

defective [dɪ'fektɪv] *adjective* not working properly

define [dɪ'faɪn] *verb* to explain the meaning of something

definition [defɪ'nɪʃn] *noun* statement of meaning, especially in a dictionary

degree of automation [dɪ'gri: ɒv ɔːtə'meɪʃn] *noun* level of use of electronic machines

de jure ['deɪ 'dʒʊəri] *adjective* by legal right, though not necessarily in fact

delay [dɪ'leɪ] **1** *noun* cause of something happening later than planned **2** *verb* to cause something to happen later than planned

delegate 1 ['delɪgət] *noun* person elected to speak for or represent others **2** ['delɪgeɪt] *verb* to give some of your responsibility to others for a period of time

delegation [delɪ'geɪʃn] *noun* **(a)** group of delegates **(b)** act of delegating

delete [dɪ'li:t] *verb* to remove information that has been written down or stored in a computer

Delphes French network of economic and business information produced by the French Chambers of Commerce

DELPHI commercial online information service

demand [dɪ'mɑːnd] **1** *noun* number of people wanting to buy something **2** *verb* to ask for something in a forceful way

demarcation [di:mɑː'keɪʃn] *noun* boundary or limit separating ideas or groups

democracy [dɪ'mɒkrəsi] *noun* system of government in which the members of the state elect their leaders

demography [dɪ'mɒgrəfi] *noun* study of changes in population

Demon Internet Systems UK ISP company that provides access to the internet for individuals and companies

demonstrate ['demənstreɪt] *verb* **(a)** to show people how to do something **(b)** to make an idea clear to people **(c)** to show that you have a skill or quality

density ['densɪti] *noun* level of darkness of an image

deny access [dɪ'naɪ 'ækses] *verb* **(a)** to refuse permission to enter **(b)** to refuse permission to use an information system

departmental information system [dɪpɑːt'mentl ɪnfə'meɪʃn 'sɪstəm] *noun* system of organizing information specific to one department

dependency level [dɪ'pendənsi 'levl] *noun* degree to which a person is dependent on another person or a system

dependent on [dɪ'pendənt 'ɒn] *adjective* needing something in order to survive or function

deploy [dɪ'plɔɪ] *verb* to place people or resources where they will be most useful

deposit [dɪ'pɒzɪt] *noun* **(a)** amount of money paid in part payment **(b)** money paid as surety against a loan which is returned when the item in question is returned undamaged **(c)** documents placed in a record office for safe keeping **(d)** legal requirement for one copy of any published book to be sent to certain libraries which are known as national deposit libraries

depth indexing ['depθ 'ɪndeksɪŋ] *noun* indexing different subjects within the body of the document

deputation [depjʊ'teɪʃn] *noun* group of people who act as representatives of a larger group

descending order [dɪ'sendɪŋ 'ɔːdə] *noun* organization of things so that each item is smaller than the one before it or comes before it in an established order; *they were arranged in descending order from Z to A*

describe [dɪ'skraɪb] *verb* to say in words what something or someone is like

description [dɪ'skrɪpʃn] *noun* words which show what something is like

descriptive list [dɪ'skrɪptɪv 'lɪst] *noun* list of holdings with a brief description of their contents to enable users to decide which they want

descriptor [dɪ'skrɪptə] *noun* code or symbol given to a document to identify it for the purposes of retrieval

desiderata [dɪzɪdə'rɑːtə] *plural noun* list of books and documents required

design [dɪ'zaɪn] *verb* to plan what something new will be like

desk [desk] *noun* writing table in an office or study; **desk accessory** = device for use on a desk such as desk light, desktop computer, etc.; **desk diary** *see* DIARY

desktop computer ['desktɒp kəm'pjuːtə] *noun* computer, usually with a keyboard and monitor, which is small enough to be used on a desk; **desktop publishing (DTP)** = design and layout of text and graphics using a small computer with a specific software application package and a printer

destination [destɪ'neɪʃn] *noun* **(a)** place where something is sent **(b)** location where data is sent on a network

detail ['diːteɪl] **1** *noun* small particular **2** *verb* to list or give full information about things

detailed enquiry ['diːteɪld ɪn'kwaɪri] *noun* investigation which lists all the small features of an event or situation

deteriorate [dɪ'tɪəriəreɪt] *verb* to become worse

determine [dɪ'tɜːmɪn] *verb* **(a)** to discover the truth about something **(b)** to control what happens; *to determine prices* **(c)** to decide or settle a discussion

develop [dɪ'veləp] *verb* to plan and produce items, ideas, etc.

developed country [dɪ'veləpt 'kʌntri] *noun* rich industrialized country

developing country [dɪ'veləpɪŋ 'kʌntri] *noun* country where industry is not yet well developed but which is moving towards it

developing market [dɪ'veləpɪŋ 'mɑːkɪt] *noun* area where the sale of goods or services is increasing

development strategy [dɪ'veləpmənt 'strætɪdʒi] *noun* policies and methods for future development

devise [dɪ'vaɪz] *verb* to design or work out a plan or system

Dewey decimal classification system ['djuːi 'desɪml] *noun* widely used system, based on a numerical structure, used in libraries for the control of stock original devised by an American librarian Melvil Dewey and copyrighted in 1876

diagnose [daɪəg'nəʊz] *verb* to identify what is wrong

diagnosis [daɪəg'nəʊsɪs] *noun* discovery of the reason for a fault or problem

diagonal [daɪ'ægənl] *adjective* slanting line from a top corner to the opposite bottom corner

dial ['daɪəl] *verb* to use a series of numbers to make a telephone connection; *see also* CODE, TONE

DIALOG online database host

dialogue ['daɪəlɒg] *noun* **(a)** written conversation in a book or play **(b)** exchange of ideas of opinions especially between those with different viewpoints

DIANE *see* EURONET

diary ['daɪəri] *noun* **(a)** detailed daily record of the events in a person's life written in a book **(b)** small book with dates and blank spaces used to record appointments, etc.; **desk diary** = book with blank pages organized by dates, which can be kept on a desk, to record appointments and commitments, etc.

dictate [dɪk'teɪt] *verb* to speak words for someone to write down or a machine to record

dictionary ['dɪkʃənri] *noun* book or compact disc containing the words of a language arranged alphabetically with their meanings; **dictionary catalogue** = catalogue in which all the entries (author, title, subject, etc.) are placed in one alphabetical sequence

Dictionary of National Biography (DNB) ['dɪkʃənri ʌv 'næʃənl baɪ'ɒɡrəfi] alphabetical listing of famous people within a country, with brief biographical details

didactic [daɪ'dæktɪk] *adjective* (speech or writing) intended to teach especially on moral issues

differ ['dɪfə] *verb* to be unlike something else in some way

differential [dɪfə'renʃl] *noun* difference between two values in a scale

difficulty ['dɪfɪkʌlti] *noun* problem

digit ['dɪdʒɪt] *noun* symbol for any of the numbers from 0 to 9

digital ['dɪdʒɪtəl] *adjective* representing physical quantities in numerical form

digitize ['dɪdʒɪtaɪz] *verb* to change analogue movement into numerical data which can be processed by a computer

diploma [dɪ'pləumə] *noun* official statement that someone has successfully completed a course or passed an examination

diplomacy [dɪ'pləuməsi] *noun* **(a)** management of relations between countries **(b)** tact in dealings with people; *librarians sometimes need to use diplomacy when dealing with library users*

direct access [daɪ'rekt 'æksəs] *noun* ability to use information without the need for an intermediary person

direct entry [daɪ'rekt 'entri] *noun* index entry in which a multi-word subject uses its normal word order instead of an inverted word sequence

director [daɪ'rektə] *noun* **(a)** top person in the management of a group, company organization **(b)** person who directs a play or film

directorate [daɪ'rektərət] *noun* board of directors of a company

directory [daɪ'rektəri] *noun* book or database which lists the names and details of people or companies in a specific geographical or subject area, such as a telephone directory

disadvantage [dɪsəd'vɑːntɪdʒ] *noun* factor in a situation which causes problems

disaster [dɪ'zɑːstə] *noun* unexpected event which causes a lot of damage or suffering; **disaster plan** = plan for what to do if a disaster occurs

discharge [dɪs'tʃɑːdʒ] *verb* to cancel the record of a loan from a library when the book or document is returned

discipline ['dɪsɪplɪn] *noun* field of academic study

discount ['dɪskaʊnt] *noun* reduction in the price of something

discover [dɪs'kʌvə] *verb* to find something out especially if it was unknown before

discovery [dɪs'kʌvəri] *noun* finding of something that nobody knew about previously

discretion [dɪs'kreʃn] *noun* ability to deal with confidential situations or information without causing embarrassment; **at someone's discretion** = when something is done because of someone's decision and not according to a fixed rule

discretionary income [dɪs'krʃənəri 'ɪŋkəm] *noun* money which is allocated to a person or a department according to the decisions of people in authority and not according to fixed rules

discussion [dɪs'kʌʃn] *noun* serious conversation; **under discussion** = topic which is being talked about but which has still to be decided

disk [dɪsk] *noun* flat, round, plastic device coated with magnetised material which can be used to store information readable by a computer; **disk drive** = slot in which to place a floppy disk so that a computer to read the data on it; **Disk Operating System (DOS)** = software which controls a computer's use of other programs; **hard disk** = electronic circuit which will store a large amount of data and which cannot usually be removed from the computer

diskette *or* **floppy disk** [dɪ'sket or 'flɒpi 'dɪsk] *noun* small portable lightweight disk which can be used in personal computers

display [dɪs'pleɪ] **1** *noun* exhibition for public viewing **2** *verb* to set up or arrange to be viewed

display case [dɪs'pleɪ 'keɪs] *noun* glass box which protects items but allows them to be seen

display stand [dɪs'pleɪ 'stænd] *noun* portable board which can be set on legs and used to display information; *see also* PACK

disposal list [dɪs'pəʊzəl 'lɪst] *noun* used in archive management to give instructions for the disposal of documents such as destruction or temporary or permanent preservation

dispose of [dɪs'pəʊz 'ɒv] *verb* to throw away or destroy

dispute [dɪs'pjuːt] *noun* disagreement or quarrel

disseminate [dɪs'semɪneɪt] *verb* to spread news and information widely

dissertation [dɪsə'teɪʃn] *noun* written account of research

distance learning ['dɪstəns 'lɜːnɪŋ] *noun* courses which can be studied at home and sent to a tutor by mail or e-mail

distort [dɪ'stɔːt] *verb* to change into a false or dishonest account of something

distribution [dɪstrɪ'bjuːʃn] *noun* delivery of goods or information to people or organizations; **distribution channel** = method by which things are sent to other people; *email, postal systems, the railway, or retail shops are all distribution channels;* **distribution list** = list of people to whom copies of a document should be sent

diversity [daɪ'vɜːsɪti] *noun* range of variation within a group of people or situations

division [dɪ'vɪʒn] *noun* department in a large organization

DNB ['diː en 'biː] = DICTIONARY OF NATIONAL BIOGRAPHY

document ['dɒkjʊmənt] *noun* any form of information in printed or electronic form, such as maps, manuscripts, computer software; *see also* CONTROL **document address class** = number or symbol indicating location of a document in store; **document image processing** *see* SCANNING **document retrieval system** = system which produces a complete copy of a document rather than a citation or reference; **document supply centre** = division of a lending library, which supplies copies of documents often through an Inter Library Loan System

documentary [dɒkjʊ'mentəri] **1** *noun* film relating true facts rather than telling a story **2** *adjective* based on written evidence in documents

domain [də'meɪn] *noun* part of an e-mail address after the

donation [dəʊ'neɪʃn] *noun* gift of something especially for a good cause

DOS [dɒs] = DISK OPERATING SYSTEM

dot matrix printer [dɒt 'meɪtrɪks 'prɪntə] *noun* printer which uses a series of closely spaced dots and prints out line by line

double check ['dʌbl 'tʃek] *verb* to check something a second time to be sure of its accuracy

double dagger ['dʌbl 'dægə] *noun* third reference mark for footnotes (dd)

double-sided ['dʌbl 'saɪdɪd] *adjective* can be used on both sides; *a double-sided disk*

down [daʊn] *adjective* used to indicate that a computer is out of action; **down cursor key** = key on a computer keyboard, marked with an arrow, which moves the cursor in a downward direction

download [daʊn'ləʊd] *verb* to move information from one electronic source to another storage device; *he downloaded the records from the main database to his own personal database*

downtime ['daʊntaɪm] *noun* time that a computer is unusable

draft [drɑːft] *noun* **(a)** rough form of something written, drawn or planned **(b)** written order for money to be transferred from one bank to another

draft copy ['drɑːft 'kɒpi] *noun* first copy of a book or document which will be changed before it becomes the final version

drag [dræg] *verb* to pull slowly along or down; *the menu on a computer can be dragged down using the mouse*

draw a conclusion ['drɔː ə kən'kluːʒn] *verb* to analyse information and decide what it means

draw up ['drɔː 'ʌp] *verb* to prepare and write out a document

drawback ['drɔːbæk] *noun* aspect of something which is a problem and makes it less acceptable

drawing pin ['drɔːɪŋ 'pɪn] *noun* pin with a flat head used for attaching notices to a board

drill [drɪl] *verb* way of learning using constant repetition

DTP = DESKTOP PUBLISHING

due [djuː] *adjective* expected to arrive or happen at a particular time; **due to** − as a result of; **due date** = date at which something on loan should be returned

dues [djuːz] *plural noun* money which is paid regularly to an organization to which you belong

dummy run ['dʌmi 'rʌn] *noun* trial or test procedure to see if something works properly

duplexing ['djuːpleksɪŋ] *noun* sending information in two directions simultaneously

duplicate 1 ['dju:plɪkət] *noun* extra copy of a book or document already in stock; **duplicate entry** = index entry of the same subject matter under two headings; **duplicate title** = used of a reprint which contains a copy of the original title page as well as its own **2** ['dju:plɪkeɪt] *verb* to make an exact copy of something; *see also* MACHINE

dust cover ['dʌst 'kʌvə] *noun* paper cover, often illustrated, which is placed over the hard binding of a book; also called dust jacket or wrapper

Ee

earmark [ˈɪəmɑːk] *verb* to put on one side for a particular purpose

ecclesiastical library [ɪkliːzɪˈæstɪkl ˈlaɪbri] *see* LIBRARY

Ecu = EUROPEAN CURRENCY UNIT

edit [ˈedɪt] *verb* **(a)** to change, correct or modify text or films **(b)** to prepare a document for publication

edited [ˈedɪtɪd] *adjective* work consisting of one or several separate items prepared for publication by someone other than the author

edition [ɪˈdɪʃn] *noun* particular version of a book, magazine, newspaper or TV or radio programme which is printed or broadcast at one time

editor [ˈedɪtə] *noun* **(a)** person who changes or corrects text or films **(b)** person in charge of publishing a newspaper or magazine who makes the final decisions about the contents and format

editorial [edɪˈtɔːriəl] *noun* main article in a newspaper, written by the editor; *see also* BOARD

educational discount [edjuːˈkeɪʃnl ˈdɪskaʊnt] *noun* amount of money taken off the price of goods when they are bought for teaching purposes

Educational Resources Information Centre (ERIC) US research centre which catalogues, abstracts and indexes educational research documents; also available on-line

educational software [edjuːˈkeɪʃnl ˈsɒftweə] *noun* set of computer programs designed to meet educational needs

effective [ɪˈfektɪv] *adjective* producing the desired results

efficient [ɪˈfɪʃənt] *adjective* using the minimum expenditure of effort and money

EIC = EUROPEAN INFORMATION CENTRES

election [ɪˈlekʃn] *noun* process of choosing representatives by voting

electoral register [ɪˈlektərəl ˈredʒɪstə] *noun* list of names of people who are eligible to vote in an election

electrical [ɪˈlektrɪkəl] *adjective* referring to anything which works by electricity

electrician [elekˈtrɪʃn] *noun* person who understands and works with electricity

electronic [ɪlekˈtrɒnɪk] *adjective* worked by or controlling electron flow; **electronic conference** = way of discussing a topic with several people simultaneously by using a computer network; **electronic funds transfer (EFT)** = using computers to transfer money to and from banks; **electronic journal** = journal that is available electronically or texts of journals transmitted via a computer network; **electronic library** = texts and documents which are available through a computer network; **electronic mail (e-mail)** = sending and receiving written messages over the telephone network using a modem and computer to read them; **electronic mailbox** = system for holding messages until the receiver is ready to use the computer to access them; **electronic point of sale** *see* EPOS **electronic publishing** = use of computer packages and laser printers to produce printed documents; **electronic record** = details of an item stored in a computer

element ['elɪmənt] *noun* **(a)** one of the single parts which make up a whole **(b)** basic and most important part of a subject

eliminate [ɪ'lɪmɪneɪt] *verb* to remove something completely

élite [eɪ'liːt] *noun* group of the most powerful, rich or talented people in a society

élitism [eɪ'liːtɪzm] *noun* belief that a society should be ruled by a group who are considered to be superior to others

e-mail ['iːmeɪl] = ELECTRONIC MAIL **e-mail address** = details of how you can be contacted through an electronic mailing system

embark on [ɪm'bɑːk 'ɒn] *verb* to start something new

emerge [ɪ'mɜːdʒ] *verb* to come out at the end of a place, experience or situation

emphasis ['emfəsɪs] *noun* extra force given to a word or activity in order to make it seem important

emphasize ['emfəsaɪz] *verb* to show that something is particularly important

empirical research [em'pɪrɪkl rɪ'sɜːtʃ] *noun* research based on experiments

employee [emplɔɪ'iː] *noun* someone who is paid by another person for the work they do

employer [ɪm'plɔɪə] *noun* someone who provides work for other people, and pays them to do it

employment [ɪm'plɔɪmənt] *noun* paid work; **employment agency** = organization that earns money by helping other people to find work; **employment statistics** = facts and figures about the number of people in and out of work in a society, often published as a government document

enable [ɪ'neɪbl] *verb* to make it possible for something to happen

encapsulate [ɪn'kæpsjʊleɪt] *verb* to capture the main points of something in a very small space or within a single object or event

enclose [ɪn'kləʊz] *verb* to send something in the same envelope

encode [en'kəʊd] *verb* to translate plain text into a code; (NOTE: in US English **encipher** or **encrypt** is used)

encourage [ɪn'kʌrɪdʒ] *verb* to support someone or something actively

encyclopaedia [ɪnsaɪklə'piːdiə] *noun* book or set of books in which facts of general knowledge are arranged in alphabetical order

end user ['end 'juːzə] *noun* user of a computer program or any electronic system

ending ['endɪŋ] *noun* final part of a document

endless ['endləs] *adjective* having no ending

endorse [ɪn'dɔːs] *verb* **(a)** to sign something on the back **(b)** to show approval or support of people or events

endpaper ['endpeɪpə] *noun* blank piece of thicker paper inserted as part of the binding; one half is pasted to the cover and the other half is partly pasted to the first or last page of the book

energy ['enədʒi] *noun* power, such as electricity, that makes machines work; **energy-saving devices** = machines that use a minimum of power

engineer [endʒɪ'nɪə] **1** *noun* person who understands how to design and construct machines, electrical devices, roads and bridges **2** *verb* to cause something to happen in a clever and indirect way

engrave [ɪn'ɡreɪv] *verb* to cut a design on metal, wood or glass

enhance [ɪn'hɑːns] *verb* to make clearer; *to enhance a photograph*

enhancement [ɪn'hɑːnsmənt] *noun* add-on device which improves the performance of a computer and so adds value

enlarge [ɪn'lɑːdʒ] *verb* to make bigger

enlargement [ɪn'lɑːdʒmənt] *noun* process or the result of making something bigger

enquiry [ɪŋ'kwaɪri] *noun* request for information; **enquiry desk** = desk in a library or information centre where people can ask for information; **enquiry service** = system for providing answers to enquiries; **enquiry work** = work of a reference librarian in finding answers to questions; (NOTE: also spelt **inquiry**)

enrich [ɪn'rɪtʃ] *verb* to improve by adding something

enrol *or US* **enroll** [ɪn'rəʊl] *verb* to sign for yourself or someone else to join a group

ensure [ɪn'ʃʊə] *verb* to make certain that something happens

enter ['entə] *verb* **(a)** to go into a room or building **(b)** to write information into to a

book or computer **(c)** to cause a computer to activate instructions

enthusiasm [ɪn'θjuːzɪæzəm] *noun* great eagerness to do something

entity ['entɪti] *noun* something which exists in its own right separate from other things

entry ['entri] *noun* single record in a database, dictionary or catalogue; **entry word** = first word of an entry in a catalogue except the articles 'the', 'a', 'an'

envelope ['envələʊp] *noun* paper cover which can be sealed and used to send a letter through the post; **airmail envelope** = lightweight envelope usually of blue paper with a red white and blue striped edging used for sending letters by air to foreign countries; **envelope window** = see-through panel in an envelope so that the address on the letter can be seen

environment [ɪn'vaɪərənmənt] *noun* natural world of land, sea, air, plants and animals; **personal environment** = everything around you that affects your daily life

environmental planning
[ɪnvaɪərən'mentl 'plænɪŋ] *noun* making decisions about the use of the environment to provide the least damage for human and natural inhabitants

ephemera [ɪ'fiːmərə] *noun* items relating to a specific event or topic which are designed to last for a very short time, such as theatre programmes, pamphlets, newspaper cuttings

epic ['epɪk] *noun* **(a)** long poem telling stories of brave actions of gods, people or the early history of a nation **(b)** long book or film telling an epic type of story

epithet ['epɪθet] *noun* descriptive additional name used to describe particular attributes of a person

epitome [ɪˈpɪtəmi] *noun* essential matter of a work contained in an abridged version of a work

EPOS [ˈiːpɒs] = ELECTRONIC POINT OF SALE such as a supermarket checkout where goods are paid for

equal [ˈiːkwəl] *adjective* same in size, amount or degree

equalize [ˈiːkwəlaɪz] *verb* to make equal

equate [ɪˈkweɪt] *verb* to say that you believe one thing is the same as another

equipment [ɪˈkwɪpmənt] *noun* machinery and furniture needed to make an office or factory work

equitable [ˈekwɪtəbl] *adjective* indicating that everyone and everything is treated equally

equivalent [ɪˈkwɪvələnt] *adjective* having the same value

era [ˈɪərə] *noun* period of time seen as a single unit because it has a common feature; *the era of apartheid in South Africa*

erase [ɪˈreɪz] *verb* **(a)** to remove marks from paper **(b)** to remove by deleting from a computer

eraser [ɪˈreɪzə] *noun* piece of rubber which is used to remove pencil marks from paper

ergonomics [ɜːgəˈnɒmɪks] *noun* study of people at work with the aim to improve safety and make machines and equipment easier to use

ergonomist [ɜːˈgɒnəmɪst] *noun* scientist who studies people at work and tries to improve their working conditions

ERIC = EDUCATIONAL RESOURCES INFORMATION CENTRE

erratum [ɪˈrɑːtəm] *noun* corrections to a printed document that are added on a separate slip of paper after publication; (NOTE: plural is **errata**)

error [ˈerə] *noun* mistake; **error detection** = using special software, such as a spell checker, to find mistakes in a document; **error rate** = number of mistakes per page or per thousand entries

ESA/IRS = EUROPEAN SPACE AGENCY INFORMATION RELAY SERVICE

essential [ɪˈsenʃl] *adjective* absolutely necessary to a person, situation or activity

establish [ɪˈstæblɪʃ] *verb* **(a)** to create something in a permanent way **(b)** to prove that something is definitely true

estimate [ˈestɪmeɪt] *verb* to calculate an amount or quantity approximately

et al. [et ˈæl] *Latin abbreviation of 'et alia'* used to mean 'and the others'

etc. [etˈsetərə] *Latin abbreviation of 'et cetera'* used to mean 'and the rest'

Ethernet [ˈiːθənet] hook up system to the Internet but with distance limitations

ethnic number [ˈeθnɪk ˈnʌmbə] *noun* number added to a classification symbol to arrange books by language or race

EU = EUROPEAN UNION

Eurolug EUROPEAN ONLINE USER GROUP

Euronet/Diane telephone networks accessible by a modem and computer covering the countries of the European Union for the transmission of information; now replaced by national PSS networks

European Currency Unit (ECU) currency unit common to all member countries of the European Union

European Information Centres (EIC) business information centres in all European Union countries sponsored by the EU

European Institute for Information Management public establishment under the Luxembourg National Ministry of Education which provides postgraduate training for specialists in information management

European Online User Group (Eurolug) association of European libraries and database users formed to encourage co-ordination in responses to developments in manufacturing

European Space Agency Information Relay Service (ESA/IRS) online database host

European Union (EU) political and economic community of European countries

Eurostat statistical office of the European Union

evaluate [ɪ'væljʊeɪt] *verb* to assess how good something is by looking at the way it works

even ['iːvn] *adjective* **(a)** multiple of two; *2, 4, 6 & 8 are even numbers* **(b)** smooth and level

evidence ['evɪdəns] *noun* things that you have seen or experienced which make you believe that something is true

evolution [iːvə'luːʃn] *noun* process of gradual change and development

examination [ɪgzæmɪ'neɪʃn] *noun* written or spoken test of ability or knowledge

example [ɪg'zɑːmpl] *noun* something which is typical of or represents a particular group

exceed [ɪk'siːd] *verb* to be greater than a limit; *he exceeded the speed limit*

exception [ɪk'sepʃn] *noun* things which are different and not included

excess [ɪk'ses] *noun* too much of something, more than is necessary or normal

exclamation mark [eksklə'meɪʃn 'mɑːk] *noun* punctuation mark (!) used to express surprise

exclude [ɪk'skluːd] *verb* to leave something or someone out deliberately

execute ['eksɪkjuːt] *verb* to carry out a plan or process

executive [ɪg'zekjʊtɪv] *noun* someone who is employed by a company or organization at a senior level

exempt [ɪg'zempt] *adjective* to be allowed not to have to perform a duty, service or payment

exercise ['eksəsaɪz] *noun* short piece of work designed to help you learn something

exhaustive search [ɪg'zɔːstɪv 'sɜːtʃ] *noun* search through a database or library which covers all known records

exhibit [ɪg'zɪbɪt] **1** *noun* item displayed in a museum, art gallery or court of law **2** *verb* to put something in a public place for people to look at

exhibition [eksɪ'bɪʃn] *noun* collection of objects displayed in a public place

exhibitor [ɪg'zɪbɪtə] *noun* person whose work is being displayed

exit ['egzɪt or 'eksɪt] *noun* way out; way of leaving, for example, a building or a computer program

ex libris [eks'liːbrɪs] *Latin phrase meaning 'from the books of'* used on book plates followed by a name to show who the owner is

expand [ɪk'spænd] *verb* to make something larger

expansion [ɪk'spænʃn] *noun* process of making something larger

expect [ɪk'spekt] *verb* to believe that something will happen

expenditure [ɪk'spendɪtʃə] *noun* total amount of money spent on something

expense [ɪk'spens] *noun* money spent while doing something connected with your work; **expense account** = arrangement with a company that they will pay for necessary work expenses

experience [ɪk'spɪərɪəns] *noun* something which happens to you or which you do; **work experience** = situation in which a student spends some time doing a job to see whether they like it

experiment [ɪk'sperɪmənt] *noun* scientific test done to prove or discover something

experimental strategy [ɪksperɪ'mentl 'strætədʒi] *noun* policy of trying out new ideas and methods to see how they work

expert system ['ekspɜːt 'sɪstəm] *noun* software which applies the knowledge of experts in a field to solve problems and replicates in part human decision making; *see also* USER

expertise [ekspə'tiːz] *noun* special skill or knowledge in a certain field

expire [ɪk'spaɪə] *verb* to reach the end of the period of time for which something is valid such as a library loan period

expiry date [ɪk'spaɪri 'deɪt] *noun* date on which a document, software, membership, etc., ceases to be valid

explain [ɪk'spleɪn] *verb* to give details of something so that it can be understood

exploratory [ɪk'splɒrətəri] *adjective* anything done in order to discover what is there, what is happening or to explore future possibilities as in exploratory talks

explosion [ɪk'spləʊʒn] *noun* (a) act of blowing something up (b) sudden large increase; *new technology has led to an information explosion*

exponent [ɪk'spəʊnənt] *noun* someone who writes and/or talks in support of an idea

exporter [ɪk'spɔːtə] *noun* person or company that sells goods and sends them to foreign countries

expose [ɪk'spəʊz] *verb* to uncover and make visible

exposé [ɪk'spəʊzeɪ] *noun* piece of writing which reveals the truth about a situation, often involving something shocking

express [ɪk'spres] *verb* to state what you think or feel; **to express concern** = to show that you care about someone or something

expression [ɪk'spreʃn] *noun* **(a)** word or phrase **(b)** mathematical formula

expurgated edition ['ekspəgeɪtɪd ɪ'dɪʃn] *noun* edition of a book which has had parts removed which are judged to be offensive

extend [ɪk'stend] *verb* to make longer or to include more

extension [ɪk'stenʃn] *noun* extra room, or longer period of time or extra telephone connected to the main line; **extension card** = second or subsequent card used in a manual catalogue when the information is too long for one card

external [ɪk'stɜːnl] *adjective* coming from outside; **external auditor** = person from outside an organization who checks its accounts; **external consultant** = expert in a field who comes in from outside an organization to give advice; **external reader** = person who is allowed to use a library which is otherwise limited to specific groups of members

extra- ['ekstrə] *prefix* indicates that something is from outside; *extra-mural studies*

extract 1 ['ekstrækt] *noun* small part of a piece of writing or music which is printed or played separately **2** [ɪk'strækt] *verb* to draw out with difficulty

extrapolate [ɪk'stræpəleɪt] *verb* to use logic applied to known facts to calculate what is likely to happen in the future

extreme [ɪk'striːm] *adjective* very great in degree or intensity often with negative feelings; **going to extremes** = extreme behaviour which is socially unacceptable; **in the extreme** = used to emphasize how bad something is

extremity [ɪk'stremɪti] *noun* very serious situation

eyestrain ['aɪstreɪn] *noun* pain in the eyes caused by looking at something, such as small print or a computer screen, for too long

Ff

fable ['feɪbl] *noun* short story which aims to teach a moral lesson

facet ['fæsɪt] *noun* in classification, the whole group of divisions when a subject is subdivided;

> COMMENT: there are five kinds of facet in a class: personality, matter, energy, space and time

facilitator [fə'sɪlɪteɪtə] *noun* someone who makes it possible for other people to do things

facility [fə'sɪlɪti] *noun* equipment or building or opportunity that makes it easy to do something

facing ['feɪsɪŋ] *adjective* opposite; *the picture was on the facing page;* **facing pages** = two pages visible when a book is open

facsimile [fæk'sɪmɪli] *noun* exact copy of an original; **facsimile transmission** *see* FAX

fact ['fækt] *noun* something which is known or accepted to be true

factual ['fæktjʊəl] *adjective* based on fact

factor ['fæktə] *noun* one aspect which affects an event, situation or decision

faculty ['fækəlti] *noun* group of departments in a university or college within the same academic area; *the library school is within the faculty of humanities and education studies*

fail [feɪl] *verb* not to succeed or not to work properly; **fail safe** = designed in such a way that nothing dangerous can happen if any part goes wrong

failure ['feɪljə] *noun* lack of success in doing something; breaking down or stopping

fair copy ['feə 'kɒpi] *see* COPY

fake [feɪk] *noun* **(a)** something or someone who is not what they pretend to be **(b)** false, and usually worthless, copy

fall back system ['fɔːl bæk 'sɪstəm] *noun* system which can be used if the one in use fails

false [fɒls] *adjective* not correct or based on wrong information; **false alarm** = warning of something bad that does not actually happen

false drop ['fɒls 'drɒp] *noun* **(a)** citation that does not relate to the subject being searched **(b)** irrelevant reference in indexing

falsify ['fɔːlsɪfaɪ] *verb* to change information so that it is no longer true or accurate

familiar [fə'mɪljə] *adjective* well known and comfortable

family ['fæmɪli] *noun* **(a)** group of people or things that are connected by a common source; *a family of typefaces;* **family name** = surname, the name which all the members of your family have in common **(b)** group of related plants, animals, languages, etc., used as the basis of classification

famous ['feɪməs] *adjective* very well known

fan [fæn] *noun* cooling device often built into electric machines so that they do not overheat

fan-fold ['fænfəʊld] *adjective* way of folding paper so that information can be printed on different parts of it as in a pamphlet

FAQ = FREQUENTLY ASKED QUESTION

far-sighted [fɑː'saɪtɪd] *adjective* good at guessing what will happen in the future

fast [fɑːst] **1** *adjective* happening quickly without delay **2** *adverb* fixed or held very firmly

fatal error ['feɪtəl 'erə] *noun* mistake that causes the death of someone or something such as a computer program

fault [fɔːlt] *noun* weakness or imperfection in something

faulty ['fɔːlti] *adjective* not working properly

favourite *or US* **favorite** ['feɪvrɪt] *adjective* something or someone that is liked more than all the others

fax [fæks] **1** *noun* exact copy of a document sent electronically to a distant receiver using the telephone network **2** *verb* to send an exact copy of a document using the telephone network

feasibility study [fiːzə'bɪlti 'stʌdi] *noun* survey and report about the usefulness and potential of a plan or policy to see if it will work

feasible ['fiːzəbl] *adjective* something that is possible, that can be made or achieved

feature ['fiːtʃə] *noun* **(a)** special characteristic of anything **(b)** special article in a newspaper or magazine or a programme of radio or TV

fee [fiː] *noun* money paid for a service

feedback ['fiːdbæk] *noun* comments from users or customers about what has been proposed or done; **negative feedback** = comments which indicate that what has been proposed, done or made is not liked by the customers; **positive feedback** = comments which indicate that what has been proposed, done or made is liked by the customers

feint [feɪnt] *noun* very light lines on writing paper

Fellow of the Library Association (FLA) highest qualification awarded by the Library Association

fiche [fiːʃ] *see* MICROFICHE

fiction ['fɪkʃn] *noun* stories about imaginary people and events

Fidonet very large worldwide e-mail server

field [fiːld] *noun* section containing individual data in a record, such as name or address; **field engineer** = maintenance worker who travels to companies or individual customers to service their machines; **field of study** = academic area of knowledge being studied in depth; **field separator** = code showing the end of one field and the start of the next; **field tested** = product or plan which is tested in a real situation

fieldwork ['fiːldwɜːk] *noun* gathering information about a subject by carrying out a

figure 53 **find**

direct investigation rather than reading or talking about it

figure ['fɪgə US 'fɪgjə]; *noun* printed and numbered line illustration, map, chart, graph, etc., in a document

file [faɪl] *noun* **(a)** cardboard holder for papers which can fit in the drawer of a filing cabinet **(b)** collection of information about a particular person or thing **(c)** *(in computing)* a set of stored, related data with its own name; **file card** *see* INDEX CARD **customer file** = details of a customer kept as a record by a company; **file maintenance** = keeping files up to date by changing, adding or deleting entries; **file management** = (computing) set of instructions used to create and maintain a file; **file protection** = software or device used to prevent any accidental deletion or overwriting of a computer file; **file recovery** = software that allows a computer file that has been accidentally deleted or damaged to be recovered; **file storage** = methods of storing files on a disc or tape; **file transfer** = moving a file from one area of computer memory to another; **on file** = kept in a list for reference

file server ['faɪl 'sɜːvə] *noun (computing)* **(a)** software used to manage and store users' files in a network **(b)** number of independent systems sharing a resource or providing a particular service within a network

filing ['faɪlɪŋ] *noun* process of putting things in order according to a set system; **filing cabinet** = metal box with several drawers used for storing files; **filing card** *see* INDEX CARD **filing code** *or* **filing rule** = explicit direction based on a recognized code for filing entries in a catalogue; **filing system** = any method of organizing documents so that they can be retrieved easily; **filing tray** = container often kept on a desk for storing documents prior to filing

fill in ['fɪl 'ɪn] *phrasal verb* to write in the information required; *to fill in a form*

film [fɪlm] *noun* **(a)** strip of light sensitive material used in a camera to take photographs **(b)** story or play, etc., recorded on film to be shown in the cinema or on television **(c)** very thin layer of powder or grease

film library ['fɪlm 'laɪbri] *noun* collection of films and video recordings, classified for easy retrieval

film strip ['fɪlm 'strɪp] *noun* strip of 16mm or 35mm film bearing up to fifty frames of still photographs with pictures and captions, sometimes with sound track attached

filter ['fɪltə] *verb* **(a)** to select information which is to be passed on **(b)** to allow information to come out very gradually

final ['faɪnl] *adjective* **(a)** which cannot be changed **(b)** which happens last

finals ['faɪnlz] *plural noun* last examinations in a university or college course

finance ['faɪnæns] **1** *noun* money needed to pay for a project; **finance department** = people in an organization who manage the accounts **2** *verb* to provide the money for a project

financial [fɪ'nænʃl] *adjective* relating to or involving money see also turnover; **financial implications** = consequences of a decision in terms of how much it will cost; **financial planning** = working out the most efficient way to use what money is available; **financial sector** = part of the economy which is involved with money transactions; **financial year** = period of twelve months which can start at any point within the calendar year, used for managing the budgets of an organization and assessing profit and loss; *the university's financial year runs from 31st July to 1st August in the next year*

find [faɪnd] *verb* to discover someone or something

finding aid ['faɪndɪŋ 'eɪd] *noun* classification scheme, catalogue, index, retrieval system, etc.

finding list catalogue ['faɪndɪŋ 'lɪst 'nætəlɒɡ] *noun* catalogue with only brief author entries

findings ['faɪndɪŋz] *plural noun* information obtained as a result of investigation or research

fine [faɪn] **1** *noun* amount of money which has to be paid as a penalty **2** *verb* to make someone pay money as a punishment; *he was fined because the library books were overdue* **3** *adjective* very thin, soft or small; **fine print** = small print in a contract or agreement, which may refer to unfavourable terms and could be overlooked when signing the contract; **fine tune** = to adjust by very small amounts

finger ['fɪŋɡə] *noun* software program that will retrieve information about a user based on their electronic mail address **2** *verb* to use the finger program to obtain information about someone

first [fɜːst] *adjective* number one; **first edition** = one of the first number of copies printed from the same type at the same time; *compare* REPRINT **first word entry** = entry under the first word of the title excepting 'the', 'a', 'an'

first class ['fɜːst 'klɑːs] **(a)** highest or best quality **(b)** best level of service in, for example, mail or travel

five laws of library science ['faɪv 'lɔːz] established by S. R. Ranganathan

COMMENT: the laws are: 1. Books are for use. 2. Every reader his book. 3. Every book its reader. 4. Save the time of the reader. 5. A library is a growing organism

fit [fɪt] **1** *verb* to be the right size or shape; **to fit someone in** = to find time to see someone

2 *adjective* to be physically capable of doing something

fixed length record ['fɪkst leŋθ 'renəd] *noun* computer record which will only accept information in a pre-set number of characters

FLA = FELLOW OF THE LIBRARY ASSOCIATION

flag [flæɡ] *verb* to use a computer code to mark a record as part of a subset

flexible ['fleksɪbl] *adjective* can be altered or changed; **flexible learning** = system of teaching which provides for people of all ages and educational backgrounds; **flexible working hours** = system whereby workers can start or stop work at hours to suit themselves so long as they work a certain number of hours in a week

flexibility [fleksɪ'bɪlɪti] *noun* ability to adapt to various situations or conditions

flier ['flaɪə] *noun* small advertising leaflet designed to encourage customers to ask for more information

flood [flʌd] **1** *noun* large number of things or a large amount of information **2** *verb* **to flood the market** = to make a very large number of a particular item available for sale at one time, usually forcing the price down

floppy disk ['flɒpi 'dɪsk] *noun* secondary storage device for computer records in the form of a portable magnetic disk

Florence Agreement ['flɒrəns ə'griːmənt] UNESCO agreement adopted in 1952 which reduces tariffs and trade obstacles to the international export and import of books, documents and other educational scientific and cultural material

flowchart ['fləʊtʃɑːt] *noun* diagram which shows the sequence of steps in a process

fluctuate ['flʌktjʊeɪt] *verb* to change in nature, amount or degree

flush with ['flʌʃ 'wɪθ] *adjective* level with; *the pages were trimmed flush with the covers*

flyleaf ['flaɪliːf] *noun* endpaper in a book

flysheet ['flaɪʃiːt] *noun* two or four page tract or circular

FM = FREQUENCY MODULATION

focus ['fəukəs] **1** *verb* to concentrate your attention on something **2** *noun* centre of interest or attention

fold [fəuld] *verb* to bend something, for example a piece of paper, so that one part covers another

-fold [fəuld] *suffix* **(a)** combines with numbers to indicate that something has a certain number of parts; *the problem was three-fold* **(b)** indicates that something has multiplied by certain number; *the number of library users rose ten-fold after the advertising campaign*

folio ['fəuliəu] *noun* **(a)** book made with paper of a large size **(b)** double page spread in an accounts book with the same number

font [fɒnt] *noun* set of characters in a typeface all the same style; **font size** = size of the characters can be changed smaller or larger; **font type** = style of the characters used in printing;

COMMENT: there are many different font types, such as Palatino and Helvetica

foolscap ['fuːlskæp] *noun* large non-metric size of paper longer than A4, about 34cm x 43cm

foot [fut] *noun* bottom part of a page; *he signed it at the foot of the page*

footer ['futə] *noun* repeated message at the bottom of every page in a document

footnote ['futnəut] *noun* note (usually in a smaller typesize) at the bottom of a page, which refers to the text above and is for reference only

forbid [fə'bɪd] *verb* to give instructions that something must not be done

force [fɔːs] **1** *noun* **sales force** = group of sales people working for one company **2** *verb* to make something happen or someone do something often unwillingly; **to force a page break** = to insert a new page which is not at the place where the word processing program would automatically place it

forecast ['fɔːkɑːst] *noun* prediction, estimate of what is likely to happen in the future; **demand forecasting** = prediction of the number of items which will be sold or used

forefront ['fɔːfrʌnt] *noun* **at the forefront of an activity** = important in its development

foreground ['fɔːgraund] *noun* front part of an illustration (as opposed to the background) which seems nearest to you

foreign ['fɒrən] *adjective* belonging to or originating from a different country; **foreign market** = other country where exports are sold

forename ['fɔːneɪm] *noun* first or given name; **forename entry** = entry in a catalogue under the author's first name instead of the surname

foreseeable future [fɔː'siːəbl 'fjuːtʃə] *noun* near future which can be reasonably predicted

foreword ['fɔːwəd] *noun* text at beginning of a book sometimes by the author, more often by another person which introduces the book and its author

forgery ['fɔːdʒəri] *noun* **(a)** false copy made with the intention to deceive **(b)** act of making things intended to deceive

form [fɔːm] *noun* pre-printed document with spaces where information can be entered; **form of knowledge** = divisions of knowledge; *science, philosophy, history are forms of knowledge for classification;* **form entry** = catalogue entry under the form in which a book is written; *form entries in the catalogue were poetry, drama, fiction, etc.*

formal ['fɔːml] *adjective* correct and official behaviour or language

formality [fɔːˈmælɪti] *noun* something which must be done but which will not change the situation; *the decision is just a formality which is not expected to affect the market*

format ['fɔːmæt] **1** *noun* size, shape and arrangement of a document **2** *verb* **(a)** to arrange text on screen as it will appear in printed form on paper **(b)** to prepare a floppy disc so that it can record data

formatted ['fɔːmætɪd] *adjective* **(a)** made ready for use by a computer; *the disks need to be formatted before use* **(b)** arranged in a particular format

formula ['fɔːmjulə] *noun* set of numbers letters or symbols which represents a mathematical or scientific rule; (NOTE: plural is **formulae**)

fortnight ['fɔːtnaɪt] *noun* period of two weeks

fortnightly ['fɔːtnaɪtli] *adjective* happening every two weeks

FORTRAN *acronym* = FORMULA TRANSLATOR computer programming language for scientific matter; *see also* ASSEMBLY LANGUAGE

forum ['fɔːrəm] *noun* place or meeting at which matters can be discussed

forward ['fɔːwəd] **1** *adjective* at or moving towards the front of something or the future **2** *verb* to send on a letter which has arrived at an address from which the recipient has moved

forwarding address ['fɔːwədɪŋ əˈdres] *noun* address which you give to someone when you move so that they can send your mail to you

foxing ['fɒksɪŋ] *noun* brown spots or stains on paper caused by poor storage, usually found on older documents or books

foyer ['fɔɪeɪ] *noun* area just inside the main entrance of a large building where people meet

frame of reference ['freɪm əv 'refrəns] *phrase* particular set of ideas or beliefs on which to base your judgement of other things

framework ['freɪmwɜːk] *noun* set of rules or ideas that can be used to decide how to behave; *they were able to contain the changes within the framework of the old system*

franking machine ['fræŋkɪŋ məˈʃiːn] *noun* machine which prints a sign on letters to show that the postage has been paid

fraud [frɔːd] *noun* deception of people or making money by dishonesty and trickery

-free [friː] *suffix* can be added to adjectives to show that they do not have the thing mentioned; *sugar-free*

free [friː] *adjective* **(a)** available for use; *is this carrel free?;* **free indexing** = natural language indexing which has no vocabulary controls; **free enterprise** = economic system where businesses compete for profit without much government control; **free market** = an economic system in which the production and sale of goods is controlled by the buyers and sellers rather than the government; **free term list** = list of terms or indicators to which others can be freely added; **free text searching** = online searching using natural language rather than a controlled vocabulary and any aspect of the record as a search term; **free trade** = buying and selling between countries without restrictions or taxes **(b)** not needing to be paid for; **free of charge** = not needing to be paid for

freedom ['friːdəm] *noun* being free to say or do what you want without restriction; **freedom of information** = having free access to all published information in any format; **freedom of speech** *or* **freedom of the press** = being free to write and publish in a newspaper, or say what you want without fear of prosecution so long as you do not break the law

freehand ['friːhænd] *adjective* (drawing) done without the help of instruments, such as a ruler or compasses

freelance ['friːlɑːns] *adverb* working for anyone who will pay for your skills

Freenet community based access to the Internet usually run by volunteers in the USA

freeze [friːz] *verb* **(a)** to stop and display a single frame from a film or TV programme or video tape **(b)** to stop funds, credits, etc., being paid

frequency ['friːkwənsi] *noun* **(a)** number of times that something happens in a certain period of time **(b)** term used to describe the wavelength of broadcast transmissions; **frequency modulation (FM)** = radio broadcasting band which reduces interference

frequent ['friːkwənt] *adjective* happening very often

frequently ['friːkwəntli] *adverb* happening very often

front [frʌnt] *noun* part of something which faces you; **front page** = first page of a newspaper which contains the most important or interesting news; **to be in front** = (i) to be leading or winning; (ii) to be in first position before anything else

frontispiece ['frʌntɪspiːs] *noun* picture at the beginning of a book opposite the title page

fugitive material ['fjuːdʒətɪv mə'tiːriəl] *noun* ephemera such as pamphlets, programmes or duplicated material produced for short-term purposes and interest

full [fʊl] *adjective* **(a)** complete, with all details; **full catalogue entry** = full details of a publication; **full stop** = punctuation mark which indicates the end of a sentence; **full text retrieval** *or* **searching** = online searching in which every word of the source document can be retrieved; **paid in full** = all the money owing has been paid **(b)** with as much inside as possible, unable to take any more; *the disk is full*

function ['fʌŋkʃn] *noun* purpose or role of something; **function key** = computer key which is used to activate a particular set of instructions

functional ['fʌŋkʃnəl] *adjective* useful or practical rather than attractive

fund [fʌnd] *noun* amount of money available for a particular purpose

funding ['fʌndɪŋ] *noun* money provided for a particular purpose

furnish ['fɜːnɪʃ] *verb* to provide or supply something

further education ['fɜːðə edju'keɪʃn] *noun* system of education for people over the official school leaving age

future policy ['fjuːtʃə 'pɒlɪsi] *noun* plans for the development of an organization in the near future

Gg

gain gein] **1** *noun* improvement or increase **2** *verb* **to gain access to** = to get into something, such as a record or file

gap [gæp] *noun* space between two things, ideas or periods of time

garbage ['gɑːbɪdʒ] *noun US* rubbish; *(in computing)* **garbage in garbage out (GIGO)** = poor data input produces poor results

gatekeeper ['geɪtkiːpə] *noun* online computer host which allows users to access a database

gateway ['geɪtweɪ] *noun* software translation device which allows users working in one network to access another

gazette [gə'zet] *noun* record of public events, a journal or newsheet or a publication of official information published periodically

gazetteer [gæzə'tiːə] *noun* index of geographical place names

gender-free language ['dʒendəfriː 'læŋgwɪdʒ] *noun* language which is deliberately used to avoid reference to either men or women, as when the leader of a committee is described as a chairperson instead of the chairman

genealogy [dʒiːni'ælədʒi] *noun* study of the history of the members of a family

genealogical tree [dʒiːniə'lɒdʒɪkl 'triː] *noun* tree structured diagram showing the relationships of the members of a family from the past to the present

general ['dʒenərəl] *adjective* for all or most people, cases or things; **general public** = ordinary people; **general purpose** = something that can be used for a variety of uses; **general reference** = reference in a catalogue directing users to a number of more specific entries

generalia class [dʒenə'reɪlɪə 'klɑːs] *noun* classification for books on a variety of subjects, such as encyclopaedias

generalization [dʒenərəlaɪ'zeɪʃn] *noun* statement that is mostly true but not based on specific facts

generate ['dʒenəreɪt] *verb* to cause something to start and develop

generation [dʒenə'reɪʃn] *noun* **(a)** stage of development in the design and manufacture of machines; *fifth generation computers* **(b)** period of time in which people can grow up and have children, usually 25 to 30 years

generic [dʒen'erɪk] *adjective* **generic relationship** = link in a classification scheme; *there is a generic relationship between the genus & species;* **generic**

searching = type of online searching using a memory to store broader and related headings to the subject being searched

Geneva Convention [dʒə'niːvə kən'venʃn] *see* UNIVERSAL COPYRIGHT CONVENTION

genuine ['dʒenjʊɪn] *adjective* real, exactly what it is said to be

genre [ʒɑːnr] *noun* type of writing style, painting or music; *science fiction is a particular genre of writing*

geographic [dʒɪə'græfɪk] *adjective* **geographic filing** = system of filing items according to their place of origin; **geographic filing method** = arranging entries or materials according to place or place names; **geographic location** = place, building, unit or site where an item is stored

get [get] *verb* to obtain or receive

get back ['get 'bæk] *verb* to have something returned to you

get down ['get 'daʊn] *verb* **(a)** to write down what someone says **(b)** to fetch from a high place; *get down a book from a high shelf*

get into ['get 'ɪntʊ] *verb* to become involved with an activity

ghost writer ['gəʊst 'raɪtə] *noun* someone who writes anonymously what someone else wishes to say

gift [gɪft] *noun* something given as a present

gilt ['gɪlt] *noun* shiny material, usually gold, used as a thin covering to other material; **gilt edge** = gold edge to a page of a book so that when the book is closed it looks like a gold block

given name ['gɪvn 'neɪm] *noun* your first name used by your family and friends

global ['gləʊbəl] *adjective* covering everything; **Global Books in Print** =

worldwide listing on CD-ROM of all books in print; **global replace** = word processing function meaning to replace a particular word, group of words, letter or symbol by a different word or words; **global search** = computing function which looks through a whole document or database, etc., for a particular word or symbol throughout the whole document

glossary ['glɒsəri] *noun* **(a)** alphabetical list and definitions of the specialist words used in a document **(b)** list of specialized terms with explanations or translations; *glossary of chess terms; an English-Chinese business glossary*

glossy ['glɒsi] *adjective* smooth and shiny

go list ['gəʊ 'lɪst] *noun* list of terms or characters to be included in a printout; *compare* STOP LIST

goal [gəʊl] *noun* **(a)** what you are trying to achieve **(b)** final state reached when a task is finished; **goal-setting** = policy discussion which agrees what a group, company or organization hopes to achieve

golf ball ['gɒlf 'bɔːl] *noun* metal ball with characters on it used to print on paper

gone to press ['gɒn tə 'pres] *phrase* indicates that text has gone for printing and it is too late to make corrections

gopher ['gəʊfə] *noun* servicing device within the Internet which allows access by allowing links between systems

gossip ['gɒsɪp] *noun* conversation or report about other people's behaviour, which is often exaggerated and not always completely true

government libraries ['gʌvənmənt 'laɪbrəriz] *plural noun* libraries that exist for all the major departments of the government, for example Dept of Employment library

government publication ['gʌvənmənt pʌblɪ'keɪʃn] *noun* publication with information which is written and published by government departments, often of a statistical nature

grade [greɪd] **1** *noun* mark given to a piece of coursework or an examination which indicates the level of success **2** *verb* to judge or measure the quality of something

graduate ['grædjʊət] *noun* person who has successfully completed a first degree course at a university; **graduate trainee** = person who has graduated in one subject and is receiving further training in a specialist skill

gram (g) [græm] *noun* measurement of weight which is used to indicate the quality of paper; *80g paper is standard copier quality*

grammar check ['græmə 'tʃek] *noun* software facility which enables the user to check the grammatical accuracy of work done on a word processor

grammatical error [grə'mætɪkl 'erə] *noun* word usage which breaks the rules of a language

graph [grɑːf] *noun* mathematical diagram which visually shows the relationship between two or more sets of variables; **graph paper** = paper which is printed with measured squares so that it can be used for drawing graphs

graphic ['græfɪk] *adjective* concerned with drawing; **graphic display** = computer screen which is able to present graphical information

graphics ['græfɪks] *plural noun* pictures or lines drawn to represent information

greater than (>) ['greɪtə 'ðæn] *adverb* mathematical term represented by the symbol (>)

Green Paper ['griːn 'peɪpə] *noun* UK government policy statement printed on green paper and issued for discussion and comment

gremlin ['gremlɪn] *noun* tiny mischievous spirit said to be the cause of a problem, so any unexplained fault in a machine or system can be called a gremlin

grey literature ['greɪ 'lɪtrətʃə] *noun* in-house publications such as parish magazines or technical reports

grid grɪd] *noun* system of numbered squares allowing points to be easily plotted or located; **grid reference** = set of numbers from the X and Y axes giving the location of a point on a map

gross [grəʊs] *noun* total amount before any deductions have been made; **gross income** = total of money earned before any deductions for tax, etc.; *see also* WEIGHT

ground floor ['graʊnd 'flɔː] *noun* in the UK the floor of a house which is level with the ground outside

ground rent ['graʊnd 'rent] *noun* rent which is paid by a tenant of a building to the owner of the land on which it is built

grounds [graʊndz] *noun* reason or justification for something

group [gruːp] *noun* collection of people or things which are in the same place at the same time and often have something in common; **group consensus** = combined feelings of a group of people about a decision, also known as 'groupthink'; **group manager** = person who has responsibility for the organization of a group of people

growth [grəʊθ] *noun* increase in the size, wealth or importance

growing demand ['grəʊɪŋ dɪ'mɑːnd] *noun* increasing number of people who want to use a product or service

Grub Street ['grʌb 'striːt] nickname of a street in London which was inhabited mainly by writers; now the general name for journalism

guarantee [gærən'tiː] *noun* written promise that any faults in a purchase which show within a given period of time will be repaired free of charge

guess [gɛs] *noun* attempt to answer a question when you do not have the information needed

guesstimate ['gɛstɪmət] *noun* approximate calculation based entirely on guesswork

guest book ['gɛst 'bʊk] *noun* book in which people write their names and addresses when they stay at a hotel or guest house

guide [gaɪd] *noun* **(a)** book of instructions **(b)** person who shows people the way; **guide letters** = large letter signs to indicate the location of items in a library

guidelines ['gaɪdlaɪnz] *noun* written code of practice about how to do things in a particular field of work

guides *or* **guiding** [gaɪdz or 'gaɪdɪŋ] *noun* system of signs to help people to find their way around a building such as a library or supermarket

guild [gɪld] *noun* association of people with similar interests or skills who join together to support each other

guillotine ['gɪlətiːn] *noun* device used for cutting and trimming paper

Gutenberg Bible ['gʊtənbɜːg 'baɪbl] *noun* first large book to be printed in Europe with movable type

gutter ['gʌtə] *noun* inside margin between two pages of type; **gutter press** = name for the tabloid newspapers which print large amounts of gossip rather than factual news; also known in some countries as the 'yellow press'

Hh

hack [hæk] **1** *verb* to gain access illegally to a computer system *or* program **2** *noun* writer who produces poor quality material only for money; (NOTE: also called **hack writer**)

hacker [ˈhækə] *noun* someone who gains access to other people's computer files without their permission

half bound [ˈhɑːf ˈbaʊnd] *adjective* style of binding common from the beginning of the 19th century: binding leathers or vellum were used on the spine and corners, the rest of the boards were covered with marbled paper or plain paper and ;cloth

half title [ˈhɑːf ˈtaɪtl] *noun* first page of a book with only the title and not the details of the publisher or author

half yearly [ˈhɑːf ˈjɜːli] *adverb* every six months

halt [hɒlt] *verb* to stop completely, although usually temporarily

hand [hænd] *noun* part of your body at the end of your arm; **by hand** = to deliver something by taking it to the recipient personally rather than using the mail service; **in hand** = something that you are currently working on; **on** *or* **off your hands** = to be or not to be your responsibility; **to hand** = ready for use as soon as you want it

handbook [ˈhændbʊk] *noun* book of advice and instructions

hand-held [ˈhændheld] *adjective* portable, small and light enough to be carried and used; *hand-held video camera*

handle [ˈhændl] **1** *noun* **(a)** computer user's nickname or screen name **(b)** *(in a graphics or DTP program)* small square that is displayed on the edge of a frame or object or image **2** *verb* to deal with or accept responsibility for a situation or people

handout [ˈhændaʊt] *noun* printed paper which supports a talk or lecture with summaries, data or diagrams, etc.

handover period [ˈhændəʊvə ˈpiːriəd] *noun* period of time when the outgoing holder of a job works with the new person to make sure they have all the necessary knowledge of the work

hands-on [ˈhændzɒn] *adjective* **hands-on experience** = used especially of computers, meaning being able to actually use the machines rather than just learning about them; **hands-on training** = method of teaching using practical experience rather than just theory

handshake [ˈhænʃeɪk] *noun* term in computing which indicates that two machines are compatible and can transfer information to each other

handwriting ['hændraɪtɪŋ] *noun* system of putting words on paper using a pen or pencil; *everyone has their own distinctive style of handwriting*

handwritten ['hændrɪtən] *adjective* written with a pen or pencil rather than a typewriter or word processor

hang up ['hæŋ 'ʌp] *verb* to end a phone call by putting the receiver down

Hansard ['hænsɑːd] written account of the proceedings of the UK Parliament

hardback ['hɑːdbæk] *noun* copy of a book with a board cover; *compare* PAPERBACK

hard copy ['hɑːd 'kɒpi] *noun* printed version of a document held on a computer

hard cover edition ['hɑːd 'kʌvə ɪ'dɪʃn] *see* HARDBACK

hard disk ['hɑːd 'dɪsk] *noun* rigid magnetic disk usually built into a computer which can store much more data than a floppy disk

hardware ['hɑːdweə] *noun* machinery of a computer rather than the programs written for it; **hardware costs** = capital costs of buying computer equipment and other machinery; **hardware resources** = amount of computer equipment and machinery available for use

hash *or* **hashmark** ['hæʃ *or* 'hæʃmɑːk] *noun* **(a)** symbol # used to indicate the word 'number' in addresses; *RD#3 (Rural District Number 3)* **(b)** symbol used on telephones for a variety of functions

head [hed] *noun* **(a)** top or most important part or person; **head librarian** = qualified librarian who is in charge of a library or district; **head of department** = person who is responsible for a group of people working in the same department; **head office** = main office of a company or organization which has branch offices in other places; **per head**

= cost or amount for each person **(b)** **to make neither head nor tail of something** = to be unable to understand it at all

headed stationery ['hedɪd 'steɪʃnri] *noun* note paper which has the name and address of the person or organization to whom they belong printed at the top of each sheet

header ['hedə] *noun* **(a)** *(in a document)* text that appears at the very top of each page; for example, the header might contain the chapter name and the page number; *see also* FOOTER **(b)** the beginning of an e-mail message with full information about the recipient's address, sender's name and address and any delivery options

heading ['hedɪŋ] *noun* word, phrase, title or name at the beginning of a page, section or catalogue entry, etc.

headline ['hedlaɪn] *noun* **(a)** title at the top of a page or article in a newspaper story **(b)** spoken list of items to be covered in a radio or TV news bulletin

headphones ['hedfəʊnz] *noun* pair of small speakers worn over your ears to listen to tape recorded information or music

headquarters [hed'kwɔːtəz] *plural noun* main administrative office of an organization

headword ['hedwɜːd] *noun* main entry word in a dictionary

help [help] *verb* to do things which make it possible for someone else to do what they want to do; **help line** = telephone numbers dedicated to a specific topic which people can ring for advice and help; **help menu** = list of options available which instruct people how to use a computer program; **help screen** = screen containing writing which explains how to use a computer program

Her Majesty's Inspectorate *or* **Inspector (HMI)** [hɜː 'mædʒəstɪz ɪn'spektərət] British government department or official responsible for inspecting teaching in schools

Her Majesty's Stationery Office (HMSO) [hɜː 'mædʒəstɪz 'steɪʃnri 'ɒfɪs] publications office of the British government

heuristic [hjuˈrɪstɪk] *adjective* solving problems by using reasoning and experience rather than standard formulas; **heuristic searching** = method of searching which modifies the search according to each piece of information as it is found; **heuristic techniques** = machine indexing which simulates human thinking and uses natural language

hidden agenda ['hɪdən əˈdʒendə] *noun* unspoken intentions behind a decision or action

hierarchy ['haɪrɑːki] *noun* system of ranking things or people according to their importance

hierarchical classification [haɪˈrɑːkɪkl klæsɪfɪˈkeɪʃn] *noun* system of classifying items with the broadest terms at the top and working down to more specific narrow terms

hierarchical database [haɪˈrɑːkɪkl 'deɪtəbeɪs] *noun* organization of information in a database so that records can be related to each other within a defined structure

hierarchical search [haɪˈrɑːkɪkl 'sɜːtʃ] *noun* search in a catalogue using an upwards chain of entries from most to least specific

hi fi ['haɪ 'faɪ] *abbreviation for* high fidelity; **hi fi (equipment)** = set of stereo equipment with speakers and amplifiers used for playing records, tapes and CDs

high density disk ['haɪ 'densɪti 'dɪsk] *noun* computer floppy disk capable of storing a quantity of data

higher education ['haɪə edjʊ'keɪʃn] *noun* also known as tertiary education, it takes place at universities or colleges usually after the age of 18 and results in gaining an academic qualification

Higher National Certificate (HNC) ['haɪə 'næʃənl sə'tɪfɪkət] awarded at British colleges in technical subjects

Higher National Diploma (HND) ['haɪə 'næʃənl dɪ'pləʊmə] advanced qualification in technical subjects

high flier ['haɪ 'flaɪə] *noun* person who is very capable, ambitious and likely to reach the top ranks of any chosen career

high level language ['haɪ 'levl 'læŋgwɪdʒ] *noun* computer programming language which is easy to use and uses natural language

high level talks ['haɪ 'levl 'tɔːks] *noun* discussions involving senior people in politics or business

highlight ['haɪlaɪt] *verb* to colour, or mark, text on a document or computer screen to make it stand out from the rest; *it is often necessary to highlight text before editing it*

high resolution ['haɪ rezə'luːʃn] *adjective* good quality, especially from a laser printer

high specification ['haɪ spesɪfɪ'keɪʃn] *adjective* having a high level of accuracy or quality

high-speed ['haɪ 'spiːd] *adjective* operating at faster than normal speed

high tech ['haɪ 'tek] *adjective* very complex and using advanced technology

histogram ['hɪstəgræm] *noun* graph on which the data is represented by vertical or horizontal bars sometimes called a bar chart

historical background [hɪs'tɒrɪkl 'bækgraʊnd] *noun* reasons why something has developed over a period of time to its present form

historical value [hɪs'tɒrɪkl 'væljuː] *noun* something which helps in the understanding of past events

hit [hɪt] *noun* successful match when searching a database; **hit list** = list of people or organizations who are most likely to do something or have something done to them; *the local council had hit lists of branch libraries which were either likely to support their projects or which they were going to close;* **hit rate** = number of relevant titles found during a database search

HMI ['eɪtʃ 'em 'aɪ] **(a)** = HUMAN MACHINE INTERFACE **(b)** = HER MAJESTY'S INSPECTORATE, INSPECTOR

HMSO ['eɪtʃ 'em 'es 'əʊ] = HER MAJESTY'S STATIONERY OFFICE

HNC ['eɪtʃ 'en 'siː] = HIGHER NATIONAL CERTIFICATE

HND ['eɪtʃ 'en 'diː] = HIGHER NATIONAL DIPLOMA

hold ['həʊld] *verb* to have *or* to keep; **to hold a meeting** = to arrange and conduct a meeting; **hold the line** = used during telephone calls when you are asked to wait to be connected

holding area ['həʊldɪŋ 'eəriə] *noun* space allocated to the temporary storage of semi-current materials

holding file ['həʊldɪŋ 'faɪl] *noun* computer file in which work waits until it can be processed

holdings ['həʊldɪŋz] *plural noun* stock of books and other items kept by a library

hologram ['hɒləgræm] *noun* three-dimensional photographic image created by laser beams

holograph ['hɒləgrɑːf] *noun* book or document written in the author's own handwriting

home computer ['həʊm kʌm'pjuːtə] *noun* stand-alone personal computer used at home

home page ['həʊm 'peɪdʒ] *noun* first page of a web site, (normally stored in a file called index.html); if you enter a web site address into your Web browser, it will automatically open the home page

homograph ['hɒməgrɑːf] *noun* word having the same spelling but different meaning, such as 'spell' (witchcraft) and 'spell' (to write words correctly);

COMMENT: homographs are to be avoided where possible as headings when indexing

homonym ['hɒmənɪm] *noun* word with the same sound and perhaps the same spelling but with a different meaning, such as 'counter' (library issue desk) and 'counter' (machine for counting)

homophone ['hɒməfəʊn] *noun* word with the same sound but different spelling and meaning, such as 'threw' (past tense of throw) and 'through' (preposition)

honorarium [ɒnə'reəriəm] *noun* payment made for professional services for which payment is not usually asked

honorary ['ɒnəri] *adjective* **(a)** (position) which is held as an honour, without payment **(b)** (title, rank or degree, etc.) given as an reward, not because it has been worked for in the usual way

hospital library ['hɒspɪtl 'laɪbri] *see* LIBRARY

host *or* **hostline** [həʊst *or* həʊstlaɪn] *noun* main computer which allows access to online databases

host computer ['həʊst kəm'pjuːtə] *noun* controlling computer in a multi-user system

hotline ['hɒtlaɪn] *noun* direct telephone line giving direct access; used, for example, for quick ordering, complaints or between heads of governments

hourly ['auəli] *adjective* happening every hour

hours [auəz] *noun* periods of sixty minutes; **opening hours** = time between opening and closing; *the library opening hours are from 9 o'clock in the morning until 9 o'clock at night;* **working hours** = time spent at work rather than at home

house journal ['haus 'dʒɜːnəl] *noun* internal magazine giving information and news to the employees of a company or organization

housekeeping ['hauskiːpɪŋ] *noun* work necessary to maintain any system of filing whether manual or computerized

House of Commons *or* **House of Lords publication** ['haus əv 'kɒmənz or 'haus əv 'lɔːdz] *noun* information document which is published by the British government

house style ['haus 'staɪl] *noun* style of writing and presentation which is specific to a particular group, company or organization

HTML ['eɪtʃtiːem'el] *(acronym)* = HYPERTEXT MARKUP LANGUAGE language used to write pages for the World Wide Web, a series of special codes that define the typeface and style that should be used when displaying the text and also allow hypertext links to other parts of the document or to other documents

HTTP ['eɪtʃtiːtiː'piː] *(acronym)* = HYPERTEXT TRANSFER PROTOCOL commands used by a browser to ask an internet Web server for information about a Web page; when you enter a site name into your browser, the browser then has a conversation with the remote Web server and asks it to send the file that contains the home page; this conversation is carried out using

HTTP commands and the remote server that is being asked questions by your browser is called an HTTP server

human ['hjuːmən] *adjective* concerning people rather than animals; **human factors** = needs of human beings which must be considered when planning automation of an office; **human machine interface** = way a computer screen looks to the user; **human resources** = staff of an organization or company, which can provide skills to do specific jobs

humanities [hjuˈmænɪtɪs] *noun* subjects of study concerned with human ideas and behaviour such as literature and philosophy; **Humanities Online Bulletin Board (HUMBUL)** = online current awareness service for the humanities

HUMBUL ['hʌmbʌl] = HUMANITIES ONLINE BULLETIN BOARD

hybrid ['haɪbrɪd] *noun* mixture of different things

hymn book ['hɪm 'buk] *noun* book containing the words, and sometimes the music, of church songs

hypertext ['haɪpətekst] *noun* system for using computers which is based on the use of icons and in which information is inserted into a pre-formed structure

hyphen ['haɪfən] *noun* punctuation mark used to join two words together as in two-sided; **hyphen stringing** = process of using hyphens to combine terms

hyphenated ['haɪfəneɪtɪd] *adjective* formed of two words joined by a hyphen

hypothesis [haɪˈpɒθɪsɪs] *noun* theory which has not yet been tested to prove its truth

hypothetical [haɪpəˈθetɪkl] *adjective* based on suggestions, not proved or tested

Ii

IAA = INTERNATIONAL AEROSPACE ABSTRACTS

I & R = INFORMATION AND RETRIEVAL SERVICE

IBA = INDEPENDENT BROADCASTING ASSOCIATION

IBIS Information Services Ltd ['aɪbɪs] company providing a subject-coded file of information about libraries and staff in academic libraries worldwide

IBM-compatible *adjective* (computer) that will run standard IBM software

ICIC = INTERNATIONAL COPYRIGHT INFORMATION CENTRE

icon *or* **ikon** ['aɪkɒn] *noun* graphic symbol used in computing to represent different functions of a program

ID ['aɪ 'di:] *noun* identity card

IDD = INTERNATIONAL DIRECT DIALLING

identical [aɪ'dentɪkl] *adjective* exactly the same

identification [aɪdentɪfɪ'keɪʃn] *noun* means used to establish who someone is such as a document, mark, number or password

identifier [aɪ'dentɪfaɪə] *noun* **(a)** grammatical term for the definite (the) and indefinite (a/an) articles in English **(b)** any tag, flag or mark put on a computer file to differentiate it from others

identify [aɪ'dentɪfaɪ] *verb* to recognize something or mark something so that it can be recognized

identity number [aɪ'dentɪti 'nʌmbə] *noun* unique number which can be used as a password for accessing a computer system

idiom ['ɪdiəm] *noun* expression which has a different meaning from the separate meanings of the words and is peculiar to a language so that it cannot be literally translated

idle [aɪdl] *adjective* waiting to be used

IFLA = INTERNATIONAL FEDERATION OF LIBRARY ASSOCIATIONS AND INSTITUTIONS

ignorance ['ɪgnərəns] *noun* lack of knowledge about something

ignore [ɪg'nɔ:] *verb* to fail to notice something deliberately

IIS = INSTITUTE OF INFORMATION SCIENTISTS

ILL = INTER LIBRARY LOAN

illegal [ɪ'liːgl] *adjective* not allowed by law

illegible [ɪ'ledʒɪbl] *adjective* so badly written that it cannot be read

illiteracy [ɪ'lɪtərəsi] *noun* inability to read or write; **computer illiteracy** = lack of knowledge about how to use a computer

illiterate [ɪ'lɪtərət] *adjective* unable to read or write

illuminate [ɪ'luːmɪneɪt] *verb* **(a)** to illustrate a medieval manuscript **(b)** to shine light on something **(c)** to make things clear by explaining them

illuminated [ɪ'luːmɪneɪtɪd] *adjective* **(a)** (manuscript) decorated with gold paint and colours **(b)** filled with light

illumination [ɪluːmɪ'neɪʃn] *noun* painting of initial letters in manuscripts with gold, silver and colours

illustrate ['ɪləstreɪt] *verb* **(a)** to draw pictures or diagrams to put into written text **(b)** to make a point clear by using examples or stories

illustration [ɪlə'streɪʃn] *noun* picture, chart or diagram, etc., which helps to explain the words of a book or talk

illustrator ['ɪləstreɪtə] *noun* person who does the drawings or pictures for a book

image ['ɪmɪdʒ] *noun* **(a)** picture or reflection of someone or something; **image enhancer** = electronic device which makes the picture clearer; **image processor** = electronic device which analyses the information in an image to enable recognition; **image scanner** = electronic device which converts pictures or drawings into machine-readable form **(b)** *(computing)* an exact replica of an area of memory

imaging ['ɪmədɪŋ] *noun* technique for creating pictures on a computer screen

immediate [ɪ'miːdiət] *adjective* happening without delay or needing to be dealt with very quickly

impact ['ɪmpækt] *noun* strong effect on something either physically by hitting or mentally by influence

implement ['ɪmplɪment] *verb* to carry out or put into action

implementation [ɪmplɪmən'teɪʃn] *noun* **(a)** carrying out of plans or systems **(b)** latest version, particularly of software

imply [ɪm'plaɪ] *verb* to suggest that something is true without actually saying so

implication [ɪmplɪ'keɪʃn] *noun* something suggested by a situation, words or events

import 1 ['ɪmpɔːt] *noun* importance of something because of the way it is likely to effect outcomes; *they discussed matters of great import* **2** [ɪm'pɔːt] *verb* **(a)** to buy goods or services in one country and bring them to your own for sale **(b)** to bring something in from outside a system; *to import a broadcast television signal from outside the normal distribution area and distribute it over a cable network*

important [ɪm'pɔːtənt] *adjective* very significant, necessary or valuable

impression [ɪm'preʃn] *noun* number of copies of a book or document printed on the same print run

imprint ['ɪmprɪnt] *noun* **(a)** publisher's or printer's name which appears on the title page of a book or document or in the bibliographical details **(b)** mark made by firmly pressing something onto a surface

improvise ['ɪmprəvaɪz] *verb* **(a)** to make something from whatever materials you have rather than using the proper ones **(b)** to carry out an activity using your initiative rather than planning it carefully in advance

impulse ['ɪmpʌls] *noun* (a) short electrical signal (b) sudden desire to do something without thinking about it or planning it first

in [ɪn] **1** *prefix* added to some words to create the opposite meaning, such as 'correct' 'incorrect' **2** *preposition* used to introduce adjectival and adverbial phrases; **in alphabetical order** = organized according to the same order as the letters in the alphabet; **in ascending order** = organized with the smallest item first and working up to the biggest; **in charge of** = in control and able to make decisions; **in descending order** = organized so that the biggest item is first and working down to the smallest; **in detail** = paying attention to all the aspects of something however small; *to describe something in detail;* **in fact** = used to emphasize the reality of a situation or to introduce more precise information; *in fact this is what really happened;* **in house** = produced internally by a company or organization and relating to internal matters; *an in-house magazine;* **in order of importance** = organized with the most important item first; **in place** = in the right position; **in practice** = what is done rather than what is talked about or theorized; *it was supposed to happen but in practice it had to be cancelled;* **in print** = (i) written down; (ii) still published; **in sequence** = organized to occur one after another according to a pre-determined order; **in stages** = done in small parts; *she learned computing in stages;* **in stock** = available for immediate purchase or loan; **in subject order** = arranged under headings which relate alphabetically to the subject of the document; **in terms of** = to talk about something specifying which particular aspects you are considering; *we discussed what was needed in terms of equipment;* **in the case of** = in the particular situation under discussion; *difficult decisions must be made in the case of closure of district libraries;* **in the long run** = eventually; *in the long run automation of the library benefited everybody;* **in the long term** = over a long period of time; *in the long term automation will be seen to be good for the library;* **in theory** = what is supposed to happen but probably will not; *in theory the librarians will be given time off for study, but more likely they will not be able to go;* **in working order** = functioning efficiently; *all the computers are in good working order now;* **in writing** = written down, not spoken; *make sure that you get the contract in writing* **3** *adverb* done internally by a company; *the work is being done in-house*

inaccessible [ɪnək'sɛsɪbl] *adjective* impossible or very difficult to reach

inaccurate [ɪn'ækjʊrət] *adjective* not correct or full of mistakes

inbuilt ['ɪnbɪlt] *adjective* included as an integral part of a system

inbuilt facility ['ɪnbɪlt fə'sɪlɪti] *noun* feature that is included in the original design

incentive [ɪn'sɛntɪv] *noun* anything which encourages extra effort; **incentive payment** = extra money that is paid to encourage someone to work harder

incident ['ɪnsɪdənt] *noun* event or happening, especially an unusual one

incidental [ɪnsɪ'dɛntl] *adjective* something happening or existing in connection with something else more important; *the librarians were allowed to claim for the incidental expenses, such as taxi fares, when they went to the conference;* **incidental music** = music written to provide the background to a play or film

include [ɪŋ'kluːd] *verb* to make one thing part of another

inclusive [ɪŋ'kluːsɪv] *adjective* counted in with other aspects; *prices are inclusive of VAT*

income-generating
['ɪŋkʌm'dʒenəreɪtɪŋ] *adjective* producing money from activities

incoming [ɪn'kʌmɪŋ] *adjective* coming in from outside; *incoming messages on the computer*

incompatible [ɪnkʌm'pætɪbl] *adjective* unable to work together

incorporate [ɪn'kɔːpəreɪt] *verb* to include one thing as part of another

increase [ɪŋ'kriːs] *verb* to make larger

incunabula [ɪnkjuː'næbjʊlə] *noun* early printed documents from before 1500 A.D.

incur ['ɪnkɜː] *verb* to cause something to happen

indent [ɪn'dent] *verb* to leave a space at the beginning of a passage of writing

indentation [ɪnden'teɪʃn] *noun* leaving a space of a set size at the beginning of a line of text

independent [ɪndɪ'pendənt] *adjective* not connected to, influenced by or needing other people or machines to be able to exist or work; **Independent Broadcasting Association (IBA)** = organization which controls all broadcasting companies in the UK except the BBC

index ['ɪndeks] **1** *noun* **(a)** alphabetical list of items contained in a book, document or computer memory; **index card** = small card containing information and usually arranged alphabetically in a card index box; **index entry** = item with bibliographic details written in an index or catalogue; **index language** = controlled vocabulary used to compile a subject index **(b)** system by which the changes in the value of something can be compared or measured; *international financial indexes compare the value of shares;* **index-linked** = linked to inflation and so changing each time inflation or the cost of living rises or falls **(c)** finding guide to

information on a specific topic **2** *verb* to compile an alphabetical list of contents

indexing ['ɪndeksɪŋ] *noun* use of alphabetical methods to organize information; **automatic indexing** = using a computer to compile an index to a document by selecting specific words or items in the text; **indexing at source** = publication of index data at the same time as a periodical article; **indexing chain** = using hierarchical steps from a subject heading to produce a chain of classification numbers; **indexing keyword** = heading word used to indicate the contents of a document and used in online searching; **indexing language** = language of the system used in compiling a library or book index

indicate ['ɪndɪkeɪt] *verb* to show

indicator ['ɪndɪkeɪtə] *noun* **(a)** something which shows whether something exists **(b)** state of a process as in closed access libraries showing the number of books 'in' and 'out'

indirect [ɪndə'rekt] *adjective* not done by the shortest or most obvious method

indirect question [ɪndə'rekt 'kwestʃən] *noun* asking for information without actually mentioning the subject; *she asked her friend an indirect question about the books she wanted to be returned*

individual [ɪndɪ'vɪdjʊəl] *adjective* relating to one single person or thing rather than to a group; **individual password** = personal code allowing access to a computer system

induce [in'djuːs] *verb* to persuade, influence or cause a situation to happen

induction course [ɪn'dʌkʃn 'kɔːs] *noun* course for new entrants to a company, organization or institution which gives basic information to help settling in

industrial archaeology [ɪn'dʌstrɪəl ɑːki'ɒlədʒi] *noun* study of buildings related to the industrial revolutions in the developed world

inexpensive [ɪnɪk'spensɪv] *adjective* cheap, not costing much money

inexperienced [ɪnɪk'spɪəriənst] *adjective* having little or no experience in a particular activity

inference ['ɪnfərəns] *noun* deduction of information from given data; **inference control** = way of determining which information can be released on a computer without disclosing personal information about an individual

influence ['ɪnfluəns] **1** *noun* power to affect people's actions **2** *verb* to cause something or someone to change

informatics [ɪnfə'mætɪks] *plural noun* collective term for the technologies concerned with the computerized collection, processing and transmission of information

information [ɪnfə'meɪʃn] *noun* knowledge given to someone in a form they can understand; **information accessibility** = how easily information is available to users; **information accuracy** = level of correctness in information; **information analyst** = person who studies information and draws conclusions; **information brokerage** = business of buying and selling information for other people; **information centre** = office where people can make enquiries; **information channel** = means by which information is distributed; **information completeness** = whether the information covers all the aspects required; **information content** = what is contained in the information; **information definition** = technique for deciding exactly what the enquirer needs to know; **information desk** = place in a library or information centre where questions will be answered; **information engineers** = computer experts who work with information systems; **information explosion** = situation in which there is so much information available because of technology; **information flow** = distribution of information; **information management** *or*

information handling = storage, searching, retrieval and updating of information; **information manager** = trained person who controls the processing and availability of information within a company or organization; **information needs** = requirements of a user or group for information on specific subjects; **information network** = group of people or computers linked together so that information can be passed around; **information officer** *see* INFORMATION MANAGER **information organizations** *see* INFORMATION SERVICES **information personnel** *see* INFORMATION SPECIALIST **information policy** = statement of policy about the provision and accessibility of information within an organization; **information presentation** = format of the information in written, spoken, computer database form, etc.; **information qualifications** = degrees or diplomas indicating a level of training in information management; **information quality assessment** = technique for assessing the level of satisfaction among users with the information provided; **information relevance** = value of the information to the enquirer; **information resource** *see* INFORMATION SOURCE **information retrieval** = technique for finding out what is required; **information science** = study of the processes for the storing and retrieving of information; **information services** = companies offering a service in the provision of information; **information skills** = ability of users to access and retrieve the information they require; **information source** = any book, document, database or person providing information; **information specialist** = trained worker in information management; **information storage** = manual or electronic methods of storing information; **information strategy** = policy of a company or organization about its use of information; **information supplier** = person or company which provides information on a specific subject; **information system** = computer system used for the provision of information and designed according to user needs; **information technology** = (i) knowledge in scientific methods and their industrial uses; (ii) the electronic equipment used for applying scientific knowledge especially in storing and distributing information; **information terms** = language used for the organization of information; **information timing** = whether the information is provided in time to be of use

infrared (IR) [ɪnfrə'red] form of invisible light, below the visible red level on the light scale

infrastructure [ɪnfrə'strʌktʃə] *noun* basic structures which enable a country, society or organization to function effectively

infringement [ɪn'frɪnʒmənt] *noun* **infringement of copyright** *or* **copyright infringement** = breaking the copyright law by illegal copying of text, ideas or patents

inhibit [ɪn'hɪbɪt] *verb* to prevent or slow down a process

initial [ɪ'nɪʃəl] **1** *adjective* happening at the start of a process; **initial phase** *or* **initial stage** = first step **2** *verb* to sign using only the first letters of your names

initialize [ɪ'nɪʃəlaɪz] *verb* to prepare a system or disk for use; *a disk needs to be initialized before the computer can make use of it*

initials [ɪ'nɪʃəlz] *plural noun* first letters of a person's names

ink [ɪŋk] **1** *noun* coloured liquid for writing or printing; **ink pad** = pad of material soaked in ink for use with official stamps; **ink-jet printer** = non-impact machine for printing the output of a computer using a system of electrically charged ink drops **2** *verb* to apply ink to; *she inked the ink pad because it had become dry*

innovation [ɪnə'veɪʃn] *noun* new thing or method of doing something

input ['ɪnpʊt] **1** *noun* information put into a computer memory **2** *verb* to enter data into a computer

inquiry [ɪŋ'kwaɪri] *noun* request for information

inscription [ɪn'skrɪpʃn] *noun* words written on stone, metal, paper, etc., as a commemoration , dedication or greeting

insert [ɪn'sɜːt] *noun* additional information printed on a separate sheet of paper and put inside a magazine or document, etc.

in-service training ['ɪnsɜːvɪs 'treɪnɪŋ] *noun* professional development training provided by an organization for its employees

insight ['ɪnsaɪt] *noun* understanding of a complex situation

INSPEC *acronym* abstracting and indexing service for electrical engineers

inspection copy [ɪn'spekʃən 'kɒpi] *noun* copy of a publication sent or given with time for a decision to purchase or return it

install [ɪn'stɔːl] *verb* to set up equipment so that it is ready for use

installation costs [ɪnstə'leɪʃn 'kɒsts] *noun* money required to put in the equipment required

instalment [ɪn'stɔːlmənt] *noun* **(a)** small amount paid at regular intervals as part of a larger total; *they paid for the expensive encyclopaedia in six monthly instalments* **(b)** part section of a book or magazine published at regular intervals

instant replay ['ɪnstənt 'riːpleɪ] *noun* feature of video recording systems which allows the viewer to see again the action which has just been recorded

institute ['ɪnstɪtjuːt] **1** *noun* organization set up for a particular group of people with a shared interest **2** *verb* to set up for the first time; *they instituted an information service in the branch library*

Institute of Information Scientists (IIS) organization for the mutual support of workers in the field of information science

instruct [ɪn'strʌkt] *verb* to teach someone how to do something

instruction [ɪn'strʌkʃən] *noun* clear and detailed information about how to do something verbal, published in a manual or typed into a computer to cause the machine to work; **instruction note** = note directing the user of a catalogue to take an unusual search step

instrumentation [ɪnstruːmən'teɪʃn] *noun* dials which display information to indicate how a machine is working

insufficient [ɪnsə'fɪʃənt] *adjective* not enough

insulate ['ɪnsjuleɪt] *verb* to protect from outside damage

insurance [ɪn'ʃuərəns] *noun* agreement to pay fixed sums of money so that if damage or injury occurs, costs will be paid by the insurance company

intake ['ɪnteɪk] *noun* people, things or quantity of anything taken into something such as an organization; *their intake of new employees each year is increasing*

integer ['ɪntɪdʒə] *noun* mathematical term to describe an exact whole number

integrated ['ɪntɪɡreɪtɪd] *adjective* combined or linked together; **integrated database** = combined database which excludes repetition or redundant terms; **integrated package** = combined applications on different topics stored on a central computer; *an integrated package can contain several programs such as a database, spreadsheet, word processing and graphics;* **Integrated Services Digital Network (ISDN)** = service which provides

high quality telecommunications such as facsimile transmission and video conferencing

integrity [ɪn'teɡrɪti] *noun* reliability, honesty; **integrity of a file** = extent to which the information on the file is reliable and not corrupted

intellectual property [ɪntə'lektʃuəl 'prɒpəti] *noun* original writing, ideas, inventions, works of art or music which are the property of the creator, and protected by copyright law

intelligent terminal *or* **workstation** [ɪnˌtelɪdʒɪnt ˌtɜːmɪnɪl *or* 'wɜːksteɪʃn] *noun* computer terminal which can be programmed independently of the central processor and which is capable of limited reasoning

intensity [ɪn'tensɪti] *noun* measure of strength of something, such as a signal

inter- ['ɪntə] *prefix* which combines with adjectives and nouns to describe the way they relate to each other; *inter-racial; inter-city*

interact [ɪntə'ækt] *verb* to work with or relate to someone or something

interactive [ɪntə'æktɪv] *adjective* **(a)** working together for the exchange of information **(b)** (computer program) which is able to be changed while working; *the computer game was interactive, so that the players could get answers to their questions;* **interactive multimedia** = systems of communication which use a variety of methods and can be controlled by the user in order to obtain information; **interactive video** = system using a computer linked to a video disk player which allows the user to answer questions in order to move on to the next picture; **interactive videotext** = system which allows the user to select pages and display the information to gain information

interchangeable [ɪntə'tʃeɪnʒəbl] *adjective* can be substituted for something else

intercom ['ɪntəkɒm] *noun* device with a microphone and loudspeaker which can be used to speak to someone in another room

interdependent [ɪntədɪ'pendənt] *adjective* dependent on each other

interdisciplinary studies

[ɪntə'dɪsɪplɪnəri 'stʌdɪz] *noun* academic studies which cross the conventional subject boundaries; *history, geography, religious studies and languages are sometimes taught together as interdisciplinary studies and called the humanities*

interface ['ɪntəfeɪs] *noun* point at which two systems contact each other

interfere ['ɪntəfɪə] *verb* to cause difficulty with other people's affairs

interference [ɪntə'fɪːrəns] *noun* unwanted signals causing difficulty in reception on a computer or broadcasting system

interim ['ɪntrɪm] *noun* part way through a process; **interim report** = report written part way through a process to show how much progress has been made

interleaved [ɪntə'liːvd] *adjective* book which has thin sheets of blank paper inserted between the pages of text

Inter Library Loan (ILL) ['ɪntə 'laɪbri 'ləʊn] *noun* **(a)** system of lending books and documents between libraries **(b)** book, photocopy or material lent between libraries for their users

interlock [ɪntə'lɒk] **1** *verb* to fit things together so that they join firmly **2** *noun (computing)* used as a security device

intermediary [ɪntə'miːdiəri] *noun* person who helps people or groups to come to an agreement

intermediate [ɪntə'miːdiət] *adjective* half way between two stages; **intermediate storage** = temporary place to store things until a more permanent place is found

intermittent [ɪntə'mɪtənt] *adjective* happening occasionally rather than continually; **intermittent error** = mistake which occurs randomly and is difficult to trace

internal [ɪn'tɜːnl] *adjective* happening inside a place, person or object; **internal consumption** = use of materials or information within a company or organization; *see also* PHONE

international [ɪntə'næʃənl] *adjective* relating to different countries; **International Aerospace Abstracts (IAA)** = summaries of research done in the field of space exploration; **International Copyright Information Centre (ICIC)** = centre based at UNESCO headquarters in Paris; **international dialling code** = numerical code which allocates specific numbers to each country to make it possible to dial directly without using an operator; **international direct dialling (IDD)** = system of telephone communication which does not need an operator; **International Packet Switching Service (IPSS)** = electronic link between terminals and computers in different countries; **International Standard Book Number (ISBN)** = system of identifying publications by specific numbers relating to publishers and titles; **International Serials Data System (ISDS)** = international network of serials libraries which promotes international standards of bibliographic description; **International Standard Music Number (ISMN)** = system for identifying editions of published music; **International Standards Organization (ISO)** = system which controls the standards of production for goods and services worldwide; **International Information Centre for Standards in Information and Documentation (ISODOC)** = centre established by UNESCO and ISO to promote the application of standards in information work; **International Standard Serial**

Number (ISSN) = system for identifying publications of journals and their publishers

internet ['ɪntənet] *noun* international network that links together thousands of computers using telephone and cable links allowing users on each computer to share information access a remote database and exchange electronic mail messages

internet service provider *see* ISP

interpret [ɪn'tɜːprət] *verb* **(a)** to change what is spoken in one language to another **(b)** to decide on the meaning of a communication

interpretation [ɪntəprɪ'teɪʃn] *noun* explanation of the meaning

interpreter [ɪn'təprɪtə] *noun* **(a)** person who is used to translate **(b)** software used to translate from one computer system to another

interrogate [ɪn'terəgeɪt] *verb* **(a)** to question formally **(b)** to work with an interactive computer program

interrogation [ɪntərə'geɪʃn] *noun* act of asking questions in order to obtain information

interrupt [ɪntə'rʌpt] *verb* to stop something happening temporarily

interval ['ɪntəvəl] *noun* short pause between two actions or activities

intervention [ɪntə'venʃən] *noun* action causing a change

interview ['ɪntəvjuː] *noun* meeting when a person is asked questions

interword spacing [ɪntə'wɜːd 'speɪsɪŋ] *noun* variable spaces between words used to justify line endings

intranet ['ɪntrənet] private network of computers within a company that provide similar functions to the internet - such as electronic mail, newsgroups and the WWW

intrinsic [ɪn'trɪnzɪk] *adjective* fundamental and important to a person or situation

introduction [ɪntrə'dʌkʃn] *noun* **(a)** first part of written text or spoken information which tells what the rest of the document or talk is about **(b)** book which provides elementary information on a specific subject; *'An Introduction to Library Management'*

intuition [ɪntjuː'ɪʃn] *noun* feeling about something for which there is no proof

invalid [ɪn'vælɪd] *adjective* not legally acceptable

inventory ['ɪnvəntri] *noun* written list of the assets owned by an organization; *the manager asked for an inventory of the library holdings*

inversion [ɪn'vɜːʃn] *noun* change something into its opposite

invert [ɪn'vɜːt] *verb* to turn upside down

inverted commas [ɪn'vɜːtɪd 'kɒməz] *noun* punctuation marks ("....") indicating speech or quotations

invest [ɪn'vest] *verb* to put money, time or energy into something or someone in the hope that it will produce more money or better results

investigation [ɪnvestɪ'geɪʃn] *noun* process by which all the facts and aspects of a situation are examined

invitation to tender [ɪnvɪ'teɪʃn] *noun* written or spoken request to a company or organization to work out their charges for doing a job

invite [ɪn'vaɪt] *verb* to ask someone formally to do something

invoice ['ɪnvɔɪs] *noun* official document listing the goods or services supplied and stating the amount of money owed

involve [ɪn'vɒlv] *verb* to include or use something

IPSS = INTERNATIONAL PACKET SWITCHING SERVICE

IR light = INFRARED LIGHT

IRC *(acronym)* INTERNET RELAY CHAT a system which allows many users to participate in a chat session in which each user can send messages and sees the text of any other user

irrelevant [ɪ'relɪvənt] *adjective* not important because it is not connected with the topic

irretrievable [ɪrɪ'triːvəbl] *adjective* cannot be found or obtained

ISBN = INTERNATIONAL STANDARD BOOK NUMBER

ISDN = INTEGRATED SERVICES DIGITAL NETWORK

ISDS = INTERNATIONAL SERIALS DATA SYSTEM

ISMN = INTERNATIONAL STANDARD MUSIC NUMBER

ISO = INTERNATIONAL STANDARDS ORGANIZATION

ISODOC = INTERNATIONAL INFORMATION CENTRE FOR STANDARDS IN INFORMATION AND DOCUMENTATION

ISP = INTERNET SERVICE PROVIDER company that provides access to the internet for a user; the user needs a modem and connects to the internet via a computer at the ISP

ISSN = INTERNATIONAL STANDARD SERIAL NUMBER

issue ['ɪʃuː] **1** *noun* particular edition of a journal or magazine; **issue card** = small card used in a manual library system of loan records; **issue desk** = counter in a library where items are recorded as on loan or returned; **issue system** = system for controlling library loan records **2** *verb* to give out or lend; *the library books were issued to the students*

italic [ɪ'tælɪk] *adjective* describes a typeface in which the characters slope to the right

item [aɪtəm] *noun* one of a collection or list of objects; **item number** = specific number which identifies an item in a collection

iterative searching ['ɪtərətɪv 'sɜːtʃɪŋ] *noun* searching for information by repeatedly asking questions until the solution is found

Jj

jacket ['dʒækɪt] *noun* paper or plastic cover for a book

jam [dʒæm] *verb* (a) to stop working because something is blocking the feeding mechanism (b) to interfere with a radio or electronic signal so that it cannot be received clearly

JANET = JOINT ACADEMIC NETWORK

jargon ['dʒɑːgən] *noun* language that uses words and expressions in specific, often technical, ways that relate to a particular field of study

jiffy bag ['dʒɪfi bæg] *noun* padded envelope used to protect goods which are sent through the post

jigsaw puzzle library ['dʒɪgsɔː 'pʌzl 'laɪbri] *see* LIBRARY

job dʒɒb] *noun* (a) any task which needs to be done; **job scheduling** = arranging the order in which jobs will be processed (b) work that is done to earn money; **job applicant** = someone who applies to be considered for a job; **job description** = official statement of what a job involves; **job specification** = detailed objectives for a job

jobbing printer ['dʒɒbɪŋ 'prɪntə] *noun* person who undertakes small printing jobs

jog [dʒɒg] *verb* to give something a small push or knock; **to jog the memory** = to remind someone of something

join [dʒɔɪn] *verb* (a) to fasten two or more things together (b) to become a member of an organization

Joint Academic NETwork
(JANET) national communication system which uses electronic mail and other systems between universities; **Super JANET** = updated version of the Joint Academic NETwork

joint author ['dʒɔɪnt 'ɔːθə] *noun* person who writes a book in collaboration with others

Joint Photographic Experts
Group *see* JPEG

journal ['dʒɜːnəl] *noun* specialist magazine

journalese [dʒɜːnə'liːz] *noun* style of writing with cliches and hackneyed phrases often used by journalists

journalist ['dʒɜːnəlɪst] *noun* person who writes for a newspaper or magazine

joystick ['dʒɔɪstɪk] *noun* lever attached to a computer which can be used to play certain types of computer games

JPEG ['dʒeɪpeg] = JOINT PHOTOGRAPHIC EXPERTS GROUP datafile for pictures and photographs on the Internet

junior ['dʒuːniə] *adjective* younger or lower in rank than another person; **junior library** *see* LIBRARY

junk [dʒʌŋk] *noun* information or hardware which is old and useless; **junk mail** = publicity and advertising materials which are sent to you through the post even though you have not asked for them

justify ['dʒʌstɪfaɪ] *verb* (a) to change the spacing between words or characters so that each line of the text ends exactly at the right-hand margin (b) to give a good reason for something; *can you justify the expenditure on children's books?*

justification [dʒʌstɪfɪ'keɪʃn] *noun* adjusting the spacing in printed text so that the text starts and ends exactly at the margins

juvenile ['dʒuːvənaɪl] *noun* young person

juxtapose [dʒʌkstə'pəuz] *verb* to put two things next to each other in order to emphasize the difference between them

Kk

k *abbreviation* one thousand; **£1k** = £1000

keep [kiːp] *verb* **(a)** to retain something or someone, or cause to remain in the same place **(b)** to do what you said you would do; **to keep track of** = to follow what is happening to someone or something; **to keep up** = to continue to supply or do something; *to keep up a constant supply of information;* **to keep up with** = to continue at the same rate as other people or things; *it was difficult to keep up with reading the large supply of information*

Keesings Contemporary Archives [ˈkiːsɪŋz kənˈtemprəri ˈɑːkaɪvz] monthly publication listing world events reported in the press

Kelly's Directories [ˈkelɪz daɪˈrektəriz] series of business directories listing products and services and the street names in Britain

kermit [ˈkɜːmɪt] *noun* file transfer protocol which enables computer programs to be transferred from one system to another

key kiː] *noun* **(a)** button on a computer or typewriter which is pressed to operate the machine; **key function** = stored command given to a specific key on a computer **(b)** something which is important; **key field** = field which identifies important entries, such as name and address, in a record; **key system** = system which controls all other functions

keyboard [ˈkiːbɔːd] *noun* set of keys arranged in a certain order and used to enter information into a computer or typewriter; **keyboard operator** = person who works with a keyboard

key in [ˈkiː ˈɪn] *verb* to enter text or commands on a computer by means of a keyboard

keynote [ˈkiːnəʊt] *noun* part of a policy or speech which is emphasized and given the most importance; **keynote speech** = speech at a conference which states the main topic for discussion

keypad [ˈkiːpæd] *noun* **(a)** set of numeric keys often used for security devices to open doors by means of a known code **(b)** numerical keys set separately on the right-hand side of a computer keyboard

keystroke [ˈkiːstrəʊk] *noun* action of pressing a key

keyword [ˈkiːwɜːd] *noun* most important word in a title or sentence; **keyword and context** *see* KWAC; **keyword in context** *see* KWIC; **keyword out of context** *see* KWOC; **keyword out of title** *see* KWOT; **keyword search** = system of searching a database by using combinations of special words connected with the subject of the search

kg *abbreviation* kilogram; **1kg** = 1000 grams

kill [kɪl] *verb* to erase or stop a computer program

kiosk ['kiːɒsk] *noun* small, often wooden building, used for selling things

kit [kɪt] *noun* set of parts which can be used to construct something or do a particular task; *it is possible to buy a bookbinding kit which has all the equipment you need to do the job*

knob [nɒb] *noun* round button which can be turned such as one on a machine which controls its working

knockdown price ['nɒkdaʊn 'praɪs] *noun* price that is much lower than normal

know-how ['nəʊhaʊ] *noun* knowledge about how to do specific tasks especially technical or scientific

knowledge ['nɒlɪdʒ] *noun* information and understanding in your mind about a subject

knowledge-base ['nɒlɪdʒbeɪs] *noun* stored instructions and commands in a computer used to develop an expert system

Kompass Directories ['kʌmpɒs daɪ'retrɪz] listings for different countries of most registered companies; in the UK these are industrial companies with more than 10 employees who trade nationally

KWAC = KEYWORD AND CONTEXT library indexing system using keywords from the title and text as the index entries

KWIC = KEYWORD IN CONTEXT library indexing system which uses the title or text to illustrate the meaning of the index entry

KWOC = KEYWORD OUT OF CONTEXT library indexing system using any relevant keywords not necessarily used in the text

KWOT = KEYWORD OUT OF TITLE indexing system using words not in the title

LI

LA = LIBRARY ASSOCIATION

label ['leɪbl] **1** *noun* **(a)** piece of paper or card attached to something giving information about it such as its price or address **(b)** word or symbol used in computing to identify a piece of data **2** *verb* to attach a label to something with information on it such as its price or address

laboratory [lə'bɒrətri] *noun* room with scientific equipment where experiments, research or teaching are carried out; **computer laboratory** = room equipped with several computers, sometimes networked together, which can be used for working in or teaching; **language laboratory** = room equipped with tape recorders and computers which can be used for learning or teaching foreign languages

lack [læk] *noun* not enough of something or none at all; *a lack of funds makes it impossible to build up our serials collection*

ladder ['lædə] *noun* **(a)** means of climbing to a high place physically; *a ladder can help you to climb up to a high shelf* **(b)** means of climbing metaphorically; *you can gain promotion up your career ladder*

lag [læg] **1** *verb* **(a)** to make slower progress than other people **(b)** to slow down so that less is produced; *production lagged and there had to be redundancies* **2** *noun* time

lag = period of waiting between two related events; *there is sometimes a time lag between speakers who are interviewed on television from another country*

laminate ['læmɪneɪt] *verb* to cover a document with a thin film of glossy plastic for protection

lampoon [læm'puːn] *noun* written satirical attack often with a humorous approach

LAN = LOCAL AREA NETWORK

landscape format ['lænskeɪp 'fɔːmæt] *noun* paper of A4 size used sideways so that the longest side is at the top

land use map ['lænd 'juːs 'mæp] *noun* map used by planners which shows the way land is used in any given district

language ['læŋgwɪdʒ] *noun* system of sounds signs or symbols used for communication; **artificial language** = man-made language for use in communicating with computers; **assembly language** = low-level computer programming language; **language laboratory** = room equipped with tape recorders and computers which can be used for learning or teaching foreign languages; **language dictionary** = book which translates words from one language into another as opposed to a monolingual dictionary, which gives synonyms within the same language

lap [læp] *noun* flat area formed by your thighs when you are sitting down

lapel microphone [lə'pel 'maɪkrəfəʊn] *noun* small microphone which can be pinned to clothing

laptop computer ['læptɒp kʌm'pjuːtə] *noun* computer that is small enough to be held on your lap but not small enough for your pocket, usually having a screen, keyboard and disk drive

lapsed [læpst] *adjective* allowed to end or become invalid; **lapsed user** = someone who used to make use of services but no longer does

large print edition [lɑːdʒ 'prɪnt ɪ'dɪʃn] *noun* book printed with a large typeface to help people with poor eyesight to be able to read it

large scale ['lɑːdʒ 'skeɪl] *adjective* large in number, amount or size

laser printer ['leɪzə 'prɪntə] *noun* high quality computer printer

launch [lɔːnʃ] *verb* to start a new activity or to make a new product, such as a new book, available to the public

laureate ['lɔːriət] *see* POET LAUREATE

law [lɔː] *noun* system of rules and regulations used by a government or society to control business agreements, social relationships and crime; **law directory** = book which lists the registered law firms in a country

LAWLIB *acronym* subscription bulletin board on the Internet for the use of lawyers

law library ['lɔː 'laɪbri] *see* LIBRARY

layout ['leɪaʊt] *noun* design of a page of printed matter including position on the page

of illustrations, text and typesizes of work, etc.

LEA = LOCAL EDUCATION AUTHORITY

lead [liːd] *verb* to be in charge of or guiding an organization or group, etc.; **lead term** = heading used for an index; **lead story** = main news item on television or in a newspaper

lead-in page ['liːdɪn 'peɪdʒ] *noun* first page in a videotext system which guides users to other pages

leader *or* **leading article** ['liːdə *or* 'liːdɪŋ 'ɑːtɪkl] *noun* **(a)** the item in a newspaper or news bulletin which is given the most space or time and which expresses the views of the editor **(b)** *(information retrieval)* the data at the beginning of a machine-readable record identifying and locating the information content

leadership ['liːdəʃɪp] *noun* state of being in control of a group or organization; **leadership styles** = methods used to lead a company or organization

leaf [liːf] **1** *noun* page of a book printed on both sides; (NOTE: the plural is **leaves**) **2** *verb* **to leaf through** = to turn the pages of a document quickly without reading them carefully

leaflet ['liːflət] *noun* small folded paper with printed information, often given away free as a form of advertising

leak [liːk] *noun* breach of security or loss of important information

learn [lɜːn] *verb* to obtain knowledge or skill through study or training

learned journal ['lɜːnɪd 'dʒɜːnəl] *noun* specialized magazine on an academic subject

learning ['lɜːnɪŋ] *noun* knowledge that has been obtained through study; **learning curve** = graphical description of the speed of learning; *if you learn a lot in a short time you are on a steep learning curve;* **learning**

environment = surrounding that is conducive to study and learning; **learning methods** = different ways in which people learn

lease [li:s] **1** *noun* written contract for letting or renting a piece of equipment for a period against payment of a fee **2** *verb* to let or rent equipment for a period

leather binding ['leðə 'baɪndɪŋ] *noun* covering of a book made from animal skin

leave [li:v] *noun* period of time when you are absent from your study or job, etc.

lecture ['lektʃə] *noun* long talk on a specific subject given to a group of people, often used as a method of teaching in higher education

left-hand corner ['lefthænd 'kɔːnə] *noun* top or bottom corners at the left side of a page or envelope

left justify ['left 'dʒʌstɪfaɪ] *verb* to use computer commands which ensure that the text on the left side of document is straight

legal ['li:gəl] *adjective* **(a)** relating to the law; *a legal discussion* **(b)** according to the law; *the contract was legal and binding;* **legal aid** = financial assistance with legal fees given by the government to someone who cannot afford a lawyer; **legal deposit** = system which entitles certain libraries to receive by law one copy of every book or publication published in that country; **legal records** = collection of legal records kept for reference purposes; **legal tender** = coins or notes which are officially part of a country's currency

legend ['ledʒənd] *noun* **(a)** caption under a picture or diagram or on a coin or medal **(b)** explanation of the symbols on a map or diagram **(c)** story based on cultural traditions handed down

legible ['ledʒɪbl] *adjective* clear enough to be read easily

legitimate [lə'dʒɪtəmət] *adjective* acceptable according to the law

lending library ['lendɪŋ 'laɪbri] *see* LIBRARY

length ['leŋθ] *noun* measurement of how long something is

lengthen ['leŋθən] *verb* to make something longer

lengthy ['leŋθi] *adjective* lasting for a long time, often with a negative feeling; *lengthy delays*

lesson ['lesən] *noun* **(a)** period of time used to teach something to an individual or a group **(b)** short extract from sacred writings, read aloud during a religious service

let [let] *verb* **(a)** to allow someone to do something **(b)** to allow someone to use your possessions in return for regular payments of rent **(c) to let off** = to allow someone not to do a task or duty; *they were let off doing weekend duties;* **to let down** = to disappoint someone by not doing what you have promised to do

Letraset ['letrəset] trade name for a system of labelling or captioning documents and illustrations

letter ['letə] *noun* **(a)** piece of writing sent from one person to another usually through the post; **business letter** = letter which is sent from one company to another about business matters; **circular letter** = letter sent to a large number of people conveying the same information; **standard letter** = letter which is sent to several different addresses without any change in the text **(b)** symbol used in writing which more or less represents one sound of a language

letterhead ['letəhed] *noun* name and address of a company or organization printed at the top of their official notepaper

level [levl] *noun* point on a scale indicating amount, importance or difficulty; *sound level; level of inflation*

lexicographer [leksɪ'kɒgrəfə] *noun* person who writes or compiles dictionaries

lexicography [leksɪ'kɒgrəfi] *noun* activity of writing and editing dictionaries

lexicon ['leksɪkɒn] *noun* **(a)** alphabetical list of words specifically related to a language or a particular subject **(b)** dictionary, especially one of an ancient language such as Latin or Hebrew

liaise [li'ɪz] *verb* to work together and keep each other informed

liaison [li'eɪzɒn] *noun* co-operation and communication between different organizations or sections of an organization

LIBNET *acronym* electronic mail service of the Australian Library and Information Association

librarian [laɪ'breəriən] *noun* **(a)** person who is in charge of a library **(b)** person who has usually been trained in librarianship and who works in a library; **subject librarian** = librarian who is a specialist in a particular subject

librarianship [laɪ'breəriənʃɪp] *noun* the study of organizing and retrieving information so that it is accessible to other people

library ['laɪbri] *noun* collection of books, documents, newspapers, and audio visual materials kept and organized for people to read or borrow; **academic library** = library which serves an academic community such as a university or college; **archive library** = library which stores and makes accessible historical materials; **branch library** = library which serves a specific area and is accountable to a main library; **chained library** = library in which books are chained to desks or shelves; **children's library** = library which specializes in providing books

usually written specially for children; **circulating library** = library in which books are sent round to members; **jigsaw puzzle library** = UK library founded in 1933 and holding over 4000 wooden handcut jigsaws; **junior library** *see* **CHILDREN'S LIBRARY law library** = library which specializes in the provision of books about the law, often to support university and college departments training lawyers; **lending library** = library which allows users to borrow items as opposed to a purely reference library; **local library** *see* **BRANCH LIBRARY mobile library** = specially adapted van which takes library books to residential areas at the same time each week; **public library** = library which serves the general public in a city, town or village; **school library** = library which is part of a school; **special library** = library which provides information for a specialist organization; **subscription library** = private library which people can join by paying a subscription; **toy library** = collection of toys which can be borrowed by young children for short periods; **Library and Information Science Abstracts (LISA)** = index of articles and of current research in Library Science; **library assistant** = person who works in a library as a helper, not qualified as a librarian; **Library Association (LA)** = UK professional body working to support librarians and information workers; **library binding** = specially strong binding of books which will withstand heavy use; **Library of Congress Catalog (LOCIS)** = catalogue of the holdings of the Library of Congress in the USA also available online; **Library of Congress Classification system** = American system of organizing documents for information retrieval; **library card** *or* **library ticket** = ticket which allows the holder to borrow library books; **library equipment** = furniture and machinery needed to run a library; **Library Information Service (LIS)** = service provided by a library to users to answer their questions on any subject; **library school** = department or college which runs courses to train library and information workers; **library supplier** = company which supplies stationery, books, equipment, and furniture needed for use in libraries; **library supply** = supply of books to libraries at a discount; **library user** = person who uses a library; **library user education** = training courses which help library users to use the library more effectively

libretto [lɪ'bretəʊ] *noun* words of an opera, musical production, etc.

licence ['laɪsəns] *noun* official document which gives you permission to use or do something

license ['laɪsəns] *verb* to give official permission for something to happen

life cycle ['laɪf 'saɪkl] *noun* stages passed through between birth and death; **life cycle of records** = the creation, storage, retrieval for use, and disposal when no longer needed, of records

light [laɪt] **1** *adjective* (a) not heavy (b) not dark; *light type appears pale on the page* **2** *noun* **light-sensitive paper** = paper which is sensitive to light such as that used for photographs; **IR light** = infrared light; **UV light** = ultraviolet light

light-pen ['laɪtpen] *noun* stylus with a light sensor used to scan bar codes

lightweight ['laɪtweɪt] *adjective* (a) not heavy (b) not thought to be of a high academic standard

Likert scale ['laɪkɜːt] *noun* system of measuring attitudes on 5 point scales from positive to negative or vice versa

limit ['lɪmɪt] **1** *noun* maximum pre-defined range used to restrict an action or thing **2** *verb* to prevent something from becoming bigger

limited ['lɪmɪtɪd] *adjective* small in amount or degree; **limited company** = company in which the shareholders are only legally responsible for debts to the amount of their shares if the company goes bankrupt; **limited**

edition = work of art, book or painting, etc., which is only produced in very small numbers

limp binding ['lɪmp 'baɪndɪŋ] *noun* binding style using flexible material usually cheaper than hard boards

Lindop Committee British government committee which investigated and made recommendations about the security of information on computers in 1978

line [laɪn] *noun* (a) row of words or figures in a text; **line by line index** = index with entries consisting of one line only; **line printer** = machine which prints out text from a computer line by line (b) type of product that a company makes or sells (c) long piece of wire used to connect communications; *a telephone line* (d) **line manager** = person in a hierarchical structure of management who is responsible for the person or people immediately below; **line management** = system of management using a hierarchical structure of jobs, so that everyone is responsible to the person immediately above them

linear ['lɪniə] *adjective* process in which things always happen one at a time following each other in a set order

linguistics [lɪŋ'gwɪstɪks] *noun* study of language, its history, grammar, structure and use

link [lɪŋk] *noun* (a) relationship between two or more things either by a physical connection or by a common idea which enables them to work together; **link word** = word which is used in writing or speaking to join ideas or sentences together; **satellite link** = use of a satellite to transmit data from one part of the earth to another; *the Olympic Games in Australia could be seen live on television in London by satellite link* (b) hypertext connection which allows users to move to another related part of the Internet. Links usually appear on screen as underlined, blue text

link up ['lɪŋk 'ʌp] *verb* to connect things to each other; *this computer can be linked up with others in the network*

LIPS *see* LIBRARY INFORMATION PLANS

LIS *see* LIBRARY INFORMATION SERVICE

LISA *see* LIBRARY AND INFORMATION SCIENCE ABSTRACTS

list [lɪst] *noun* (a) series of items written down usually one under the other; **black list** = list of companies, countries or people who are banned from trading or using goods or services; *the library has a black list of borrowers who are not allowed to use the library services;* **mailing list** = (i) list of names and addresses of people which can be used for sending out specific types of mail; (ii) list of subscribers to an e-mail network (b) catalogue; *there is a price list for cars of different ages and models;* **list price** = the price of a commodity according to a printed list

list owner ['lɪst 'əʊnə] *noun* person who controls an electronic mailing list

LISTSERV very large electronic mailing list manager

literal ['lɪtərəl] **1** *adjective* following the exact meaning of a word or phrase, without any additional meanings **2** *noun* mistake made when keyboarding so that characters are transposed

literate ['lɪtərət] *adjective* able to read and write; **computer literate** = able to understand and use computers

literacy ['lɪtrəsi] *noun* the ability to read and write; **adult literacy** = measure of the number of adults in a society who can read and write

literary ['lɪtrəri] *adjective* related to literature; **literary prize** = award given for a piece of writing judged to have literary value

literature ['lɪtrətʃə] *noun* (a) novels, plays and poetry especially those considered to have artistic quality (b) printed information on a specific subject; **literature search** = preliminary investigation when studying a subject to find all other related writing; **literature survey** = bibliography listing material on a given subject or sometimes in a given location

lithography [lɪ'θɒgrəfi] *noun* method of printing in which the ink sticks to greasy areas of treated metal, stone or film and is then transferred to paper

load [ləʊd] **1** *noun* (a) large amount to be carried (b) work to be done; **load sharing** = using more people to even out the workload; **work load** = amount of work to be done by a certain person or group **2** *verb* to load a file = to call a computer file so that it can be seen on screen and worked with

loan [ləʊn] *noun* something which is lent and must be returned; **loan collection** = collection of books and materials available for borrowing (as opposed to a reference collection which cannot be taken away from the library); **loan fee** = sum of money paid to borrow an item; **loan period** = period of time before a document which has been borrowed must be returned; **long loan** = extended period for borrowing library items; **on loan** = being borrowed; *the book is on loan from the library;* **short loan** = restricted period for borrowing library items

local ['ləʊkl] *adjective* belonging or relating to the specific area where you live or work; **local collection** = books and documents about a specific area close to where the collection is held; **local directory** = collection of information about businesses and residents in a specified area arranged in alphabetical order of street names and also with classified trade entries; **local history** = history of a small area of a country; **local maps** = maps which give detailed information about a particular area; **local newspaper** = newspaper which reports on local events and people; **local radio** *or* **local TV** = broadcasting stations which concentrate on the news and issues relevant to a small local area; **local record office** = archive store which keeps information about the particular area in which it is situated; **Local Area Network (LAN)** = system linking computers, terminals and printers, within a restricted geographical area, which share the same stored information in the network memory; **Local Education Authority (LEA)** = administrative body which controls the supply of education through schools and colleges in a local area of the UK

locate [ləˈkeɪt] *verb* (a) to place or position something (b) to find something

location [ləˈkeɪʃn] *noun* place where something is situated or happens; **on location** = (filming) done in natural surroundings rather than in a studio

LOCIS = LIBRARY OF CONGRESS CATALOGUE

lock [lɒk] *verb* to fasten something to prevent access; **to lock a file** = to prevent anyone from making changes to a computer file

log [lɒg] *verb* to record something officially; **to log in** *or* **on** = to enter data, such as a password or code, in order to gain entry to a computer system; **to log off** *or* **out** = to enter data, in order to close down and leave a computer system

log book [ˈlɒg ˈbʊk] *noun* (i) book in which entry and departure times to a particular place are recorded; (ii) book in which someone writes records of their activities especially related to travelling; *a ship's log book shows distance travelled and any places visited, etc.*

logic [ˈlɒdʒɪk] *noun* way of thinking and reasoning which takes account of previous steps

logistics [ləˈdʒɪstɪks] *plural noun* organization of something very complicated especially moving people and things from one place to another

logo [ˈlɒgəʊ] *noun* special design which identifies the products and publicity material of a company or organization

long-distance [ˈlɒŋ ˈdɪstəns] *adjective* applies to journeys, communications or places which are far apart

long-term [ˈlɒŋ ˈtɜːm] *adjective* concerning a long period of time; *the long-term plans include the development of a music library;* **long-term needs** = what people will need for a long time in the future; **long-term planning** = making plans for the future; **long-term project** = project which will take a long time to complete; *see also* IN THE LONG RUN

look [lʊk] *verb* to turn your eyes to see something or someone; **to look after** = to take care of someone or something; **to look at** = to read, consider or examine something; **to look for** = to search for something or someone; **to look into** = to find out about something or someone; **to look like** = to have a similar appearance to someone or something else; **to look through** = to examine a document to find what you want; **to look up** = to find information by looking in a book, journal or document

loop [luːp] *noun* series of actions that are performed repeatedly until the procedure has been completed

loose-leaf [ˈluːs ˈliːf] *adjective* (book) which has pages which can be removed or replaced

loss [lɒs] *noun* (a) having less of something (b) having nothing left; **loss leader** = commodity which is sold at a low price which makes no profit in order to encourage people to buy more of other things from the same company; **to cut your losses** = to stop doing something in order to prevent a bad situation becoming worse

loudspeaker [laʊdˈspiːkə] *noun* device that turns electrical signals into recognizable sound

low level language [ˈləʊ ˈlevl ˈlæŋgwɪdʒ] *noun* computer programming language that is similar to the machine language and difficult for non expert users to understand

lower case [ˈləʊwə ˈkeɪs] *adjective* describes small letters such as a, b, c, as opposed to upper case A, B, C

lyric [ˈlɪrɪk] *noun* short poem which expresses strong feelings in a songlike form

Mm

mb *abbreviation* megabyte

machine [məˈʃiːn] *noun* piece of equipment which uses power to carry out work; **dictating machine** = recording machine which records what someone says so that it can be typed later; **duplicating machine** = machine which produces duplicate copies; **machine-readable** = (text) which is stored on a disk or tape in machine language, so that it can read by a computer without the need for translation

Machine Readable Catalogue
(MARC) automated system of cataloguing books and documents in a library

machinery [məˈʃiːnri] *noun* machines in general

machinist [məˈʃiːnɪst] *noun* person whose job is to work a machine

magazine [mægəˈziːn] *noun* **(a)** regular weekly, monthly or quarterly publication containing articles, stories, photographs and advertisements **(b)** radio or television programme made up of several different items **(c)** container for slides to be used in an automatic projector

magnetic [mægˈnetɪk] *adjective* something which uses electrical magnetism to record and store information to be read by a computer; **magnetic strip** = data strip attached to card and read by a machine; *credit cards have a magnetic strip to identify the legitimate owner;* **magnetic tape** = tape coated with a magnetic material so that electrical signals can be recorded on to it for speech, film or computer information

magnetised [ˈmægnɪtaɪzd] *adjective* converted into a magnet; *the library uses magnetised strips inside books to prevent theft*

magnify [ˈmægnɪfaɪ] *verb* to make something appear bigger or more important than it really is

magnitude [ˈmægnɪtjuːd] *noun* level, degree or importance of a signal or situation; *they did not appreciate the magnitude of the task*

mail [meɪl] *noun* letters and parcels delivered by the Post Office; **mail-box** = (i) box outside your house for the delivery of letters as opposed to a letter box which is a covered hole in the front door of your house; (ii) electronic mail personal storage location identified by a name and ;address **direct mail** = system of selling goods by sending publicity material about them through the post; **electronic mail** = messages sent on a computer using a modem and telephone lines to other users of a network or bulletin board; **junk mail** = unwanted publicity and advertisements sent to you through the post;

mail merge = word processing program which allows a standard letter to be sent out to a series of different names and addresses; **mail order** = shopping by choosing items from a catalogue and having them delivered to your house; **mail shot** = large number of information or publicity leaflets sent out to a selected group of prospective customers

mailbase ['meɪlbeɪs] *noun* UK electronic mailing list service used by discussion groups; *see also* BULLETIN BOARD

mailing list ['meɪlɪŋ 'lɪst] *noun* **(a)** list of names and addresses kept by an organization so that it can send people information or regular publications **(b)** electronic list of e-mail addressees or subscribers who usually have an interest in the same topic;

mailserver ['meɪlsɜːvə] *noun* computer on the Internet which stores incoming mail and sends it to the correct user, and stores outgoing mail and transfers it to the correct destination server

main [meɪn] *adjective* most important; **main catalogue** = full list of all the holdings in a library; **main class** = major division of a general classification scheme; **main entry** = fullest entry in a catalogue often with a tracing of related references; **main heading** *see* MAIN ENTRY **main index** = general index which guides users to more specific entries; **main processor** *see* MAINFRAME

mainframe ['meɪnfreɪm] *noun* large high powered computer, which is the central processing unit that can be used to service many other devices

mainstream ['meɪnstriːm] *adjective* normal or conventional; **mainstream research** = research that follows on from previous work done in the field

maintain [meɪn'teɪn] *verb* to keep something in good condition and up to date

maintenance ['meɪntənəns] *noun* process of keeping something in good condition by giving it regular care and attention; **maintenance contract** = arrangement with a repair company to make regular checks and repairs at special prices; **maintenance costs** = money put into a budget for carrying out regular maintenance; **maintenance of records** = process of updating information or keeping records up to date

major ['meɪdʒə] *adjective* very important; **major contributor** = person who has supplied the most information or written text for a publication or meeting

majority [mə'dʒɒrɪti] *noun* the larger part, more than half

make up ['meɪk 'ʌp] *phrasal verb* **(a)** to form or create something; *the various groups that make up society* **(b)** to add to a sum of money to provide the amount required; **to make up time** = to work or travel so that time that has previously been lost is saved; *they were told that they could make up the time lost by arriving late, by staying later in the evening*

malfunction [mæl'fʌŋkʃən] **1** *noun* failure to work properly **2** *verb* to fail to work properly

man [mæn] **1** *noun* adult male human being, an ordinary worker **2** *verb* to provide the workforce for something; *they manned the exhibition stand all day*

man-made ['mænmeɪd] *adjective* made by people rather than formed naturally

manage ['mænɪdʒ] *verb* to direct or take responsibility for controlling someone or something

manageable ['mænɪdʒəbl] *adjective* can be controlled easily because it is not too big or complicated

management ['mænɪdʒmənt] *noun* process of controlling an organization, company or group; **Management By Objectives (MBO)** = system of managing a company by stating the aims of the organization as the basis of policy; **Management Information System (MIS)** = system designed to collate all the information collected by an organization and supplied to support anyone involved in decision making; **management of records** = process of creating, storing, retrieving and disposing of records; **management styles** = different ways of controlling, organizing and motivating groups of people; **management training** = training of managers by making them study the principles and practices of management; **middle management** = level of management which has responsibility for a part within the structure of the whole organization; *heads of departments are middle managers*

manager ['mænɪdʒə] *noun* person who is responsible for running a company, organization or group

managerial ['mænɪ'dʒiːərial] *adjective* relating to the work of a manager

mandatory ['mændətri] *adjective* must be done; *it is mandatory to pay taxes*

manifesto [mænɪ'festəu] *noun* written statement of the intentions of a person or group of people who are standing for election

manipulate [mə'nɪpjuːleɪt] *verb* to control people, data or situations to produce a specific result

manpower ['mænpauə] *noun* workforce or labour force which produces goods; **manpower resources** = number of people available for work

manual ['mænjuəl] **1** *noun* document or book containing instructions about the operation of a system or machine **2** *adjective* done by hand rather than by machine; **manual systems** = information control systems which use handwritten rather than computerized records

manufacture [mænjuː'fæktʃə] *verb* to make something in a factory

manufacturer [mænjuː'fæktʃərə] *noun* company which makes a product

manuscript (MS) ['mænjuːskrɪpt] *noun* typed or handwritten text such as a book before it is printed; **manuscript music book** = book of paper ruled with five line staves for the writing of music

map [mæp] *noun* diagrammatic representation of an area of land; **local map** = map showing the area near to where you live or work; *see also* PIN

marbled paper ['maːbld 'peɪpə] *noun* multi-coloured paper used by book binders usually for the endpapers of books

MARC = MACHINE READABLE CATALOGUE

margin ['maːdʒɪn] *noun* blank space around a section of printed text between the printed text and the edge of the paper; **margin of error** = number of mistakes which are considered to be acceptable in a document or calculation

mark [maːk] **1** *noun* **(a)** sign or symbol written on a page; **proof correction marks** = special marks written on a proof text to show where and how it should be corrected; *see* SUPPLEMENT **(b)** score or grade achieved for an assignment or examination **2** *verb* to assess work and award it a grade or score; **to mark up** = to prepare copy for printing by indicating such things as font size, typeface, and layout

marker ['maːkə] *noun* object which is used to show the position of something; **marker pen** = coloured pen used to indicate or highlight sections of text

market ['maːkɪt] **1** *noun* number of people wishing to buy a product or the area of the world where it is sold; **market penetration** = how much of the chosen market is reached by the product; *they estimated a 50% market penetration for the information service;* **market research** *or* **market analysis** =

investigation into what people want, need, think and buy **2** *verb* to organize the sale of a product by deciding the price, the areas where it will be sold, and how it will be advertised

marketing plan ['mɑːkɪtɪŋ 'plæn] *noun* strategy for selling a product or service by planning the advertising and distribution within a selected market

marketplace ['mɑːkɪtpleɪs] *noun* **(a)** potential number of people who will buy a product, or use a service **(b)** place where goods or services can be sold or offered

mass media ['mæs 'miːdiə] *see* MEDIA

mass production ['mæs prə'dʌkʃən] *noun* manufacture of large quantities of the same product

master ['mɑːstə] **1** *noun* **(a)** original document from which copies are made; **master file** *or* **master catalogue** = one in which every entry contains full bibliographical information **(b)** most important person or device within a system; **master plan** = detailed plan to organize several difficult tasks **2** *verb* to learn something so that you can do it well

mastermind ['mɑːstəmaɪnd] *verb* to plan a complicated activity in detail and make sure it happens successfully

masterpiece ['mɑːstəpiːs] *noun* original creation in the arts which is of exceptional quality

match [mætʃ] **1** *noun* thing which is equal to another in physical or mental characteristics; *the two chess players were a perfect match for each other so the game ended in a draw* **2** *verb* to find an item which has equal characteristics; *he had to match them for size and colour;* **to match a record** = to search a database or record for a similar piece of information to the record you have

material [mə'tiːriəl] *collective noun* equipment or items needed for a particular

activity; **display material** = items which can be used for an exhibition; **material requirements planning** = detailed statement of the equipment required for a specific task and its cost

matt [mæt] *adjective* surface which is not shiny; usually used of paper for photographs

matter ['mætə] *noun* **(a)** situation which you have to deal with; *this is a matter which the library committee must decide;* **matter for discussion** = topics which need to be discussed in order to make decisions **(b)** **printed matter** *or* **reading matter** = anything such as books, journals, newspapers that is printed and can be read; **publicity matter** = advertisements or printed publicity material; **subject matter** = subject of book or talk, etc.

maximize ['mæksɪmaɪz] *verb* **(a)** to make the most possible use of something **(b)** to make something as large or important as possible; *they aimed to maximize their profits*

maximum ['mæksɪməm] *adjective* **(a)** largest amount possible **(b)** highest achievement possible

MBO = MANAGEMENT BY OBJECTIVES

mean [miːn] **1** *noun* average of a set of numbers **2** *verb* to signify or explain something; *'the computer is down' means that is not working*

means [miːnz] *plural noun* **(a)** method of doing something; *we have the means to store a large number of documents* **(b)** money that someone has to spend; *he has the means to buy a large house*

measure ['meʒə] **1** *verb* to discover the size or quantity of something by using a calibrated instrument such as a ruler **2** *noun* **(a)** set of scales or strip for measuring; **tape measure** = flexible strip of metal or cloth marked with divisions of length **(b)** action taken to bring about a specific result;

measures have been taken to reduce the loss of books; **safety measure** = action or regulation to ensure that activities do not endanger anyone

measurement ['meʒəmənt] *noun* size in centimetres or inches, etc.

mechanical [mɪ'kænɪkl] *adjective* something which has moving parts and uses power to perform tasks

mechanics [mɪ'kænɪks] *plural noun* way something works or is done; *the mechanics of reading are difficult for children to learn*

mechanism ['mekənɪzm] *noun* **(a)** piece of machinery **(b)** method of doing something

media [mi:diə] *collective noun* means of communication as in radio, television or newspapers; **audio-visual media** = means of communication that can be heard or watched; **media coverage** = number of reports about a situation or event in the newspapers or radio or television; **media resource officer** = person who is in charge of the management of audio-visual resources; **media storage systems** = systems for storing and retrieving non-book materials such as audio tapes, video tapes, films, illustrations, etc.

medieval manuscript ['medii:vəl 'mænju:skrɪpt] *noun* written manuscript dating from between 1100 and 1500 A.D.

medical ['medɪkl] *adjective* relating to the treatment and prevention of illness and injuries; **medical abstracts** = collection of summaries of medical articles in journals; **medical directory** = list of medical institutions, practitioners and specialists; **medical indexes** = list of bibliographical references to articles on medical subjects; **medical journal** = specialist magazine for medical practitioners; **medical library** = special library to support medical work

Medical Literature Analysis and Retrieval Service (MEDLARS) collection of databases operated by the national library of medicine

medium ['mi:diəm] **1** *adjective* neither large or small; middle-sized **2** *noun* means that is used to communicate or express yourself; *they communicated through the medium of the written word;* (NOTE: plural is media)

MEDLARS = MEDICAL LITERATURE ANALYSIS AND RETRIEVAL SERVICE

MEDLIB *acronym* subscription bulletin board mainly used by doctors

Medline *noun* information database mainly used by workers in medical professions

meet [mi:t] *verb* **(a)** to make contact with someone face to face **(b)** to deal with a situation, need or requirement

meeting ['mi:tɪŋ] *noun* event when people come together to discuss things

mega- ['megə] *prefix* literally meaning one million but often used simply to express the idea of very large size; **megabyte** = measure of the data storage capacity of a device, equal to 1,048,576 bytes

membership ['membəʃɪp] *noun* state of belonging to an organization, group, etc.; **membership ticket** *or* **membership card** = card or ticket stating someone's name and the name of the organization of which they are a member; **membership list** = list of names and addresses of members of an organization, group, etc.

memo ['meməʊ] *see* MEMORANDUM

memoir ['memwɑ:] *noun* story of someone's life, especially one who has been well known in public life

memorandum [memə'rændəm] *noun* abbreviated as memo; note sent internally within a company or organization; **memo pad** = pad of headed paper used for internal messages (NOTE: plural is **memoranda**)

memorial volume [mɪ'mɔ:riəl 'vɒlju:m] *noun* **(a)** book containing the names of people to be remembered **(b)** book written in memory of someone

memory ['memri] *noun* **(a)** your ability to remember things **(b)** *(computing)* the capacity to store information

memorize ['meməraɪz] *verb* to learn something so that you can remember it exactly

mention ['menʃn] **1** *noun* reference to something or someone **2** *verb* to say something about a topic very briefly

menu ['menju:] *noun* list of options displayed on screen for the user of a computer program; **menu-driven** = computer program where the user can choose options from a menu; **pull-down menu** = list of options displayed on the computer screen temporarily overwriting other work

merchandise ['mɜːtʃəndaɪz] **1** *noun* goods that are bought, sold or traded **2** *verb* to sell goods and services

merge [mɜːdʒ] *verb* combine two data files on a computer; *see also* MAIL MERGE

MERIT US regional gateway with access to commercial services such as CompuServe

metaphor ['metəfɔː] *noun* expression used to describe one thing in terms of another, without using the words 'like' or 'as', as in 'the librarian was a fountain of knowledge'

MESH *acronym* Medical Subject Headings for Medline

message ['mesɪdʒ] *noun* piece of information that you send or leave for someone; **message heading** = title given to information to indicate its contents; **message numbering** = identification of messages using a numerical system

meteorological office
[miːtiərə'lɒdʒɪkl 'ɒfɪs] *noun* government office which records the forecasting and occurrence of weather conditions world-wide

meteorology [miːtiə'rɒlədʒi] *noun* study of weather formation and conditions

method ['meθəd] *noun* particular planned way for doing something

methodical [me'θɒdɪkl] *adjective* careful, planned and ordered way of working

methodology [meθə'dɒlədʒi] *noun* system of ways and principles for doing something, for example in teaching or research

metre ['miːtə] *noun* unit of length equal to 100 centimetres

micro- ['maɪkrəʊ] *prefix* used to indicate a very small version of anything; **micro computer** = small computer usually used as a stand-alone machine, i.e. one not connected to a network; **micro image** = stored graphical image which is too small to be seen with the naked eye

microcopy ['maɪkrəʊkɒpi] *noun* copy of a document which has been reduced in size

microfiche ['maɪkrəʊfiːʃ] *noun* small sheet of photographic film on which information is stored in very small print; **microfiche reader** = machine which magnifies the writing on microfiche film and displays it in readable form on a monitor

microfilm ['maɪkrəʊfɪlm] **1** *noun* material for making microfiches **2** *verb* to make microfiches

microphone ['maɪkrəfəʊn] *noun* electronic device used to record sounds on to tape or to make them louder

microprocessor ['maɪkrəʊprəʊsesə] *noun* micro chip which can be programmed to do a large number of tasks or calculations

Microsoft Disk Operating System
see MS/DOS

mid-user ['mɪd 'juːzə] *noun* operator who retrieves relevant information from a database for a customer or end-user

millennium [mɪ'leniəm] *noun* **(a)** period of one thousand years **(b)** future time in which everyone will be perfectly happy

mini- ['mɪni] *prefix* combines with nouns to indicate a smaller version of something; *mini-computer*

miniature ['mɪnɪtʃə] *noun* **(a)** coloured picture in an illuminated manuscript **(b)** much reduced copy of a document **(c)** small, very detailed drawing or painting especially on ivory or vellum

minimize ['mɪnɪmaɪz] *verb* to reduce to the smallest possible amount or to make something seem unimportant

minimum ['mɪnɪməm] *noun* smallest amount possible

ministry ['mɪnɪstri] *noun* government department; **ministry publication** = published report of the proceedings of a government department

Minitel ['mɪnɪtel] *noun* national information database in France accessible by telephone and home computer

minority [maɪ'nɒrɪti] *noun* group of people who form less than half of the total population of an area in terms of race, religion, opinion, etc.; **minority sampling** = method of surveying the needs and opinions of a minority group

mint [mɪnt] **1** *adjective* new; **mint condition** = same condition as when new; *the books were in mint condition* **2** *verb* to make, especially coins

minuscule ['mɪnəskjuːl] *adjective* extremely small

MIS = MANAGEMENT INFORMATION SYSTEM

mis- [mɪs] *prefix* combines with verbs or nouns to indicate that something is done badly or wrong; *misuse; mismatch*

miscalculate [mɪs'kælkjuːleɪt] *verb* **(a)** to add up incorrectly **(b)** to make a mistake in judging a situation

miscellaneous [mɪsə'leɪniəs] *adjective* collection of items which are all very different from each other

miscellany [mɪ'seləni] *noun* collection of written texts on a variety of subjects in one book

misleading title [mɪs'liːdɪŋ 'taɪtl] *noun* one which does not indicate the subject matter or the form of the work

mismatch ['mɪsmætʃ] *noun* situation where two things are not correctly linked

misprint ['mɪsprɪnt] *noun* mistake in printing

misquote [mɪs'kwəut] *verb* to state incorrectly what someone else has said or written

misread [mɪs'riːd] *verb* **(a)** to read something incorrectly **(b)** to read someone's intentions incorrectly

misses ['mɪsɪz] *plural noun* documents not retrieved by a computer search

missing ['mɪsɪŋ] *adjective* not in the expected place; **missing data** = information which is not available, so that a task cannot be completed; **missing link** = missing piece of information in a chain of data, which makes it difficult to use the information

mission statement ['mɪʃn 'steɪtmənt] *noun* statement of the aims and objectives of an organization

missive ['mɪsɪv] *noun* letter especially a long and detailed one

misspelt [mɪs'spelt] *adjective* spelt wrongly

mistake [mɪs'teɪk] *noun* error, something which is done incorrectly

mix [mɪks] *verb* to combine two or more things together to form something else

mixed ability class ['mɪkst ə'bɪlɪti 'klɑːs] *phrase* class in a school or college where pupils have different levels of learning ability

mnemonic [nɪ'mɒnɪk] *noun* word, rhyme or sentence which helps you to remember other things, as, for example, 'Richard Of York Gave Battle In Vain' which has the same first letters as the colours of the rainbow - Red, Orange, Yellow, Green, Blue, Indigo, Violet

mobile ['məʊbaɪl] *adjective* can be moved easily or can move by itself; **mobile library** *see* LIBRARY **mobile phone** *see* PHONE **mobile storage files** = files that can be moved physically or electronically; **mobile unit** = complete set of filming and editing equipment which can be transported in a van for purposes such as outside broadcasts

mock-up ['mɒkʌp] *noun* model of a new product, building, etc., which can be used to show to potential customers

modal verb ['məʊdl 'vɜːb] *noun* grammatical term to describe verbs in English such as can, might, ought, which express an element of doubt or uncertainty

mode [məʊd] *noun* way of doing or operating something

model ['mɒdl] *noun* **(a)** three-dimensional smaller copy of something **(b)** theoretical statement of how a system will work which people can copy to achieve the same results

modem ['məʊdem] *noun* electronic device which converts binary to analogue signals so that data can be transmitted over the telephone network

modify ['mɒdɪfaɪ] *verb* to change something, often in only a small way, usually in order to improve it

modification [mɒdɪfɪ'keɪʃn] *noun* small change to something usually made to improve it

module ['mɒdjuːl] *noun* small section of a larger programme which can also function as a unit in its own right

modular ['mɒdjʊlə] *adjective* describes a method of organizing and teaching courses as a series of independent modules

modus operandi ['məʊdəs ɒpə'rændaɪ] *singular noun* particular and often personal way of working

MOMI = MUSEUM OF THE MOVING IMAGE

money ['mʌni] *noun* coins or bank notes that can be used to buy things

monitor ['mɒnɪtə] **1** *noun* visual display unit used to show the text and graphics generated by a computer **2** *verb* to make regular checks to see how something or someone is working

mono- ['mɒnəʊ] *prefix* used with nouns that have 'one' or 'single' as part of their meaning

monograph ['mɒnəgrɑːf] *noun* book on one specific subject

monolingual [mɒnə'lɪŋgwəl] *adjective* using only one language; *a monolingual dictionary has words in only one language*

montage [mɒn'tɑːʒ] *noun* combination of photographs, drawings or parts of pictures used for display or advertising

month [mʌnθ] *noun* period of four weeks, or about 31 days; **lunar month** = period of time between one new moon and the next, usually about 28 days

monthly ['mʌnθli] **1** *adjective* coming out regularly once a month **2** *noun* magazine published once a month

moon type ['mu:n 'taɪp] *noun* system of reading for the blind more easily learned than Braille and so often used by people who go blind late in life

morgue [mɔ:g] *noun* *(journalism)* collection of miscellaneous reference material

morocco binding [mə'rɒkəʊ 'baɪndɪŋ] *noun* fine leather book covering made from goat skin

morse code ['mɔ:s 'kəʊd] *noun* international system of short and long sounds or written dots and dashes used to send messages

mosaic [mə'zeɪɪk] *noun* picture made up of small dots as in a videotext system

mother tongue ['mʌðə 'tʌŋ] *noun* first language learned as a child

motif [məʊ'ti:f] *noun* **(a)** often repeated pattern or design **(b)** main subject which acts as the base for a work of art or music

motion picture ['məʊʃn 'pɪktʃə] *noun* film made to be shown in the cinema

motivate ['məʊtɪveɪt] *verb* encourage people to do something or behave in a positive way

motivation [məʊtɪ'veɪʃn] *noun* feeling that you want to work hard

motive ['məʊtɪv] *noun* strong reason for doing something

mount [maʊnt] *verb* **(a)** to organize an event and ensure that it happens **(b)** to fix something in a certain place; **mounted picture** = picture which is fixed on to a background to make it look better

mouse [maʊs] *noun* small hand device used to control the cursor on a computer screen; (NOTE: plural is: **mice**)

move [mu:v] *verb* **(a)** to change position **(b)** to propose an motion or amendment at a meeting

movement ['mu:mənt] *noun* **(a)** gradual change in attitude or opinion **(b)** group of people who share the same beliefs or ideas

movie ['mu:vi] *noun* *(US)* film shown in a cinema

MPEG ['empeg] = MOVING PHOTOGRAPHIC EXPERTS GROUP datafile for moving pictures on the Internet

MS = MANUSCRIPT (NOTE: plural is **MSS**)

MS/DOS = MICROSOFT DISK OPERATING SYSTEM operating system on personal computers

muddling through ['mʌdlɪŋ 'θru:] *phrase* to manage to do something even though you are not sure how to do it properly

multi- ['mʌlti] *prefix* used to form adjectives describing things which have many parts; **multi-cultural** = community or philosophy which draws from many different races and cultures; **multi-level indexing** = indexing of a document by both broad and narrow terms; **multi-lingual dictionary** = dictionary which uses several different languages; **multi-lingual thesaurus** = collection of words providing synonyms in a variety of languages; **multi-media** = using several different communication channels; **multi-tasking** = doing many things at the same time; **multi-user** *or* **multi-access system** = computer system that allows several users to access a program at the same time; **multi-value words** = words which have different meanings in different contexts

multiple ['mʌltɪpl] *adjective* having many parts, or users or uses; **multiple index** = listing of contents from several documents on a related theme

museum [mju'zi:əm] *noun* building where old, interesting and valuable objects are stored and displayed to the public; **museum catalogue** = organized list of the contents of a museum; **museum yearbook** = listing of the museums in a country and their special collections and interests

Museum of the Moving Image
(MOMI) museum in London concerned with the history of the film industry

music ['mju:zɪk] *noun* combination of sounds made by people singing or playing musical instruments; **music dictionary** = reference book which gives information about music and musicians; **music index** = reference list of articles and research about music; **music paper** = paper ruled with staves of five lines for writing out music; *see also* MANUSCRIPT MUSIC BOOK

music department   ['mju:zɪk dɪ'pɑ:tmənt] *noun* **(a)** teaching department in a college or university for the study of music theory and performance **(b)** section of a library which holds music scores, cassettes, discs, etc. **(c)** department in a shop which sells products connected with music

muted ['mju:tɪd] *adjective* describes a weak reaction to a situation

mutual ['mju:tjuəl] *adjective* something such as an interest that is shared in common between two people

myth [mɪθ] *noun* story made up a long time ago to explain natural phenomena or to justify religious beliefs

Nn

n.d. *abbreviation for* 'no date': indicates that the date of publication is not known

n.p. *abbreviation for* 'no place of publication', 'no printer's name', 'no publisher's name', 'new paragraph', 'no price'

name [neɪm] *noun* word or words used to identify a person place or object; **brand name** = name of a particular make of product; **corporate name** = name of a large corporation; **name catalogue** = catalogue arranged alphabetically by the names of people or places; **name entry** = index entry under the name of a person, place or institution; **name plate** = small sign on or next to a door to show the name of the person or company who works in that room or building

narrative [ˈnærətɪv] **1** *noun* story or poem which gives an account of a series of events **2** *adjective* told as a story

narrow term [ˈnærəʊ ˈtɜːm] *noun* indexing term to indicate a specific field which is a subsection of a broader field

NASA [ˈnɑːsə] = NATIONAL AERONAUTICS AND SPACE ADMINISTRATION US government organization concerned with space exploration and development; *NASA database contains space travel information, and can be accessed through the Internet*

national [ˈnæʃnl] *adjective* belonging to one's own country; **National Aeronautics and Space Administration** *see* NASA **national archive** = storage library for keeping records of national importance; **National Book League** *see* BOOK TRUST **National Book Council** = Australian organization founded to bring together and support all who have in interest in books whether personal, commercial or educational; **National Discography** = central online database of all commercially recorded audio materials; **National Educational Resources Information Services (NERIS)** = database of educational and curriculum information; **National Federation of Abstracting and Indexing Services (NFAIS)** = American-based confederation of all the major abstracting and indexing services; **National Film Archive** *see* BRITISH FILM INSTITUTE **National Foundation for Educational Research (NFER)** = government-funded body in the UK which undertakes research into school education; **National Health Service (NHS)** = system of public healthcare which operates in the UK; **National Information Systems (NATIS)** = international body under the guidance of UNESCO which encourages the standardization of information services for all categories of users; **national libraries** =

government funded libraries which hold copies of all books published in that country; **National Library for the Blind** = principal source in Britain of materials published in Braille and Moon; **National Record Office** = store in the UK of non-current and semi-current government records which have restricted access for 30 years; **National Register of Archives** = collection of lists of holdings of historical documents in private collections, libraries and record offices; **National Sound Archive (UK)** = formed by a merger in 1983 of the British Institute of Recorded Sound and the British Library sound archive; **national statistics** = government produced facts and figures about various aspects of national life; *there is a quarterly government publication of national statistics called Social Trends;* **National Union Catalogue** = cumulative author list of holdings in the USA, catalogued using Library of Congress printed cards; **National Vocational Qualification (NVQ)** = certificate which can be gained in the UK after following a work based course of after school training in a specific skill

NATIS = NATIONAL INFORMATION SYSTEMS

Native Speaker (NS) ['neɪtɪv 'spiːkə] *noun* person who speaks a language as a mother tongue

natural language ['nætʃrl 'læŋgwɪdʒ] *noun* language that is used and understood by humans

NBA = NET BOOK AGREEMENT

NCR paper ['en'siː'ɑː 'peɪpə] no carbon required paper, which will produce copies on paper underneath it without the use of carbon paper

need to know ['niːd tə 'nəʊ] *phrase* basic security principle which restricts access to classified materials to essential users

needs [niːdz] *plural noun* what people require in order to do what they want to do; *a library must cater for all its users' needs*

negative ['negətɪv] **1** *noun* developed film in which the colour tones are reversed and used to produce a positive print **2** *adjective* not positive; **negative feedback** = bad response to a product, book, event or idea

negotiated environment [nɪ'gəʊʃieɪtɪd ɪn'vaɪrənmənt] *noun* working conditions agreed between employer and employee

negotiation [nɪgəʊʃi'eɪʃn] *noun* discussions between people who have different viewpoints in which they try to reach an agreement

NERIS = NATIONAL EDUCATIONAL RESOURCES INFORMATION SERVICES

net [net] *adjective* describes a final amount when everything has been deducted; *a net profit or a net result after deductions;* net **book agreement (NBA)** = formerly, the agreement between publishers and booksellers, that books would be sold at an agreed price with no discounting allowed (abandoned in 1995/6)

Net [net] *see* INTERNET

netsearch ['netsɜːtʃ] *noun* program which allows the used to search for information on the Internet

network ['netwɜːk] **1** *noun* large number of people, organizations or machines that work together as a system; **Network Information System (NIS)** = electronic 'Yellow Pages' on the Internet **2** *verb* to join computers together so that they work as a system

new [njuː] *adjective* recently produced; **new book number** = temporary number assigned to a book which is required for borrowing before it is processed fully; **new edition** = book which has just been reprinted with some updating and changes; **new technology** =

electronic communication machines which have been recently invented, such as computers and fax machines

newsgroup *or* **Usenet** *noun* feature of the internet that provides a discussion forum in which any user can contribute a comment

newsletter ['njuːzletə] *noun* brief publication issued by an organization to its members with internal news and information

newspaper ['njuːzpeɪpə] *noun* number of large sheets of folded cheap paper containing printed articles and pictures and published daily or weekly; **newspaper cutting** = article on a specific subject cut out of a newspaper page; **newspaper index** = index to articles in past copies of newspapers, now usually held on a database, which can be accessed by keyword searching

newsprint ['njuːzprɪnt] *noun* cheap paper on which newspapers and magazines are printed

news-sheet ['njuːzʃiːt] *noun* small paper, with only a few pages, giving information and news to a limited number of people

newsworthy ['njuːzwɜːði] *adjective* considered to be important enough to be reported as news by the media

next [nekst] *adjective* coming immediately after the present one; **next field** = following area of information in a computer record; **next sequential record** = following record in a sequence

next of kin ['nekst əv 'kɪn] *noun* nearest relative or relatives to someone

NFAIS = NATIONAL FEDERATION OF ABSTRACTING AND INDEXING SERVICES

NFER = NATIONAL FOUNDATION FOR EDUCATIONAL RESEARCH

NHS = NATIONAL HEALTH SERVICE

niche [niːʃ] *noun* situation which exactly fits the needs of people, companies or markets etc.; *they found a niche in the market for their product so it sold well*

nickname ['nɪkneɪm] *noun* alphabetical list of frequently used names on e-mail, giving the corresponding full and official names and easy access to addresses

nil ['nɪl] *noun* **nil number** = means the same as nought (0), often used for sports scores; **nil response** = reply to a survey question which indicates that there is nothing to record as opposed to a non response which means the question is not answered

NIS = NETWORK INFORMATION SYSTEM

NNS = NON-NATIVE SPEAKER

Nobel prize ['nəʊbel 'praɪz] *noun* annual international prize for excellence awarded in various different fields such as literature, science and peace work

noise [nɔɪz] *noun* **(a)** electronic interference in an online search resulting in nonsensical responses **(b)** electronic signal present in addition to the wanted signal resulting in noisy interference

nom de plume [nɒm də 'pluːm] *noun* assumed name used by a writer for professional purposes

non- [nɒn] *prefix* not; **non-book media** *or* **non-book materials** = information which can be seen or heard but is not in printed form; **non-current record** = record which is no longer required for current business and so is assessed for storage or destruction; **non-essential record** = information that is additional to the essential facts; **non-fiction** = writing about real events and facts; **non-native speaker** (NNS) = person who speaks a language after having learned it as a second or subsequent language later in life; **non-numeric** = expressed in letters or words; **non-paper record** = record kept in electronic format; **non-preferred terms** = indexing term for sub-headings; **non-verbal communication** = messages that are given by the use of body language rather than words

norm [nɔːm] *noun* average standard by which other behaviour can be judged

normal ['nɔːməl] *adjective* usual, expected and happening regularly; *normal procedure in this company is to work;* **normal distribution** = statistical term indicating that the majority of results will appear towards the centre of a graph with smaller amounts towards the top and bottom

notation [nəʊ'teɪʃn] *noun* system of symbols used to communicate ideas such as music or mathematics

note [nəʊt] *noun* additional information in a catalogue or bibliography

note pad ['nəʊt 'pæd] *noun* memo pad, pad of headed paper used for internal messages

notice ['nəʊtɪs] **1** *noun* written announcement displayed so that everyone can read it **2** *verb* to become aware of something

noticeboard ['nəʊtɪsbɔːd] *noun* board fixed to a wall so that information can be displayed for people to read

novel [nɒvl] *noun* long fiction narrative story

novella *or* **novelette** [nə'velə or nɒvə'let] *noun* short novel

novice user ['nɒvɪs 'juːzə] *noun* person who has little or no previous experience of using a system

NS = NATIVE SPEAKER

Nuffield Talking Book Library for the Blind (NTBL) *see* BRITISH TALKING BOOK SERVICE FOR THE BLIND

number ['nʌmbə] **1** *verb* to place the call number or the charging symbol on or in a book **2** *noun* symbol representing quantity, such as 1, 20, 64, 103; (NOTE: also written **no. (no. 15)** plural: **nos. (nos. 2-20)**)

numerate ['njuːmərət] *adjective* able to calculate using numbers

numeric *or* **numerical** [njuː'merɪk or njuː'merɪkl] *adjective* using numbers; **numeric classification system** = system of organizing information for retrieval by using numbers in sequence

NVQ = NATIONAL VOCATIONAL QUALIFICATION

Oo

obiit ['ɔʊbɪɪt] *Latin word meaning* 'died'; usually abbreviated to 'ob.'; *ob. 1791*

obituary [ə'bɪtʃuəri] *noun* piece of writing about the character and achievements of someone who has just died

objective [əb'dʒektɪv] **1** *noun* what you are trying to achieve by a certain course of action **2** *adjective* outside the mind, not concerned with thoughts or feelings

oblique [ɒ'bliːk] *adjective* **(a)** indirect and difficult to understand **(b)** (line) which slopes at an angle to the right

obscene [ɒb'siːn] *adjective* shocking or offensive usually because of pictures or references to naked people, sexual acts or bodily functions; **obscene publications** = books, films or any publications which offend against an accepted standard of decency

observation [ɒbzə'veɪʃn] *noun* action of watching someone or something very carefully especially for the purpose of research or study

obsolescence [ɒsə'lesəns] *noun* becoming obsolete; **built-in obsolescence** = deliberate features of the design which will cause a piece of equipment to become out of date and needing to be replaced

obsolete ['ɒbsəliːt] *adjective* no longer needed because something newer or more efficient has been invented or designed

obtain [ɒb'teɪn] *verb* to get or achieve something

obtainable [ɒb'teɪnəbl] *adjective* easily available

obverse ['ɒbvɜːs] *noun* **(a)** opposite opinion in an argument or situation looked at from the opposite point of view **(b)** front of a coin as opposed to the reverse

obvious ['ɒbviəs] *adjective* easily seen and understood; **stating the obvious** = saying things which everyone ought to know already

occasional publication [ə'keɪʒənl 'pʌblɪkeɪʃn] *noun* document which does not appear on a regular basis

occasional user [ə'keɪʒənl 'juːzə] *noun* person who does not use a service or system very often

occidental [ɒksɪ'dentl] *adjective* relating to the countries of Europe and America, commonly known as the Western world

occupation [ɒkju'peɪʃn] *noun* job or profession

occupational hazard [ɒkju'peɪənl 'hæzɑːd] *noun* something unpleasant or even dangerous that you may encounter as a result of doing your job

occur [əkɜː] *verb* to happen or take place; *data loss can occur because of power variations*

OCR = OPTICAL CHARACTER RECOGNITION

octavo (8vo) [ɒk'teɪvəʊ] *noun* page made when a sheet of paper is folded three times, giving a 16-page section

odd [ɒd] *adjective* (a) strange or unusual (b) **odd number** = number which cannot be divided by 2 to give a whole number; *5 and 7 are odd numbers*

OED ['əʊ 'iː 'diː] = OXFORD ENGLISH DICTIONARY

offcut ['ɒfkʌt] *noun* scrap paper left over when a sheet is trimmed to size

off-duty ['ɒf 'djuːti] *adjective* not working for a period of time; often used of people who do part-time or shift work like librarians; *compare* ON-DUTY

offer ['ɒfə] *noun* statement of willingness to do something; **special offer** = goods or services being sold at a specially low price usually for a short period of time

office automation ['ɒfis ɔːtə'meɪʃn] *noun* use of machines and computers to carry out normal office tasks

official catalogue [ə'fiʃl 'kætəlɒg] *noun* union catalogue for the use of library staff only

official name [ə'fiʃl 'neɪm] *noun* legal name

official publication [ə'fiʃl pʌblɪ'keɪʃn] *noun* document produced and published by official bodies, often kept by libraries as reference material

official title [ə'fiʃl 'taɪtl] *noun* title used by the cataloguer and appearing on the title page

offline [ɒf'laɪn] *adjective* processor or printer or terminal which is disconnected from the network or central computer, usually temporarily

offset litho ['ɒfset 'laɪθəʊ] *noun* printing process where the ink sticking to the image areas on film is transferred to rubber rollers for printing onto paper

off the record ['ɒf ðə 'rekɔːd] *phrase* used to indicate that something that is said should not be recorded or made public

OHP = OVERHEAD PROJECTOR

OK informal word meaning 'correct' or 'yes', sometimes used as a computer prompt to ask if you want to continue; (NOTE: also spelt **Okay**)

old stock ['əʊld 'stɒk] *noun* books or documents that have been withdrawn from public use and either disposed of or kept in reserve

Olympic Games [ə'lɪmpɪk 'geɪmz] *plural noun* international sports competitions at a very high level held every four years in a different country

omission factor [ə'mɪʃn 'fæktə] *noun* number of relevant documents missed in a search

omission marks [ə'mɪʃn 'mɑːks] *noun* three dots ... used in a quotation to show that something in the original has been left out

omit [ə'mɪt] *verb* (a) to leave something out or not put something in (b) to fail to do something; *he omitted to transfer the new books to the acquisitions register, so no-one knew they had arrived*

omnibus ['ɒmnɪbəs] *noun* collection of stories and/or articles by one or more authors bound into one book

on [ɒn] *preposition* (a) placed on top of something (b) done by a machine or instrument; *done on a computer* (c) to be a member of a council or committee; *she was on three committees* (d) **on approval** = describes goods which are kept for a short time by a customer without payment, so that they can decide to buy or return them; **on demand** = providing something only when it is asked for; *video tapes were provided on demand;* **on disk** = held on a computer floppy disk which can be transferred to other machines; **on hand** = readily and immediately available; **on screen** = displayed on a computer screen rather than printed out; **on site** = in the building where the user is working

on-duty ['ɒndjuːti] *adjective* at work for a certain period of time; *compare* OFF-DUTY

online ['ɒnlaɪn] *adjective* connected to a mainframe computer often by a remote terminal; **Online Public Access Catalogue (OPAC)** = electronic system for cataloguing library stock which can be used at a computer terminal to search for specific items; **online search** = searches of catalogues and databases for bibliographic records by direct computer contact with national, international or inter-library databases; **online storage** = data stored on a computer

on-the-job ['ɒnðə'dʒɒb] *adjective* done while you are working; *on-the-job training*

one-off ['wɒn 'ɒf] *noun* something that happens or is made only once

one to one ['wɒn tə 'wɒn] *adverb* working or talking with one person only

onerous ['ɔunərəs] *adjective* difficult or unpleasant work

onus ['ɔunəs] *noun* duty or responsibility to do something; *the onus was on me to finish the job*

OP = OUT OF PRINT

op. cit. Latin phrase meaning opere citato; used in references after an author's name, to refer to a book by the same person which has already been cited

op. no. = OPUS NUMBER

OPAC = ONLINE PUBLIC ACCESS CATALOGUE

opaque [ə'peɪk] *adjective* difficult to see through or understand

open ['ɔupən] *adjective* not closed; **open access** = direct access for library users to documents on the shelves; *compare* CLOSED ACCESS **open back file** = box file in the shape of a book for holding pamphlets and papers, with a back which can be easily opened; **open day** = special day when the public are allowed to visit an institution; **open entry** = catalogue entry which leaves room for additions; *the library did not have all the items in the set, so it used an open entry to allow for additions later;* **open learning** *see* DISTANCE LEARNING **open question** = question which can be answered by an opinion or expression of views; *compare* CLOSED QUESTION **Open University (OU)** = institution of higher education in the UK which does most of its teaching by distance learning materials and the use of the national broadcasting networks

opening hours ['ɔupnɪŋ 'auəz] *plural noun* hours during which a company, organization or service is open to the public

operate ['ɒpəreɪt] *verb* to work or to make work

operating instruction ['ɒpəreɪtɪŋ ɪn'strʌkʃn] *noun* command which explains how to work a machine

operating system ['ɒpəreɪtɪŋ 'sɪstəm] *noun* basic software which controls the running of the computer

operating time ['ɒpəreɪtɪŋ 'taɪm] *noun* time required to carry out a task

operational [ɒpə'reɪʃnl] *adjective* in working order

operational indicators [ɒpə'reɪʃnl 'ɪndɪkeɪtəz] *noun* statistics which indicate how a system or organization is functioning

opinion [ə'pɪnjən] *noun* advice, belief or judgement

opportunity [ɒpə'tjuːnɪti] *noun* situation which makes it possible to do something

oppose [ə'pəʊz] *verb* (a) to express strong disagreement (b) to contrast one thing to another deliberately in order to emphasize a particular point of view; **as opposed to** = contrasting two things when you want to emphasize the first one

opposite ['ɒpəzɪt] *adjective* next to something, but facing the other way; **opposite number** = person who does the same job as you in another department or institution

optical character recognition (OCR) ['ɒptɪkl 'kærəktə rekəg'nɪʃn] *noun* technique for machine reading which uses special forms of type

optical information system ['ɒptɪkl ɪnfə'meɪʃn 'sɪstəm] *noun* encoded format for information storage; *CD-ROM and Video disk are forms of optical information systems*

optimism ['ɒptɪmɪzm] *noun* feeling that the future will be successful

optimization [ɒptɪmaɪ'zeɪʃn] *noun* making the very best possible use of a situation or asset

option ['ɒpʃn] *noun* (a) action or situation which can be chosen (b) freedom to choose something

opus ['əʊpəs] *noun* work of music or art; often abbreviated and used with an opus number to indicate the chronology of the work within a composer's total work; *Beethoven Op 23*

ORACLE teletext system used by the UK Independent Broadcasting Authority

ORBIT Infoline database host specializing in patents, science, engineering, health & safety

order ['ɔːdə] **1** *verb* **(a)** to arrange things according to a system, such as first, second, third **(b)** to ask for something to be brought or sent to you which you will then pay for **2** *noun* **in order** = (i) in sequence; (ii) working properly

ordinal number ['ɔːdɪnəl 'nʌmbə] *adjective* which tells the position in a sequence; *second and third are ordinal numbers*

Ordnance Survey map (O.S.) ['ɔːdnəns 'sɜːveɪ] *noun* detailed map of Britain or Ireland known as the Ordnance Survey, originally used for military purposes

organization [ɔːgənaɪ'zeɪʃn] *noun* **(a)** company or group of people doing things together **(b)** structure of something, especially the way in which different parts are related to each other

oriental [ɔːri'entl] *adjective* of the East especially India, China, Japan, Korea, etc.

orientation [ɔːrien'teɪʃn] *noun* **(a)** information or training that is necessary in order to understand a new subject, job, activity or situation **(b)** interests and aims of an organization

oriented ['ɒrientɪd] *adjective* describes the direction of the interests of a person or organization

origin ['ɒrɪdʒɪn] *noun* **(a)** place or time of the beginning of something **(b)** country, place or social class of a person's parents or ancestors

original [ə'rɪdʒɪnl] *noun* **(a)** first document from which copies have been made **(b)** piece of writing or music that is genuine and not a copy

orphan ['ɔ:fən] *noun* first line of a paragraph when it is printed by itself at the bottom of a column or page

orthodox ['ɔ:θədɒks] *adjective* believed or accepted by most people

-ory [əri] *suffix* forming adjectives with the sense of 'the nature of'; *advisory*

OS = OUT OF STOCK

O.S. = ORDNANCE SURVEY

-ose [əuz] *suffix* forming adjectives with the sense of 'characterized by'; *grandiose*

-osity ['ɒsɪti] *suffix* forming nouns from adjectives with the meaning of 'the quality of being'; *curiosity*

OU = OPEN UNIVERSITY

out- [aut] *prefix* used with verbs to show that you can do the action better than another person; *they were outbid at the auction by someone with more money;* out of date = no longer in general use, past the date for legal use; **out of order** *or* **out of action** = not working properly; **out of print (OP)** = describes a book of which the publisher has no copies left and which is not going to be reprinted; **out of stock (OS)** = describes a publication of which the supplier or retailer has no copies at present

outcome ['autkʌm] *noun* result of an action or process

outlay ['autleɪ] *noun* amount of money paid especially at the beginning of a project

outlet ['autlət] *noun* market for a product, or shop or organization which sells commodities (including information)

outline ['autlaɪn] **1** *noun* **(a)** edge round an image **(b)** rough draft or summary **2** *verb* to describe the main features of something

outlying ['autlaɪɪŋ] *adjective* (places) that are far away from the main cities in a country

outnumber [aut'nʌmbə] *verb* to have more people or things than another group

output ['autput] **1** *noun* amount which a person, organization or machine produces **2** *verb* to print work done on a computer

outside broadcast ['autsaɪd 'brɔ:dka:st] *noun* programme made for radio or television outside the studio

outside supplier ['autsaɪd sə'plaɪə] *noun* person who provides information from outside the company or organization

outsource ['autsɔ:s] *verb* to send work out to be done by freelance workers outside the company or organization

outstanding [aut'stændɪŋ] *adjective* **(a)** excellent **(b)** still to be done or completed; *outstanding invoices are those which still have to be paid*

outweigh [aut'weɪ] *verb* to be more important or significant than something else

overall [əuvə'ɔ:l] *adjective* including everything in general but not considering the details; *an overall view*

overcharge [əuvə'tʃa:dʒ] *verb* to ask for more money than is reasonable for a product or service

overdue [əuvə'dju:] *adjective* past the due date; *the library book was overdue because the date for returning it had past;* overdue notice = written request to a reader to return books or materials

overhead projector (OHP) [əuvə'hed prə'dʒektə] *noun* machine for displaying an image of transparent artwork on a screen usually for the purposes of teaching or presentations

overink [əuvə'ɪŋk] *verb* to cover in too much ink so that the printing image is unclear

overlap ['əuvəlæp] *noun* point at which things start to be duplicated; *the periods of library duty overlapped by ten minutes*

overlay ['əʊvəleɪ] *noun* transparent sheet used with overhead transparencies to add information at a specific time and place

overleaf [əʊvə'liːf] *adjective* on the other side of the page

overseas [əʊvə'siːz] *adjective* used in the UK to describe anyone from other countries (now thought to be politically incorrect and being replaced by 'international'); *they are not called overseas students now but international students*

oversee [əʊvə'siː] *verb* to supervise a person or task

oversight ['əʊvəsaɪt] *noun* omission or a careless mistake because of failure to notice something

oversize [əʊvə'saɪz] *adjective* books and other printed materials that are larger than the standard book sizes and are often stored in a special area

overstock [əʊvə'stɒk] *verb* to keep more books, documents, information than is necessary for the users being served

overtime ['əʊvətaɪm] *noun* time that is worked in addition to contracted hours and for which you are usually paid extra

overworked [əʊvə'wɜːkt] *adjective* describes someone who is working too hard and beginning to look and feel unwell

own brand ['əʊn 'brænd] *adjective* packaged and marketed under a name belonging to the company selling them

ownership ['əʊnəʃɪp] *noun* position of owning something; *the ownership of information is a difficult matter to determine*

Oxford English Dictionary (OED) complete collection of words and definitions for the English language; also available on CD-ROM

Pp

p *abbreviation for* page; *table 6 is on p23 and tables 7-9 are on pp24 & 25;* (NOTE: plural is **pp**)

pack [pæk] **1** *noun* packet of information containing such items as leaflets, maps, etc. relevant to a particular topic **2** *verb* to put things into containers or parcels so that they can be sent to another address

packet ['pækɪt] *noun* small parcel; **Packet Assembler/Dissembler** *see* PAD **packet switching** = method of dividing data into small packets for transmission between terminals and networks

packing list *or* **packing slip** ['pækɪŋ 'lɪst *or* 'slɪp] *noun* note sent with goods to say that the goods have been checked against the order

pad [pæd] *noun* several pieces of paper joined together at one edge so that each piece can be torn off after use; **memo pad** = pad of headed paper used for internal messages; **phone message pad** = pad specially printed so that information such as the time and telephone number of the caller can be recorded

PAD Packet Assembler/Disassembler; a device for making up the packets in a packet switching system

padding ['pædɪŋ] *noun* **(a)** soft material put inside something to provide protection or change the shape **(b)** unnecessary information put into a speech or written document to increase the length

padded envelope ['pædɪd 'envələup] *noun* container which has a soft lining to protect goods sent through the post

page [peɪdʒ] **1** *noun* **(a)** one side of a sheet of paper in a book, newspaper or magazine **(b)** computer text which will fill one sheet of paper when printed out; **page break** = line on the screen of word processed text which shows where the end of the printed page will occur; **page layout** = word processing facility which allows the text to be formatted in different ways; **page preview** = word processing facility which allows the shape of the text to be seen before printing **(c)** document, or item of information, on the Internet available through the World Wide Web; **2** *verb* to call for someone over the public address system in a large building such as a hotel or airport

pager ['peɪdʒə] *noun* small device carried in the pocket which allows someone to be called from a telephone in a central office by using a radio signal

pagination [pædʒɪ'neɪʃn] *noun* system of numbering the pages in a document

paleography [pæli'ngrəfi] *noun* study of ancient writing and documents

palimpsest ['pælɪmsest] *noun* manuscript in which the first text has been partly erased and replaced by the second text

pamphlet ['pæmflət] *noun* small thin book, with at least 6 but not more than 48 pages and a paper cover, used to convey information; **pamphlet box** = box specially designed to hold pamphlets within in a storage system

panel ['pænəl] *noun* group of people chosen to do something or make a decision

panellist ['pænəlɪst] *noun* person who sits with a group of other people to perform a group task; *the librarian was one of the interview panellists*

paper ['peɪpə] *noun* **(a)** material that you write on or wrap things in; **carbon paper** = paper with a blue or black surface, which enables copies to be made when it is placed between sheets of writing paper; **duplicating paper** = special quality paper used for photocopying; **paper deterioration** = effect of age or damage on paper which causes it to discolour, tear or become brittle **(b)** newspaper **(c)** part of a written examination **(d)** long essay on an academic subject

paperback ['peɪpəbæk] *noun* book with a paper or light card cover

paperbased record ['peɪpəbeɪst 'rekɔ:d] *noun* record kept on paper or card rather than a computer

paperless office ['peɪpələs 'nfɪs] *noun* office which uses only electronic means of working, without any hard copy of materials

papers ['peɪpəz] *plural noun* your papers are official documents, such as your passport or identity card

paperweight ['peɪpəweɪt] *noun* small heavy object, often decoratively designed, which can be placed on piles of paper to stop them blowing away

paperwork ['peɪpəwɜ:k] *noun* routine part of a job which involves dealing with items written on paper such as letters and reports

paradigm ['pærədaɪm] *noun* model or typical example of something

paragraph ['pærəgra:f] *noun* section of writing which contains one main idea, always starts on a new line, and is usually indented

parallel ['pærəlel] *adjective* used to describe an event or situation that happens at the same time as another similar one; **parallel edition** = publication in which different editions of the same work are published side by side, i.e. the same text in different languages; **parallel processing** = computer operations which occur simultaneously; **parallel publishing** = simultaneous production of a text in printed and electronic format

parameter [pə'ræmɪtə] *noun* limit which affects how something is done or made

paraphrase ['pærəfreɪz] *noun* to summarize someone's ideas in your own words

parchment ['pa:tʃmənt] *noun* writing material made from thinly stretched skin of sheep or goats

parent ['peərənt] *noun* mother or father; **parents' association** = group of parents who meet to discuss issues of importance to their children's schools

parentheses [pə'renθɪsi:z] *plural noun* round brackets () as opposed to square brackets []

parliament ['pa:ləmənt] *noun* group of people who are elected to represent the citizens, and can make or change the laws of a country

parliamentary [pa:lə'mentri] *adjective* **parliamentary directory** = list of the members of parliament with details about their careers; **parliamentary paper** = policy statement issued by parliament either as a proposal for law (white paper) or for consultation (green paper); **parliamentary publication** = information or report published by the government; in the UK these are published by HMSO (Her Majesty's Stationery Office); **parliamentary record** = record of what is said in the debates in parliament published as Hansard; *see also* HANSARD

part [pɑːt] *noun* section of a larger item; **part order** = one or some of the items in a group of items ordered together; **two part** *or* **three part stationery** = invoices or receipts which have a top sheet with copy sheets attached

part-time ['pɑːttaɪm] *adjective* working for only a part of normal full working hours

participate [pɑːˈtɪsɪpeɪt] *verb* to take part or become involved in something

participant [pɑːˈtɪsɪpənt] *noun* someone who takes part in an activity or event

partition [pɑːˈtɪʃn] *noun* screen or temporary wall used to separate one part of a room from another

partnership ['pɑːtnəʃɪp] *noun* relationship in which people or organizations work together with equal status

partwork ['pɑːtwɜːk] *noun* long work published in smaller parts at regular intervals

party line ['pɑːti 'laɪn] *noun* **(a)** telephone line shared with other subscribers **(b)** policy followed by political parties

pass [pɑːs] *noun* document which allows you to do something; *the student pass allowed them to get cheap tickets at the cinema*

password ['pɑːswɜːd] *noun* secret word or phrase which allows you to use a computer system or get into a building

patent ['pætənt] **1** *noun* official right given to the inventor or originator of a product to control the making and sale of it, for a period of time; **patent file** = patent specifications and drawings indexed either by country and number or by name of patentee or by subject; **patent office** = government office in the UK which controls the issuing of patents **2** *verb* to register an invention with the patent office

patentee [peɪtənˈtiː] *noun* person in whose name the patent is registered

patently ['peɪtəntli] *adjective* very obvious; *it is patently obvious that she was best*

Patents Information Network Bulletin (PIN Bulletin) electronic information service of the Science Reference and Information Service of the British Library

path [pɑːθ] *noun* particular course of action; *here are many paths to success*

patron ['peɪtrən] *noun* person or group that encourages and supports an activity, sometimes with money

pattern ['pætən] *noun* particular way something is done or organized; *the work patterns need to be changed*

pay [peɪ] **1** *noun* money received in return for work **2** *verb* **(a)** to give someone money in exchange for goods or services **(b)** to be profitable; *these days there is a move towards making some library services pay*

pay factor ['peɪ 'fæktə] *noun* effect of wages on the demand for work

payment ['peɪmənt] *noun* sum of money given to someone in return for goods or services; **payment date** = date by which a bill must be paid

payphone ['peɪfəʊn] *noun* public telephone in which the user can pay for calls by coins, or cards

payroll ['peɪrəʊl] *noun* list of employees who are paid wages or salaries by a company

PC ['piː 'siː] **1** = PERSONAL COMPUTER **2** = POLITICALLY CORRECT

peak [piːk] *adjective* describes the highest point or maximum value of a variable; **peak demand** = highest level of demand from users for services; **peak time** *or* **peak period** = time of day when most people do something; *peak viewing time for television in the UK is from 7 - 10 pm*

peer [piːə] *noun* person of the same age or social status

peg [peg] *verb* to fix the value or level of something and prevent it from changing

pending ['pendɪŋ] *adjective* awaiting attention, which will be dealt with soon; **pending file** = file for keeping papers about matters which cannot be dealt with immediately

PEN International international fellowship of writers in any genre which aims to promote freedom of expression and international cultural understanding

per [pɜː] *preposition* used to express ratio; *the rent was £250 per month; the speed limit is 50 km per hour;* **per annum** = each year; *she earns £25,000 per annum;* **per capita** *or* **per head** for each person; *what is the average per capita income?;* **per cent** = describes a number which represents a part of a hundred; *10 per cent (10%) means 10 in every 100*

percentage [pə'sentɪdʒ] *noun* amount shown as a fraction of 100; *the percentage of library users is about 10% of the population;* **percentage point** = one per cent

perception [pə'sepʃn] *noun* **(a)** ability to notice things that are not obvious **(b)** opinion about someone or something

perfect 1 [pə'fekt] *verb* to improve something until is completely correct **2** ['pɜːfɪkt] *adjective* without any mistake; **perfect binding** = method of binding a paperback book by glueing the pages to the cover, without sewing them **3** ['pɜːfɪkt] *noun* grammatical term to describe the tenses of a verb formed with the auxiliary verb 'to have' together with the past participle, such as 'he has written'

perfector [pə'fektə] *noun* printing machine which prints on both sides of a sheet of paper

perforate ['pɜːfəreɪt] *verb* to make holes in something so that it can be torn easily; *sheets of stamps are perforated*

perforated edge ['pɜːfəreɪtɪd 'edʒ] *noun* irregular edge left after tearing perforated paper such as round the edge of postage stamps

perforating stamp ['pɜːfəreɪtɪŋ 'stæmp] *noun* device which punches a mark by making a pattern of holes through the pages of a book

perforation [pɜːfə'reɪʃn] *noun* very small hole made to help to tear paper at a certain point

perform [pə'fɔːm] *verb* to do a task or action

performance [pə'fɔːməns] *noun* way in which something is done; **performance indicator** = record which shows how well or badly an organization is functioning

period ['pɪəriəd] *noun* **(a)** particular length of time; **accounting period** = time at the end of which a company's accounts are closed for checking; **holiday period** = time of year during which most people take their annual holidays; **period of notice** = time which must be worked after giving notice of leaving a job

(b) *US* used to mean full stop; also to emphasize that there is no more to be said about a subject

periodic *or* **periodical** [pi:ri'ɒdɪkl] *adjective* happening occasionally but fairly regularly

periodical [pi:ri'ɒdɪkl] *noun* magazine or journal especially a serious academic one; **periodical control** = system for organizing journals in a library; **periodical index** = (i) index to one or more volumes of a periodical; (ii) cumulative subject index issued at stated intervals

peripheral [pə'rɪfərəl] **1** *noun* piece of equipment attached to a computer, such as a printer or monitor **2** *adjective* not essential, attached to the edge of something else

perk [pɜːk] *noun (short for 'perquisite')* goods or advantages additional to expected ones; *a perk of writing book reviews is that you can keep the review copy*

permanent ['pɜːmənənt] *adjective* expected to last for ever or very long lasting

permeate ['pɜːmieɪt] *verb* to spread through and affect every part

permit 1 ['pɜːmɪt] *noun* official document which allows you to do a particular thing; *you have to have a permit to study in this library* **2** [pə'mɪt] *verb (formal)* to allow something to be done

permutation [pɜːmju:'teɪʃn] *noun* one of a set of ways in which things can be arranged; *there were so many permutations to the combination for the lock that it was very secure*

persist [pə'sɪst] *verb* to continue doing something even though it is very difficult or time consuming

persistent [pə'sɪstənt] *adjective* continuing to exist for a very long time

person to person ['pɜːsən tə 'pɜːsən] *US see* REVERSED CHARGES

personal ['pɜːsnəl] *adjective* belonging to you; **personal attention** = dealing with a matter by yourself

personal computer (PC) ['pɜːsnl kʌm'pju:tə] *noun* small computer designed mainly for home or light business use

Personal Identification Number (PIN number) given to people for use with electronic cards such as credit cards

personalized ['pɜːsənəlaɪzd] *adjective* printed with a person's name and/or address

personnel [pɜːsə'nel] *noun* people who work for an organization

phase [feɪz] **1** *noun* particular stage in the development of something **2** *verb* to do something in stages; **to phase out** = to stop using something gradually; **to phase in** = to introduce something gradually

phased changeover ['feɪzd 'tʃeɪndʒəʊvə] *noun* change which takes place in stages over a period of time

Ph.D *see* DOCTOR OF PHILOSOPHY

phone [fəʊn] **1** *noun* electronic device which enables two people who each have a phone to talk to each other over a distance; **internal phone** = telephone on a network so that you can communicate with other offices within an organization; **phone book** *see* TELEPHONE DIRECTORY **phone card** = electronically coded card which enables the user to pay for calls on a public phone without using coins; **phone message pad** = pad specially printed so that information such as the time and telephone number of the caller can be recorded; **phone number** = set of figures which identifies the phone line which is being used **2** *verb* to use a phone to contact another person

phone back ['fəʊn 'bæk] *verb* to make a telephone call to someone who has just called you

phoneme ['fəuni:m] *noun* single item of sound used in speech; *the letters 'd' and 't' are two different phonemes*

phonetics [fə'netɪks] *noun* study of speech sounds; **phonetic script** = system of writing the sounds of language by using one symbol for each sound

photocopy ['fəutəkɒpi] **1** *noun* exact copy of a document produced by a photocopier, in black and white or colour **2** *verb* to make a copy of a document by using a photocopier

photocopier ['fəutəkɒpiə] *noun* machine that copies documents by photographing them very quickly

photograph ['fəutəgrɑːf] *noun* picture formed by exposing light sensitive paper to light by using a camera; **photograph directory** = list of photographs held by a special photo library such as one in a newspaper office or broadcasting company, often catalogued by subject

photographic [fəutə'græfik] *adjective* used to describe anything to do with photography or photographs

photography [fə'tɒgrəfi] *noun* art or skill of producing photographs including use of a camera and the processing of the films

photogravure [fəutəugrə'vjuə] *noun* printing method in which the paper is pressed directly on to the printing plate

photoprint ['fəutəprɪnt] *noun* final proof of a typeset copy

photostat ['fəutəstæt] *noun* *see* PHOTOCOPY

phototext ['fəutətekst] *noun* characters and text produced by a phototypesetter

phototypesetter [fəutəu'taɪpsetə] *noun* person who works with a computer and light sensitive film to produce text ready for printing

physical ['fɪzɪkl] *adjective* something which can be seen or touched, as opposed to a theoretical idea; **physical record** = manual form of a record rather than electronic

pica ['paɪkə] *noun* measurement of typeface equal to 12 point

pick [pɪk] *verb* to choose something or someone; **to pick out** = to select from a group

pick up ['pɪk 'ʌp] *verb* **(a)** to learn a skill or an idea easily **(b)** to improve; *the working conditions for the library staff picked up last month*

picture ['pɪktʃə] *noun* drawing, painting or photograph; **picture file** = collection of small pictures, cuttings, illustrations, etc. usually arranged by subject; **picture library** = storage system for pictures, which can be borrowed; **picture researcher** = someone who looks for pictures relevant to a particular topic, so that they can be used as illustrations in a book, newspaper, TV programme, etc.

pie chart ['paɪ 'tʃɑːt] *noun* statistical diagram where the ratios are shown as sections of a circle

pigeonhole ['pɪdʒənhəul] *noun* small open section in a wall mounted rack used as a temporary storage space or for delivery of personal mail

pilot ['paɪlət] **1** *verb* to use a small-scale test to investigate whether a larger scale operation will work **2** *adjective* small test of a larger project; *a pilot scheme in a temporary building was used to see if a library was needed in the area*

pin [pɪn] *noun* **(a)** sharp piece of metal used for holding material or paper together **(b)** part of an electric plug which fits into the hole in the socket; **drawing pin** = sharp metal object with a large flat head used for attaching notices to a board; **map pin** = sharp metal object with a small round coloured head used to indicate places on a map

PIN Bulletin = PATENTS INFORMATION NETWORK BULLETIN

PIN number = PERSONAL IDENTIFICATION NUMBER

pipeline ['paɪplaɪn] *noun* system for the dissemination of information; **in the pipeline** = something which has already been started but has not yet produced an answer or result

piracy ['paɪrəsi] *noun* act of illegal copying

pirate ['paɪrət] *verb* to copy a patented or copyright work and sell it; **pirate copy** = illegal copy of a patented or copyright work

pitch [pɪtʃ] *verb* to set a talk or instruction at a particular level

pixel ['pɪksəl] *noun* smallest unit of display on a computer screen whose colour or brightness can be controlled; *the picture was made up of several hundred pixels of different colours*

place [pleɪs] **1** *noun* position **2** *verb* to put something in a particular position; *place the reserved books on a special shelf;* **to place an order** = to ask for particular goods to be sent to or obtained for you

place name ['pleɪs 'neɪm] *noun* name by which a location is identified; **dictionary of place names** = alphabetical list of places often with historical notes about their names

plagiarize ['pleɪdʒəraɪz] *verb* to copy someone else's work and publish it as your own

plagiarism ['pleɪdʒərɪzm] *noun* copying and publishing someone else's work as your own

plagiarist ['pleɪdʒərɪst] *noun* person who copies other people's work without admitting what they have done

plagiary ['pleɪdʒəri] *noun* work which has been plagiarized

plaintext ['peɪntekst] *noun* (i) term used in word processing to mean text that is in the standard font for that document without commands such as bold or italics, etc. (ii) an electronic mail message or document before it is encrypted

plan [plæn] **1** *noun* (**a**) carefully worked out method of achieving objectives; **contingency plan** = decision about what to do if the first arrangements cannot be implemented; *there was a contingency plan to move the book store to the first floor in case of flood danger;* **economic plan** = policy for economic development in a country (**b**) map; **floor plan** = diagram showing the layout of a building; **seating plan** = diagram showing where people should sit at a formal function such as a dinner; **street plan** *or* **town plan** = map of the streets in a particular town **2** *verb* **to plan for** = to make plans for a future event

planner ['plænə] *noun* person who works out in detail what needs to be done in the future; **wall planner** = chart with empty spaces marked with the dates for each day of the year so that events can be written in

planning ['plænɪŋ] *noun* process of working out in detail how to do something before starting to do it; **planning department** = local government department which decides how land in a given area will be used and what buildings may be put on it; **long-term planning** = decisions about what will be done several years ahead; **short-term planning** = decisions about what will be done in the near future

plastic ['plæstɪk] *noun* artificial waterproof material which can be both soft or hard

plasticize ['plæstɪsaɪz] *verb* to put a plastic cover over a book jacket for protection

plate [pleɪt] *noun* illustration in a book often on better quality paper than the text; **plate camera** = camera which uses glass plates instead of film

platen ['plætən] *noun* roller which supports the paper in a typewriter or printer

playback ['pleɪbæk] *verb* to operate a machine so that it can reproduce the sound or video pictures previously recorded

Play Matters working title of the UK National Toy Library

plenary ['pliːnəri] *adjective* attended by everyone who should be there; *the conference ended with a plenary session for all the participants*

plot [plɒt] **1** *noun* secret plan **2** *verb* to mark the co-ordinates and draw a graph

plotter ['plɒtə] *noun* computer device that draws straight lines between two co-ordinates

plug [plʌg] **1** *noun* device with metal pins which can be inserted into an electrical socket to provide power for a machine; **plug board** = board with several electrical sockets so that they are all connected to the same; **plug compatible** = (machines) that can be joined together because they use the same size plugs **2** *verb* **(a)** to publicize something by praising it thus encouraging people to buy it **(b) to plug in** = to push a plug into an electrical socket power source

plural ['pluərəl] *adjective* grammatical term to describe words which refer to two or more things

plus [plʌs] *noun* **(a)** mathematical sign for addition (+) **(b)** benefit or advantage; *the effect of the new library was to provide several pluses for the user*

pocket ['pɒkɪt] *noun* part of clothing, a small bag for carrying things which is attached to a jacket or skirt, etc.; **pocket diary** *or* **pocket calculator** *or* **pocket dictionary** = diary, calculator or dictionary which is small enough to be carried in your pocket; **be out of pocket** = to have less money than you should have because you have paid for something out of your own

money instead of asking for it to be paid for by your employer

poem ['pəʊɪm] *noun* imaginative writing which is arranged in a particular pattern of lines and sounds

poet ['pəʊɪt] *noun* person who writes poems; **Poet Laureate** = poet appointed by the British Queen to write poems for official occasions

point [pɔɪnt] **1** *noun* **(a)** place or position in time; *starting point;* **to be on the point of** = to be just about to start doing something; **up to a point** = partly, not completely; *it is true up to point;* **point of sale** = place where things sold in a shop are paid for **(b)** idea or opinion; *he made a good point in the discussion* **(c) decimal point** = dot which separates whole numbers from fractions; in many countries this is a comma; *2.75 or 2,75;* **percentage point** = 1 per cent **(d)** *(in typography)* **point size** = the size of printed letters; *9 point, 14 point* **2** *verb* **to point out** *or* **to point to** = to use a finger or stick to draw attention to something

point of presence *see* POP

pointer ['pɔɪntə] *noun* stick used to indicate something

policy ['pɒlɪsi] *noun* set of plans used as a basis for decisions

political [pə'lɪtɪkl] *adjective* concerned with the government or state; **political correctness** = use of gender free language and behaviour

politically correct (PC) [pə'lɪtɪkli kə'rekt] *adjective* (language) that is gender free and will not offend anyone

politics ['pɒlɪtɪks] *noun* art or science of government; **internal politics** = relationships within an organization which affect the way it works; *the internal politics of promotion within the library caused a lot of arguments*

polysemy [pɒ'lisimi] *noun* quality of having two or more overlapping meanings

poll [pəʊl] *noun* **(a)** survey in which a selected sample of people are asked their opinions about something **(b)** voting at a political election

polling station ['pəʊlɪŋ 'steɪʃn] *noun* place where people go to vote at an election

POP = POINT OF PRESENCE telephone access number that a user dials with his modem to connect to the internet via an ISP

pop-up book ['pɒpʌp 'bʊk] *noun* book, usually for children, in which the pictures are cut out from the page so that they stand up when the book is opened

POP3 standard method of sending electronic mail messages from a user's computer via the internet *see also* SMTP

popular edition ['pɒpjʊlə ɪ'dɪʃn] *noun* book with poorer paper and lighter cover, sold at a cheaper price

population [pɒpjʊ'leɪʃn] *noun* **(a)** all the inhabitants of a particular area or country **(b)** selected sample for a survey; **population coverage** = selection of a survey population which considers all the different aspects to be covered

pornography [pɔ:'nɒgrəfi] *noun* publications of an obscene nature, usually in a sexual sense

portable ['pɔ:təbl] **1** *adjective* easily carried **2** *noun* easily carried machine such as a small computer or television

portfolio [pɔ:t'fəʊliəʊ] *noun* **(a)** collection of original works **(b)** area of responsibility held by a government minister **(c)** thin flat case for carrying drawings and papers

portrait ['pɔ:treɪt] *noun* painting, drawing or photograph of a person or group

position [pə'zɪʃn] *noun* job or status within a company

positive ['pɒzɪtɪv] *adjective* good, useful and forward looking; **positive discrimination** = policy which deliberately treats one group of people better than others because they have previously been unfairly treated; **positive feedback** = response to an event or product which shows approval

post- [pəʊst] *prefix* combines with nouns, adjectives and dates to indicate that something has happened after the given time; *post-war; post-audit;* postdated = dated later than the day of issue; *the cheque was postdated to the end of the month so that her salary would have been paid in to the bank*

post [pəʊst] *verb* **(a)** to send letters and parcels through the mailing system; **post & packing (p&p)** = cost of wrapping goods and paying for them to be delivered; **post office** = national organization which controls the postal services within a country **(b)** to add the accession number to an index entry

postage stamp ['pəʊstɪdʒ 'stæmp] *noun* small official piece of paper which is stuck on to a letter or parcel to show that the cost of the postage has been paid

postal survey ['pəʊstəl 's3:veɪ] *noun* survey which is conducted by sending questionnaires through the post

postcard ['pəʊstkɑ:d] *noun* card, often with a picture on one side, which can be written on and sent to someone without an envelope

postcode ['pəʊstkəʊd] *noun* system of letters and numbers used by the post office to identify towns and roads to aid the delivery of letters

post-coordinate indexing system

[pəʊstkəʊ'ɔ:dɪnət 'ɪndeksɪŋ 'sɪstəm] *noun* system in which information is organized under simple main headings but with devices whereby the user can combine them to produce compound subjects

poster ['pəustə] *noun* large notice or advertisement stuck to a wall or board

postgraduate [pəust'grædjuət] *noun* **(a)** student who already has a first degree and who is studying or doing research at a higher level **(b)** *US* graduate

postings list ['pəustɪŋz 'lɪst] *noun* alphabetical list of descriptors with the identification numbers of documents using them

postpone [pəs'pəun] *verb* to rearrange for something to be done at a later date or time

potential [pə'tenʃl] **1** *noun* having the possibility to develop into something or someone better; *the library needed a lot of work but had the potential to become a very efficient service* **2** *adjective* capable of becoming something better in the future; *there is a large potential market for electronic information*

power ['pauə] *verb* to provide a source of energy especially by electricity

power supply ['pauə 'sʌplaɪ] *noun* supply of electricity to a building or work site

powered ['pauəd] *adjective* worked by electricity or another source of energy such as gas; *gas-powered central heating*

pp = PAGES

ppm = PAGES PER MINUTE

practical ['præktɪkl] *noun* lesson or examination in which you are asked to do tasks rather than just read or write about them

practice ['præktɪs] *noun* **(a)** repeated performance of something to learn to do it well **(b)** regular or standard course of action; *it is standard practice to keep reference books in a separate area of the library; see also* IN PRACTICE

pre- [pri] *prefix* combines with adjectives to indicate something done before; **pre-paid** = paid for in advance of delivery; **pre-printed form** *or* **pre-printed stationery** = form or notepaper which has some information already printed on it; **pre-recorded** = recorded at an earlier time; *a message on a telephone answering machine is pre-recorded;* **pre-requisite** = something that must be done before something else; *a reasonable standard of English is a pre-requisite to studying in an English speaking country;* **pre-set** = set to specific levels before using; *the temperature of the heating in the library was pre-set to a comfortable level*

precede [prɪ'siːd] *verb* to happen before something else happens

preceding record [prɪ'siːdɪŋ 'rekəd] *noun* record which comes before the current one

PRECIS indexing ['preɪsi 'ɪndeksɪŋ] *acronym* PREserved Context Index System: a technique for subject indexing originally developed for the British National Bibliography

precise [prɪ'saɪs] *adjective* exact and accurate

precision equipment [prɪ'sɪʒn ɪ'kwɪpmənt] *noun* machines that are made to very accurate specifications

Pre-coordinate Indexing System [prikəu'ɔːdɪnət 'ɪndeksɪŋ 'sɪstəm] *noun* system whereby the terms are combined at the indexing stage; used by the British National Bibliography

preface ['prefəs] *noun* author's note which comes before the introduction and after any dedication

preferment [prɪ'fɜːmənt] *noun* promotion to a better job

preferred order [prɪ'fɜːd 'ɔːdə] *noun* set order in which the items in a classification scheme are arranged; **preferred term** = term chosen in a catalogue to gather together all synonymous and otherwise scattered entries; *publications is the preferred term for books, documents, monographs, etc.*

prefix ['pri:fiks] *noun* word or letters added to the front of another word, which can change its meaning, such as 'undone', 'misread'

prejudice ['predʒudɪs] *noun* unfair and often negative feeling based on incomplete knowledge and information

premise ['premɪs] *noun* something that is supposed to be true and therefore used as the basis for an argument

premises ['premɪsɪz] *plural noun* land and buildings occupied by a business

prepare [prɪ'peə] *verb* to make something ready for use or for consideration; *the librarians were asked to prepare a report for the management meeting*

preparation [prepə'reɪʃn] *noun* work done before in order to be ready for something; *they made careful preparation for the open day;* **preparation of text** = making text ready for printing by editing and checking it

preposition [prepə'zɪʃn] *noun* grammatical term for words such as 'by' 'with' 'on' 'under', etc. which indicate place or direction

prescription [prɪ'skrɪpʃn] *noun* instruction or plan for what needs to be done in a particular situation

prescriptive [prɪ'skrɪptɪv] *adjective* describes rules and regulations for what should or should not be done

present 1 ['prezənt] *noun* something given to a person as a gift **2** [prɪ'zent] *verb* to introduce a person, idea, information, etc. **3** ['prezənt] *adjective* now, at this moment; *the present situation*

presentation [prezən'teɪʃn] *noun* talk about a specific subject given to provide information

preservation [prezə'veɪʃn] *noun* provision of suitable environmental conditions to ensure the condition of library stock

PREserved Context Index System *see* PRECIS INDEXING

press [pres] **1** *noun* double-sided bookcase of not less than four tiers **2** *collective noun* newspapers and the people who write for them; **local press** = newspapers which cover news relevant to a local area and which are printed and sold in one small area of the country; **national press** = newspapers which cover more general news and are sold in all parts of the country; **press coverage** = amount of space or time given in newspapers or TV and radio news bulletins to one topic; **press cutting** = one item cut from a newspaper; **press guide** = reference book which lists the main newspaper publications throughout the world; **press release** = statement given by an organization to the media to explain a situation from their point of view **3** *verb* **(a)** to try to persuade someone to do or say something **(b)** to put pressure on something; *to press a key or switch or button to make it work something*

Prestel ['prestel] *noun* viewdata system used in the UK marketed by British Telecom

prevent [prɪ'vent] *verb* to make sure something does not happen

prevention [prɪ'venʃn] *noun* action which stops something from happening

preventive maintenance [prɪ'ventɪv 'meɪntənəns] *noun* regular checks and repairs to small faults so that they do not develop into large problems

preview ['pri:vju:] *noun* opportunity to see something before it is released to the general public

previous ['priːviəs] *adjective* describes the one before the one being discussed

price [prais] *noun* amount of money needed to buy an item; **price bracket** = limited range of prices; *the goods were in the cheaper price bracket;* **price label** = piece of paper or card attached to something to show its price; **price list** = list of the prices of everything in stock

pricing strategy ['praisɪŋ 'strætɪdʒi] *noun* company policy about how much to charge for goods or services in order to make a reasonable profit

prima ['priːmə] *noun* first word of the next page printed at the bottom of a page

primary ['praiməri] *adjective* first, original, basic or most important; **primary colours** = three colours, red, yellow and blue, from which all other colours can be made; **primary education** = first period of schooling usually up to the age of 11 years; **primary operator** = first person to operate a machine; **primary records** = first records on a subject; **primary sampling** = unit the first selected population for a survey; **primary school** = school for young children usually for about the first 6 years of schooling; **primary source** = original source of the information; **primary user** = first person to use a service

prime [praim] **1** *adjective* most important or a typical example of something; **prime time** = time of day when most people are expected to be watching television or listening to the radio **2** *verb* to give someone information about something

primer ['praimə] *noun* **(a)** manual or simple instruction book **(b)** basic, simple school book for children

print [print] *verb* to produce a book, magazine, newspaper, leaflet, etc. by a mechanical process; **in print** = (i) appearing in a book or journal; (ii) available in the bookshops; **out of print** = not being reprinted

and so no longer available for purchase because stocks have run out; **print style** = typeface and fonts used in any particular document

printed catalogue card ['printid 'kætəlɒg 'kɑːd] *noun* pre-printed card containing the bibliographical details of a book for inclusion in a library catalogue

printed ephemera ['printid ɪ'fiːmərə] *plural noun* items such as theatre programmes, leaflets, advertising fliers, etc. which would normally be read and thrown away

printed index ['printid 'indeks] *noun* alphabetical list of words used in a text

printed matter ['printid 'mætə] *noun* anything which is in printed form

printer ['printə] *noun* **(a)** machine which converts electronic data into readable form on paper **(b)** person or company who prints books, stationery, etc.

printing press ['printiŋ 'pres] *noun* machine which presses the paper on to type and prints text fast

printout ['printaʊt] *noun* hard copy of a computer file

print run ['print 'rʌn] *noun* pre-determined number of copies of a book produced at one time

prior ['praiə] *adjective* **(a)** (something) that has happened previously; *to be unable to go somewhere due to a prior engagement* **(b)** (something) that is given priority over something else

priority [prai'ɒriti] *noun* something which must be dealt with first

privacy ['privəsi] *noun* state of being left alone to do things; **privacy of information** = keeping documents secret so that only authorized people are allowed to read them

private ['praɪvət] *adjective* for the use of one person or group only; **private sector** = services or industries that are owned by individuals or groups rather than by the state

privilege ['prɪvɪlɪdʒ] *noun* special right that gives someone advantages over other people

probability [prɒbə'bɪlɪti] *noun* likelihood of something happening often expressed as a fraction or percentage

probe [prəʊb] *verb* to investigate a situation by asking a lot of questions

problematic [prɒblə'mætɪk] *adjective* describes any situation that involves difficulties and needs a solution

problem solving learning ['prɒbləm 'sɒlvɪŋ 'lɜːnɪŋ] *noun* method of teaching which sets problems for students to solve so that they learn how to reason

procedure [prə'siːdʒə] *noun* method of doing something which is generally accepted as being efficient

proceedings [prə'siːdɪŋz] *plural noun* published record of a meeting of a society or institution

proceeds ['prəʊsiːdz] *plural noun* money that is made by an activity or event

process ['prəʊses] *verb* (a) to manipulate into the required format; *(printing)* **process colours** = cyan, magenta and yellow (b) to perform the necessary routines to a book before it can be borrowed, such as classifying, cataloguing, stamping, labelling, numbering, etc.

processor ['prəʊsesə] *noun* computer that is able to manipulate data according to given instructions; *see also* WORD PROCESSOR

produce [prə'djuːs] *verb* to make, create or show something; *he produced evidence to support his argument*

product ['prɒdʌkt] *noun* (a) something that is made to be sold often in large quantities (b) result of previous actions or discussions; **product development** = improving a product to meet the needs of the market; **product life** = length of time that a product is likely to be saleable

production [prə'dʌkʃn] *noun* creation of something; **on production of** = when something is shown; *goods can only be exchanged on production of a receipt*

productivity [prɒdʌk'tɪvɪti] *noun* rate at which goods are manufactured

profession [prə'feʃn] *noun* job which requires advanced education or training

professional [prə'feʃənl] **1** *noun* person who works in one of the professions **2** *adjective* (a) relating to work requiring a high level of training and done to a very high standard; **professional ethics** = conduct and behaviour expected of members of a professional organization; **professional judgement** = ability of someone who has special knowledge or skill to assess a situation and recommend a course of action; **professional organization** = group of people in the same profession who act to support other workers and to set standards for the way they work; *the Library Association is a professional organization for all information workers* (b) done for money rather than as a hobby

profit ['prɒfɪt] **1** *noun* amount of money that you gain when you sell something for more than you paid for it **2** *verb* **to profit by** *or* **from** = to gain advantage or benefit from something

proforma ['prəʊ 'fɔːmə] *noun* standard layout of a form; **proforma invoice** = invoice sent to the purchaser of mail order goods which must be paid before the goods can be despatched

program ['prəʊgræm] *noun* set of instructions for a computer

programme ['prəʊgræm] *noun* series of actions or events planned in advance

programmer ['prəʊgræmə] *noun* person who designs and writes instructions for a computer

programming language

['prəʊgræmɪŋ 'læŋgwɪdʒ] *noun* software which allows someone to write instructions for a computer which it can then translate into a workable program

progress ['prəʊgres] *verb* to improve or become more advanced

prohibit [prə'hɪbɪt] *verb* to forbid by law

project 1 ['prɒdʒekt] *noun* **(a)** detailed study of a subject written up by a student **(b)** planned course of action; *they were involved in a large building project;* **project leader** *or* **project manager** = person in charge of a project; **project team** = group of people working together on a project **2** [prə'dʒekt] *verb* to plan ahead

projection [prə'dʒekʃn] *noun* forecast of a future amount from a set of data

projector [prə'dʒektə] *noun* mechanical device that displays films or slides on a screen

PROLOG computer language used in the development of expert systems

prologue ['prəʊlɒg] *noun* **(a)** introduction to a play, book, long poem, film, etc. **(b)** events which lead up to more serious consequences

promote [prə'məʊt] *verb* **(a)** to advance someone to a higher position within an organization **(b)** to encourage something to develop or succeed

promotion [prə'məʊʃn] *noun* **(a)** upgrading someone to a higher position **(b)** marketing activity to persuade people to buy goods or use a service; *the library had a special children's book promotion during the school holidays*

prompt [prɒmt] **1** *adjective* done on time, without delay **2** *noun* symbol on a computer screen to remind the user to do something

pronunciation [prənʌnsi'eɪʃn] *noun* way in which the sounds of a language are said and stressed

-proof [pru:f] *suffix* added to nouns to show that something cannot be damaged; *the table surface was heatproof so hot pans could be put on it*

proof [pru:f] *noun* **(a)** facts or evidence to show that something is true **(b)** impression made from type before being finally prepared for printing; **proof correction marks** = marks written in the margin of a text by a proof reader to indicate errors; *see also* SUPPLEMENT

proofread ['pru:fri:d] *verb* to read a text and mark any errors for correction before it is printed

proofreader ['pru:fri:də] *noun* person whose job it is to proofread texts

propaganda [prɒpə'gændə] *noun* information which is often untrue and biased, published and disseminated to influence people

proper noun ['prɒpə 'naʊn] grammatical term for a word which is the name of a person place or institution which should always be written with a capital letter

property ['prɒpəti] *noun* something that is owned, especially a building

proportion [prə'pɔ:ʃn] *noun* size, shape and position of something compared to other parts of the whole

proportional [prə'pɔ:ʃnl] *adjective* in proportion to the other parts; **proportional spacing** = printing system where each letter takes the space proportional to the character width so 'm' takes more space than 'i'

proposal [prə'pəʊzl] *noun* suggestion or plan, often written down and put forward as a discussion document

proposed system [prə'pəʊzd 'sɪstəm] *noun* system which has been designed and suggested for use, but is not yet installed

prospectus [prə'spektəs] *noun* document produced by an academic institution giving details about it for the information of potential students

protect [prə'tekt] *verb* to keep safe and free from damage

protection [prə'tekʃn] *noun* action of keeping something free from harm or damage

protective [prə'tektɪv] *adjective* designed to keep things free from harm; *the books were covered in protective plastic*

protocol ['prəʊtəkɒl] *noun* (a) written record of a treaty agreed between two or more countries (b) system of rules about the correct way to behave in formal situations

prototype ['prəʊtətaɪp] *noun* first model of something that is completely new

provenance ['prɒvənəns] *noun* place of origin; **provenance order** = document which proves that the origin of an item is genuine; *when genuine antiques are sold they require a provenance order or certificate*

provide [prə'vaɪd] *verb* to make something available

provider [prə'vaɪdə] *noun* **provider company** = which provides public Internet access links via the telephone network see also public service providers; **information provider** = company or user who acts as a source of information, such as for a videotext system

provisional [prə'vɪʒənl] *adjective* (a) only for a short time (b) likely to be changed

pseudo- [sju:dəʊ] *prefix* used with nouns and adjectives to describe things that are not really what they claim to be

pseudonym ['sju:dənɪm] *noun* name used by a writer which is not his or her real name

PSTN = PUBLIC SWITCHED TELEPHONE NETWORK

public ['pʌblɪk] *adjective* open for anyone to use; **public address system** = loudspeaker and microphone which enables a speaker to be heard by a large group of people; **public archives** = historical records which are accessible by the general public from a records office; **public domain** = information which is unrestricted and accessible by the general public; **public library** *see* LIBRARY **public librarian** = trained information worker in the public library service; **public record office** = collection of historical archives organized for retrieval and use by the public; **public sector organization** = company or organization which is owned by the government rather than a private body; **public service announcement** = government information announcement usually broadcast nationally; **public service broadcasting** = radio and television programmes which are accessible by everyone as opposed to satellite and cable channels which require a subscription to be paid; **public service provider** = electronic hosts providing interactive access to Telnet, e-mail and Usenet news; **public speaking skills** = ability to speak well and retain the interest of large groups of people; **Public Switched Telephone Network (PSTN)** = form of automatic telephone exchange interconnecting worldwide

publication [pʌblɪ'keɪʃn] *noun* (a) book, newspaper or magazine which can be sold (b) leaflet which is given out to provide information (c) act of printing and distributing a book, newspaper or magazine; **publication data** = information about the date, publisher, ISBN, etc., printed on the back of the title page in a book

publicize ['pʌblɪsaɪz] *verb* to make something widely known to the general public

publicity [pʌb'lɪsɪti] *noun* advertisements and information materials which make something generally known; *see also* MATTER

publish ['pʌblɪʃ] *verb* to arrange to have a book or article printed and usually distributed for sale; **publishing house** = company that publishes books, magazines and newspapers

publisher ['pʌblɪʃə] *noun* person or company that publishes books, magazines and newspapers

pull-down menu ['puldaun 'menju:] *noun* list of options in a computer program which can be displayed on screen over work that is already being done

pull-out ['pulaut] *noun* inserted pages into a magazine which can be easily removed and retained for reference

punch [pʌnʃ] *verb* (a) to hit something hard (b) to make holes in something so that it can be inserted into a ring file

punched card *or* **punched tape** ['pʌnʃd 'ka:d or 'teɪp] *noun* materials with holes in them in patterns which contain instructions or data for computers

punctuation [pʌŋktʃu'eɪʃn] *noun* system of symbols such as full stops, commas and question marks which enable a reader to make sense of written texts

pupil ['pju:pəl] *noun* person who is undertaking a course of education usually at a school

purchase ['pɜ:tʃəs] *verb* to buy

purchaser ['pɜ:tʃesə] *noun* buyer; **purchaser of information services** = person who pays for information to be provided

purport [pə'pɔ:t] *verb* to claim to be or have something; *the service purports to have a full range of business information*

push [puʃ] *verb* to apply force to something in order to move it; **push button** = switch which is worked by pushing; **to push for** = to try hard to persuade people to do what you want; **to push through** = to apply pressure in order to, for instance, get a proposal accepted

put put] *verb* to place something or someone in a certain position; **to put someone or something off** = to postpone until a later date; **to put someone through** = expression used on the telephone when you are connecting someone to another speaker

Qq

quad [kwɒd] *noun* sheet of paper four times as large as a basic sheet

qualification [kwɒlɪfɪ'keɪʃn] *noun* proof that a person has passed examinations or reached a certain level of skill

qualifier ['kwɒlɪfaɪə] *noun* word or phrase added to an index heading to differentiate it from other headings with the same spelling but different meaning

qualitative research ['kwɒlɪtətɪv rɪ'sɜːtʃ] *noun* research which examines the quality of something rather than its quantity

quality ['kwɒlɪti] *noun* measure of how good or bad something is; **quality assessment** = method of measuring how well a company is performing in achieving its stated aims; **quality control** = work of a department in a company that checks that its products are of satisfactory standard; **quality newspapers** = newspapers which are considered to have well written and thoughtful views about topics

quango ['kwæŋgəʊ] *noun* independent advisory body set up by the government, but having separate legal powers within a restricted area of activity

quantify ['kwɒntɪfaɪ] *verb* to represent something in terms of figures so that it can be counted or measured

quantitative research ['kwɒntɪtətɪv rɪ'sɜːtʃ] *noun* research which examines the effects of something by using numbers and statistics

quantity ['kwɒntɪti] *noun* amount or number of items; **in quantity** = in large amounts; **unknown quantity** = someone or something about which nothing is known

quarter ['kwɔːtə] *noun* a fourth part of a whole; **quarter day** = last day of a quarter, every three months, when payments are due: Lady Day 25th March, Midsummer Day 24th June, Michaelmas 29th September, Christmas Day 25th December

quarterly ['kwɔːtəli] *noun* anything which is issued or paid every three months

quarto ['kwɔːtəʊ] *noun* paper size made when a full sheet is folded twice to make eight pages (approx. 20 x 26 cm)

quasi- ['kweɪzaɪ] *prefix* used with adjectives or less frequently with nouns, to describe things which are very like other things but not actually the same; **quasi-official** = appears to be official, but is not really so; **quasi-synonym** = word which appears to be similar in meaning but actually is not

query language ['kwɪəri 'læŋgwɪdʒ] *noun* computing programming language in a database management system which allows a search to be done quickly and easily

question ['kwestʃn] **1** *noun* **closed question** = question which can be answered by yes or no; **open question** = question which can be answered by stating an opinion or fact in full sentences; **question mark** = punctuation mark (?) used to show that a question is being asked **2** *verb* **(a)** to ask a lot of questions **(b)** to imply doubt about the truth of something

questionnaire [kwestʃə'neə] *noun* written list of questions given to people to answer to provide the information for a survey; **questionnaire design** = technique of writing questionnaires in order to avoid bias in the answers

queue [kju:] *noun* line of people or tasks waiting to be dealt with

quick reference ['kwɪk 'refrəns] *noun* system of finding answers to queries which provides rapid but not very detailed answers

quicksort ['kwɪksɔ:t] *noun* method of sorting and ordering information very quickly on a computer

quit [kwɪt] *verb* to leave a computer program

quorum ['kwɔ:rəm] *noun* smallest number of members of a committee which must be present before a meeting can be held

quorate ['kwɔ:reɪt] *adjective* having the minimum required number of people at a meeting

quota sampling ['kwəʊtə 'sɑ:mplɪŋ] *noun* method of selecting the population for a survey by choosing a fixed proportion of people from certain groups

quotation [kwə'teɪʃn] *noun* exact words said or written by someone and used by another person; **quotation dictionary** = collection of famous sayings and writings arranged alphabetically according to the authors; **quotation marks** = punctuation marks both single quotes (' ') or double quotes (" ") which mark the beginning and end of a written quotation; *(also known as 'inverted commas')*

quote [kwəʊt] **1** *verb* to repeat the exact words written or said by someone else **2** *noun (informal)* **in quotes** = written inside quotation marks

quotidian [kwə'tɪdɪən] *adjective* daily

quotient ['kwəʊʃnt] *noun* level or degree; *the stress quotient in that job is very high*

qwerty keyboard ['kwɜ:ti 'ki:bɔ:d] *noun* set of keys on an English typewriter or computer; the first six letters on the top row from the left are QWERTY which give it its name

Rr

R & D = RESEARCH AND DEVELOPMENT

rack [ræk] *noun* a frame for holding things often used for display purposes

radio ['reɪdiəʊ] *noun* **(a)** equipment used to broadcast speech, sounds and data over long distances **(b)** broadcasting; *radio is a powerful medium for information;* **radio phone** = mobile two-way communications system that can access the public telephone network; **radio station** = place from where a particular broadcasting company transmits it programmes

ragged margin ['rægɪd 'mɑːdʒɪn] *noun* uneven or unjustified right margin to a block of writing

RAM [ræm] = RANDOM ACCESS MEMORY a computer system which allows access to any part of the data in any order

random ['rændəm] *adjective* done without any definite plan; **random access** = method of accessing a computer file where all the parts are directly accessible so do not have to be searched sequentially; **random access memory** *see* RAM **random number** = number which cannot be predicted; **random sampling** = sampling used to compile unbiased samples in a survey population

Ranfurly Library Service *see* BOOK AID INTERNATIONAL

rank [ræŋk] *verb* to put into order according to size or merit

rapid ['ræpɪd] *adjective* very quick; **rapidly developing field** = an area of development that is growing very quickly; *information brokerage is a rapidly developing field*

rare book ['reə 'bʊk] *noun* book which has only very few copies still in existence

rate [reɪt] *noun* speed or level at which something happens

ratings ['reɪtɪŋz] *plural noun* a measurement of size of the audience for TV programmes

raw data ['rɔː 'deɪtə] *noun* data which has not yet been processed by a computer to provide information to the user

re [riː] *preposition* used in business English to refer to something which is to be discussed; *re your letter of 12th Sept, I can now tell you ...*

re- [riː] *prefix* used with verbs and nouns to indicate repetition; *to re-order something when it becomes available*

react to [ri'ækt tʊ] *verb* to act in a certain way in response to an earlier event

reaction [ri'ækʃn] *noun* human or chemical response to previous activity

read [ri:d] *verb* to look at and understand what is written down

readable ['ri:dəbl] *adjective* capable of being read, also implies well written and interesting

reader ['ri:də] *noun* a person or a device which can read written or printed texts

readership ['ri:dəʃip] *noun* number of people who read a certain publication

reading list ['ri:diŋ 'list] *noun* a list of recommended books on a specific subject

reading matter ['ri:diŋ 'mætə] *noun* anything which can be read

reading room ['ri:diŋ 'ru:m] *noun* room in a library where users can sit and read quietly

read only memory ['ri:d 'əunli 'memri] *see* ROM

Readme file *noun* computer information file containing instructions about how to use a program or information on latest developments

ready ['redi] *adjective* prepared and able to be used or to do something; **ready money** = cash in notes and coins rather than cheques, cards or other electronic transfer forms; **ready reference** = easily accessible information

real time ['riəl 'taim] *noun* something which happens without any delay between the action and its effect

realize [riə'laiz] *verb* (a) to understand what is happening (b) to make a physical representation of an idea as in a design

ream [ri:m] *noun* 500 sheets of paper in a pack

recall [ri'kɔ:l] **1** *noun* retrieval of a document from an information store **2** *verb* (a) to request the return of a library book (b) to bring back data or text on to the screen of a computer

receive [ri'si:v] *verb* to accept things that are sent or given to you

received opinion [ri'si:vd ə'pinjən] *noun* an opinion or method that is generally accepted as correct

Received Pronunciation (RP) [ri'si:vd prənʌnsi'eiʃn] standard accent of spoken British English with no regional variations

recent ['ri:sənt] *adjective* happening only a short time earlier

recently ['ri:səntli] *adverb* not long ago; *her recently-published book...*

reception [ri'sepʃn] *noun* (a) quality of radio or TV signal received (b) area for receiving visitors to a building

receptionist [ri'sepʃənist] *noun* person who works in a reception area, greeting and advising people who arrive

recession [ri'seʃn] *noun* weak period in a country's economy when bankruptcy and unemployment rates rise

reciprocal [ri'sirəkəl] *adjective* agreed because it is mutually beneficial; *a reciprocal arrangement which meant they both made a profit*

recode [ri:'kəud] *verb* to change the coding in a retrieval system so that it will work in another system

recognize ['rekəgnaiz] *verb* to see something and to remember that it has been seen before

recognition [rekəg'niʃn] *noun* process that allows something to be recognized; **optical character recognition (OCR)** = recognizing and converting printed or written characters to computer readable form

recognized fact ['rekəgnaɪzd 'fækt] *noun* fact which is generally accepted as true

recommend [rekə'mend] *verb* to advise that something is good or useful because you have experience of using it

reconfigure [riːkən'fɪgə] *verb* to alter the structure of data within a system

record 1 ['rekəd] *noun* written account either on paper or in electronic format; **record analysis** = an analysis of the information contained in a set of records; **record clerk** = person who has the job of filing records; **record control** = a system for organizing records so that they can be traced, referred to or disposed of as necessary; **record disposal** = process of destroying records when they are no longer needed; **record inventory** = list of all the records held in a system; **record management audit** = an official check on the efficiency and effectiveness of the record management within an organization; **record management manual** = book of instructions for users of the record management system; **record management program** = computer program for storing and retrieving records; **record management programme** = company policy programme for the control of records; **record management software** = computer software which enables records to be stored and retrieved; **record office** = form of archive library; **record retrieval** = process of finding and making documents available; **record retrieval management** = organization and control of record retrieval; **record storage** = system of storing records so that they can be retrieved easily; **record supply** = provision of records as required; **record transfer** = process of transferring records from one system to another; **record transfer document** = form which gives details of the record to be transferred and is used for record control; **record update** = system of keeping records up to date by changing data as necessary; **record vault** = secure room where confidential records can be kept safely **2** [rɪ'kɔːd] *verb* to write down

or preserve something on film or tape so that it can be used for later reference; **recorded information** = information which has been recorded on tape or disk

records information officer ['rekədz ɪnfə'meɪʃn 'ɒfɪsə] *noun* **(a)** archivist who works in a records office **(b)** company information specialist who manages the record supply

recover [rɪ'kʌvə] *verb* **(a)** to replace a cover on a document or book which has been damaged **(b)** to get back something that has been lost

recoverable [rɪ'kʌvrəbl] *adjective* able to be returned to normal after being lost

recovery procedure [rɪ'kʌvri prə'siːdʒə] *noun* methods of finding what has been lost especially when using a computer

rectify ['rektɪfaɪ] *verb* to correct a mistake

recto ['rektəʊ] *adjective* right-hand page of a book

recur [rɪ'kʌr] *verb* to happen again once or several times; **recurring subject** = item in a record system that appears many times

redefine [riːdɪ'faɪn] *verb* to change the function or value assigned to a variable

redirect [riːdaɪ'rekt] *verb* **(a)** *(in computing)* to send a message to its destination by an alternative route **(b)** to send mail to a new address after it has been delivered to the old one

red tape ['red 'teɪp] *noun* official rules and regulations which seem to have no obvious value

reduce [rɪ'djuːs] *verb* to make smaller

reduction [rɪ'dʌkʃn] *noun* act of reducing anything such as size or cost; *they were able to make a 75% reduction of the document on the photocopier so fewer copies were needed and the cost was less*

redundant [rɪ'dʌndənt] *adjective* **(a)** no longer needed because it has been replaced by a more up-to-date version **(b)** something that can be removed without losing any information such as extra data or some words in spoken English

redundancy [rɪ'dʌndənsi] *noun* words or symbols that do not add to meaning

reel [riːl] *noun* a circular holder around which tape can be wound; **reel to reel** = playing data on one tape on to another without enclosing it in a cassette

reel off ['riːl 'ɒf] *verb* to repeat information quickly from memory

refer [rɪ'fɜː] *verb* **(a)** to mention *or* to deal with *or* to write about something; *he referred to an article which he had seen in the 'Times'* **(b)** to pass a question on to someone else to decide

referee [refə'riː] *noun* person who provides information about whether someone known to them is suitable for a particular job

reference ['refrəns] *noun* **(a)** a letter written by someone to support someone else's application for a job **(b)** coded information which tells you where to find a document or stored item **(c)** an acknowledgement of someone else's work quoted in a written document; **reference book** = information book such as a dictionary, encyclopaedia or directory in which you can look things up; **reference collection** = books in a library which are used for reference only and cannot be borrowed; **reference database** = large database which can be searched for information on a particular subject; **reference interview** = discussion between a user and the reference librarian to ascertain exactly what information is required; **reference librarian** = qualified person who works in a reference library to control the retrieval systems and supply information; **reference library** = library where the books and documents can only be used within the building and cannot

be borrowed; **reference manual** = book of instructions about how to use a machine which can be referred to when learning how to use the machine or when problems occur; **reference material** = books, documents and materials kept in a reference library or designated area; **reference request form** = form which users fill in to give details of exactly which reference books or documents they require to be fetched from stock; **reference source** = any source of information which can be searched; **reference tool** = index or retrieval system which help the user to search for information

referral [rɪ'fɜːrəl] *noun* act of sending something or someone to a person who is better able to deal with them

referral centre [rɪ'fɜːrəl 'sentə] *noun* organization which directs researchers to information and appropriate sources but does not supply documents

reflect [rɪ'flekt] *verb* to think deeply about something

reformat [riː'fɔːmæt] *verb* to reformat a computer floppy disk and so erase any data on it

refusal [rɪ'fjuːzəl] *noun* deliberate statement that you will not do, say, allow, give or accept something

regenerate [rɪ'dʒenəreɪt] *verb* to reactivate something after a period of decline, so that it is improved

register ['redʒɪstə] **1** *noun* **(a)** official list of names, events, etc.; **electoral register** = list of names of the people in a country eligible to vote **(b)** ribbon attached to the binding of a book to act as a bookmark **2** *verb* to make a record of something on an official list; **to register for** = to put your name on to an official list for something

registration [redʒɪs'treɪʃn] *noun* act of recording something on an official list

registration card [redʒɪs'treɪʃn 'kɑːd] *noun* card which is filled in with personal details to register for membership of something

regress ['riːgres] *verb* to return to a former bad position

regular ['regjʊlə] **1** *noun* person who frequently uses the same services **2** *adjective* happening at equal intervals

regulate ['regjʊleɪt] *verb* to control the behaviour of a situation or a machine

reimburse [riːɪm'bɜːs] *verb* to pay back money spent by someone else while they were doing something for you

reinforce [riːɪn'fɔːs] *verb* to provide more information to strengthen a case

reinstate riːɪn'steɪt] *verb* to give someone back a job that has previously been taken away

reissue [riː'ɪʃuː] **1** *noun* book or document which is made available again after a period of time; *the book was reissued after being unavailable for five years* **2** *verb* to produce or publish again something that has not been available for a long time

reject 1 ['riːdʒekt] *noun* product that is not up to standard, so sold cheaply or not at all **2** [rɪ'dʒekt] *verb* to refuse to accept something

relate [rɪ'leɪt] *verb* to show the connection between two things

related work [rɪ'leɪtɪd 'wɜk] *noun* document which has some connection with another such as a supplement or sequel

relational database [rɪ'leɪʃnl 'deɪtəbeɪs] *noun* set of data in which everything is connected so that it can be searched to show different relationships

relational index [rɪ'leɪʃnl 'ɪndeks] *noun* index which shows the relationship between works by the use of symbols

relationship [rɪ'leɪʃnʃɪp] *noun* way in which two things are connected or linked together

relative ['relətɪv] *adjective* describes the qualities of something by comparing it with something else

relatively ['relətɪvli] *adverb* in comparison to; *a relatively small number applied this year compared to last year*

relay ['riːleɪ] *verb* to transmit, broadcast or repeat what has been said or written

release [rɪ'liːs] *verb* to make available; **to release records** = to make records accessible to the public

relevance ['reləvəns] *noun* relationship to the subject; **relevance ratio** = number of documents wanted in relation to the number retrieved which are relevant to the subject searched

relevant ['reləvənt] *adjective* connected with and appropriate for what is being discussed or written about

reliability [rɪlaɪə'bɪlɪti] *noun* quality of being reliable

reliable [rɪ'laɪəbl] *adjective* can be trusted or depended on to function or behave as expected

relocate [riːlə'keɪt] *verb* to move data, people or an organization from one place to another

reluctant user [rɪ'lʌktənt 'juːzə] *noun* someone who is forced to use a service but does not want to; *some children are reluctant users of the school library*

remainder [rɪ'meɪndə] **1** *noun* **(a)** something left when demand has fallen **(b)** book sold cheaply to clear stock **2** *verb* to deal with a book as a remainder; **remaindered publication** = book that will not be reprinted because demand has almost ceased and so the stock is sold cheaply

remedial [rɪ'miːdiəl] *adjective* designed to correct a damaged situation or previous learning failure

remedy ['remədi] *noun* a successful way of dealing with a difficult situation

remind [rɪ'maɪnd] *verb* to say something that causes another person to remember something

remote control [rɪ'məʊt kən'trəʊl] *noun* a system of controlling a device from a distance by means of radio or electronic signals; *using remote control she could listen to her answerphone messages when she was away from the office*

removable [rɪ'muːvəbl] *adjective* (something or someone) which can be taken away; *the records which were no longer needed were removable*

rename [riː'neɪm] *verb* to give a different name to someone or something; *they renamed all the computer files when they reorganized the system*

renew [rɪ'njuː] *verb* to extend the period of time for which a contract or a loan is valid; *they were told that they could not renew their books because they had been reserved by another reader*

renumber [rɪ'nʌmbə] *verb* to change the numbers on items or within a system

repaginate [rɪ'pædʒɪneɪt] *verb* to change the numbers on the pages in a document

repeat [rɪ'piːt] *verb* to do or say exactly the same thing again

repertoire [repə'twɑː] *noun* range of activities or functions that a person or a machine is capable of doing

repetitive [rɪ'petɪtɪv] *adjective* repeated many times; **repetitive letter** = standard letter which is reprinted with a different name and address each time

replace [rɪ'pleɪs] *verb* **(a)** to put something back where it was before **(b)** to put a new item in the place of one that is broken or worn out

replacement [rɪ'pleɪsmənt] *noun* something or someone that takes the place of another; *the new library book was a replacement for the one that was lost*

replicate ['replɪkeɪt] *verb* to make an exact copy of something, such as an action, research method, etc.

report [rɪ'pɔːt] *noun* formal document that discusses a particular subject or states exactly what happened

report generator [rɪ'pɔːt 'dʒenəreɪtə] *noun* word-processing facility for producing business reports on personal computers

repository [rɪ'pɒzɪtri] *noun* book or archive store

represent [reprɪ'zent] *verb* **(a)** to act as a symbol or typical example of something **(b)** to act for someone; *he was asked to represent his users' group at the public meeting*

representations [reprɪzen'teɪʃnz] *plural noun* formal requests, complaints or statements made to an official body

representative [reprɪ'zentətɪv] *noun* a person who acts on behalf of another or of a group

reprint 1 ['riːprɪnt] *noun* more copies of a book made from the original but with a note in the publication details of the date of reprinting and possibly a new title page and cover design **2** [riː'prɪnt] *verb* to print more copies of a book after all the others have been sold; **reprinting (RP)** = note indcating that a book cannot be supplied because it is being reprinted

reproduce [riːprə'djuːs] *verb* to produce copies of an item

reprography [rɪ'prɒgrəfi] *noun* technique of producing copies; **reprographic equipment** = machines such as photocopiers used to produce copies of documents and materials

request [rɪ'kwest] *verb* to ask formally for something; **request document** = (i) form which must be filled in asking for a restricted document; (ii) document which has been requested for use in a closed access system; **request form** = form that is filled in to ask for an item which is not immediately available

require [rɪ'kwaɪə] *verb* **(a)** to need something **(b)** to demand something from someone; **to be required to do** = to have to do something because of a rule or regulation

requirement [rɪ'kwaɪəmənt] *noun* something that is essential in order to do what you want to do

requisite ['rekwɪzɪt] *adjective* necessary for a particular purpose; *they needed time to collect the requisite number of references*

re-run ['riːrʌn] *noun* a film or programme that is shown again; *the film was re-run on TV a year after the first showing*

research [rɪ'sɜːtʃ] **1** *noun* work that is done to investigate something; **research and development** = work in an organization which researches new products or services and makes recommendations; **research establishment** = an institution devoted to the work of research in a particular subject area; **research tool** = system of discovering or measuring facts such as a questionnaire or a standard measure in a given field **2** *verb* to investigate a field of study and to discover new facts about it

reserve [rɪ'zɜːv] *noun* supply of things kept for use if the regular supplies have been used before replacements can be obtained; **reserve collection** = (i) books for which there is little demand and are kept in a closed store; (ii) books for which there is heavy demand as in

an academic library and which are put in a short loan collection for limited period ;loan

reserved book [rɪ'zɜːvd 'bʊk] *noun* a book which has been specially requested as it is not available at the time of the request

reset [riː'set] *verb* to return a system to its original state so that it can start again

resident ['rezɪdənt] *adjective* someone who works permanently for one company; *the resident engineer is always available if things go wrong*

residual [re'zɪdjuəl] *adjective* remaining after everything else has been used

resist [rɪ'zɪst] *verb* to refuse to accept or do something and even try to prevent it happening

resistance to change [rɪ'zɪstəns] *phrase* refusal to accept changes often in working conditions or practices

resolution [rezə'luːʃn] *noun* **(a)** formal decision taken at a meeting by means of a vote **(b)** solving of a problem; *the resolution of her difficulties with the immigration authorities took a long time*

resource [rɪ'zɔːs] *noun* information in a variety of formats which is useful and available; **resource-based learning** = method of teaching in which the student is allowed free access to resources in order to solve problems or undertake research on set topics

respond [rɪ'spɒnd] *verb* to reply or react to something said or done

response [rɪ'spɒns] *noun* reaction or reply to an event, action or statement; **response rates** = percentage of people who reply to a questionnaire or survey

responsible [rɪ'spɒnsɪbl] *adjective* independent and important, involving the need to make decisions; **be responsible to** = to work under a controlling person or body and to have to report to them

responsibility [rɪspɒnsɪ'bɪlɪti] *noun* **have responsibility for** = having the duty to deal with a situation or person because of your position

restart [rɪ'stɑːt] *verb* to begin again, often used as an option in computer systems

restore [rɪ'stɔː] *verb* to return things to their previous state or position or owner

restrict [rɪ'strɪkt] *verb* to limit something so that only a specific person or group can have access to it

restricted [rɪ'strɪktɪd] *adjective* limited to certain uses or people; **restricted access** = can only be seen or used by certain people; *if the information is classified as restricted access, only members can use it*

result [rɪ'zʌlt] *noun* outcome of a set of events or activities; *the results of his exams were so good that he was given a scholarship for further study*

retailer ['riːteɪlə] *noun* person who sells goods to the public

retain [rɪ'teɪn] *verb* to keep something which you have already had for some time

retainer [rɪ'teɪnə] *noun* fee paid to someone so that they will be available to work for you when required

retention schedule [rɪ'tenʃn 'ʃedjuːl] *noun* list of documents held for reference

retouch [riː'tʌtʃ] *verb* to improve a photograph or painting or surface by painting over parts of it

retrieve [rɪ'triːv] *verb* to get something back from where it has been stored

retrieval [rɪ'triːvəl] *noun* process of finding items which have been stored; **retrieval system** = a system of organizing items so that information can be found quickly and easily

retrospective [retrə'spektɪv] *adjective* concerned with things that take effect from an earlier date than when the decision is made; *the changes in the salary structure will be retrospective to last April*

return [rɪ'tɜːn] **1** *noun* **(a)** giving back of something; *the date for the return of all the library books is next week;* **return on investment (ROI)** = profit made by investing money in something which is financially successful **(b) return key** = key on a computer keyboard which gives the instruction for the machine to process the data entered **2** *verb* to give something back or to change it so that it is in its former state again; *to return the company to its former position by investing a large amount of capital*

reveal [rɪ'viːl] *verb* to uncover something so that it can be seen

reverse [rɪ'vɜːs] *verb* **(a)** to go in the opposite direction **(b)** to organize a set of things so that the first item becomes the last

revert [rɪ'vɜːt] *verb* to return to a former state or system; *although they spoke slowly to the foreigner at first they soon reverted to their normal speed of talking*

review [rɪ'vjuː] **1** *noun* evaluation of a book, publication printed in a journal, etc.; **review copy** = copy of a book given to the reviewer **2** *verb* to look again at a situation or difficulty to assess what can be done

revise [rɪ'vaɪz] *verb* **(a)** to change something so that it is more accurate **(b)** to go over work done before in order to learn it more thoroughly; **revised edition** = book which has been reprinted with some changes usually to bring it up to date; **revised plan** = plan that has been changed after consideration in order to make it more suitable for the task to be done

revision [rɪ'vɪʒn] *noun* **(a)** improvement and correction of a text **(b)** re-learning work in order to do an examination

revisions [rɪ'vɪʒnz] *plural noun* changes that are made to improve something

reward [rɪ'wɔːd] *noun* something given in return for doing something well

rewrite ['riːraɪt] *verb* to write again with improvements

rhetorical question [re'tɒrɪkl 'kwestʃn] *noun* question that is used as a statement and does not expect an answer, such as 'who knows when we will find the answer?'

rhyming dictionary ['raɪmɪŋ 'dɪkʃənri] *noun* a dictionary which organizes words in groups of rhymes so that they are useful for writers of poetry

ribbon ['rɪbən] *noun* long, thin, flat piece of plastic coated with powdered ink used for printers or typewriters

right [raɪt] *adjective* **(a)** correct and acceptable **(b)** opposite to left; **right aligned** = with the right-hand margin straight; **right justification** = process of aligning the right-hand margin on a piece of text so that the edge is straight; **right justify** = to use a computer program to ensure that the right-hand margins of text are straight; **right-hand corner** = top or bottom corners at the right side of a page or envelope, etc.

rights [raɪts] *plural noun* things that you are entitled to by law

rigmarole ['rɪgmərəʊl] *noun* a long misleading collection of stories; *she told me some rigmarole about having lost her ticket*

ring up ['rɪŋ 'ʌp] *verb* to telephone someone; **ring back** = to telephone someone after they have telephoned you first; **ring off** = to finish a telephone call and replace the receiver

risk [rɪsk] **1** *noun* danger, chance of loss or injury; **at your own risk** = to do something with understanding of the danger and accepting the responsibility for the outcome **2** *verb* to do something even though you know it may have dangerous or unpleasant results

RLOGIN *noun* gateway to Internet files; *see also* TELNET

road atlas *or* **road map** ['rəʊd 'ætləs *or* 'mæp] *noun* map which shows the roads which are passable by motor traffic but does not include very small roads or paths

road plan ['rəʊd 'plæn] *noun* map which shows all the roads in an area

role [rəʊl] *noun* function or position within an organization; **role playing** = acting out the behaviour of someone different from yourself as part of a training exercise

roll [rəʊl] *noun* **(a)** official list of names; **roll call** = check of people present by calling out their names and waiting for them to answer **(b) roll of film** = length of film wound round itself and ready for use in a camera

rolling header *or* **rolling footer** ['rəʊlɪŋ 'hedə *or* 'fʊtə] *noun* title which is repeated at the top or bottom of every page in a document

ROM [rɒm] = READ ONLY MEMORY a computer system which allows data to be read but not edited; *see also* CD-ROM

roman numeral ['rəʊmən 'njuːmərəl] *noun* letter used as a number, such as V for 5; *see* SUPPLEMENT

romance language [rə'mæns 'læŋgwɪdʒ] *noun* language which is almost entirely based on Latin, such as Italian, Spanish, Romanian, Portuguese and French

roster ['rɒstə] *see* ROTA

rota ['rəʊtə] *noun* list of people who take turns to do a job; *according to the rota it will be my turn to work late at the library on Friday*

rotate [rəʊ'teɪt] *verb* **(a)** to move in a circular way **(b)** to take turns to do a job until everyone has had a turn and then to start again with the first one

round up ['raʊnd 'ʌp] *verb* to approximate a number to a slightly higher one, so that 1.9 becomes 2; **round off** *or* **round down** = to approximate a number to a slightly lower one, so that 1.2 becomes 1

roundup ['raʊndʌp] *noun* summary of everything that has been said and shown before; *the newscaster on the television gave a roundup of the evening's news*

routeing ['ruːtɪŋ] *noun* distribution of written information among members of staff according to a routeing list; **routeing list** = list of names attached to the front cover of a document which is passed round several people to be read

routine [ruː'tiːn] **1** *adjective* done everyday as a regular part of your job **2** *noun* procedure which, if followed, helps to perform tasks in an efficient and organized way

row [rəʊ] *noun* horizontal line in a table as opposed to columns which are vertical

RP *see* REPRINTING, RECEIVED PRONUNCIATION

rubber band ['rʌbə 'bænd] *noun* thin circle of elastic which you can use to hold a bundle of things together

rubber stamp ['rʌbə 'stæmp] *verb* to agree to something without discussion or thought

rubric ['ruːbrɪk] *noun* set of rules or instructions such as those at the beginning of an examination paper

rule [ruːl] **1** *noun* set of regulations which tell you what you are and are not allowed to do **2** *verb* **ruled paper** = paper which has lines printed on it for writing on

ruler ['ruːlə] *noun* long flat object calibrated in inches or centimetres which is used for measuring or drawing straight lines

ruling ['ruːlɪŋ] *noun* official decision which must be obeyed

run [rʌn] **1** *verb* **(a)** to take charge of and be responsible for an organization or activity; *the head librarian will be running the next course* **(b)** to make a machine work; *they run the computer every day* **(c) to run risks** = to do things even though you realize the result may be dangerous or not what you expect **2** *noun* **in the long run** = over a long period of time; **in the short run** = in the near future

run down ['rʌn 'daʊn] *verb* **(a)** to reduce the amount of work done by a department or organization **(b)** to criticise someone very aggressively

run-down ['rʌndaʊn] *adjective* in poor condition

running title ['rʌnɪŋ 'taɪtl] *noun* title which appears throughout a book or document at the top of each page

Ss

sabbatical [sə'bætɪkl] *noun* period of time during which a teacher or lecturer is allowed to leave their normal duties for the purpose of study or travel

safe [seɪf] *noun* secure metal cupboard with special locks to keep valuables; **safe deposit box** = box for the safekeeping of personal documents, usually stored in a bank

safety measure ['seɪfti 'meʒə] *noun* action or regulation to ensure that activities do not endanger anyone

saga ['sɑːgə] *noun* **(a)** long story about a particular time in history or group of people **(b)** story written between the 12th and 14th century about the Norwegian Vikings

salary ['sæləri] *noun* money that is paid, usually monthly, to someone for their job

sales [seɪlz] *plural noun* quantity of a product or service that is sold; *sales of information are becoming more common nowadays;* **sales department** = department in a company which organizes the sales of its products

sample [sɑːmpl] *noun* small quantity of a product to show what it is like

sans serif ['sænz 'serɪf] *noun* way of printing letters with all lines of equal thickness and no serifs

satellite ['sætəlaɪt] *noun* device sent into space to collect information or to be part of a communications system; **satellite link** = satellite which enables the transmission of live sound and images to another; **weather satellite** = satellite which collects meteorological information enabling the weather to be forecast

satire ['sætaɪr] *noun* writing which aims to make readers or an audience recognize the foolishness of people, organizations or events in an amusing way

satirical [sə'tɪrɪkl] *adjective* using satire

satisfy ['sætɪsfaɪ] *verb* to give enough of something to make a person feel happy and comfortable

satisfaction [sætɪs'fækʃn] *noun* feeling of contentment that comes from having what you want

satisfactory [sætɪs'fæktri] *adjective* acceptable or good enough for your purpose

save [seɪv] *verb* to keep something for later use

saving *or* **savings** ['seɪvɪŋ] *noun* reduction in the amount of time or money needed to accomplish your purpose

scale [skeɪl] *noun* **(a)** set of marks or standards for measuring things **(b)** size or level of something in relation to what is usual; *scale of development was very difficult to estimate;* **economies of scale** = achieving savings by producing very large quantities; **large scale** = size or level of company, activity or object which is larger the norm

small-scale [ˈsmɔːlˈskeɪl] *adjective (company or activity or object)* which is limited in size and extent; *a small-scale map shows a larger area than a large scale map; the library's evening activities were kept small-scale to reduce costs*

scan [skæn] *verb* **(a)** to look at something very quickly in order to see what it is about **(b)** to examine periodicals routinely in order to keep users informed of new material **(c)** to use a machine to read coded data

scanner [ˈskænə] *noun* machine that converts documents, drawings or photographs into machine-readable form

scatter [ˈskætə] *verb* to distribute things widely and without any order

scatter graph [ˈskætə ˈɡrɑːf] *noun* plot of individual points or values on a two-axis graph

scenario [sɪˈnɑːriəʊ] *noun* way in which a situation is likely to develop; *the planners took account of the worst possible scenario*

schedule [ˈʃedjuːl] **1** *noun* **(a)** written list of information such as prices, conditions, dates, and times **(b)** detailed written programme of events and times **2** *verb* to include an activity in a plan or list; **job scheduling** = process of allocating specific tasks to certain people and times

schema [ˈskiːmə] *noun* an outline of a process, plan or database structure

school library [ˈskuːl ˈlaɪbri] *noun* small library specially designed and stocked to cater for the needs of the pupils and staff of a school

School Library Association (SLA) sub-section of the Library Association specially for the support of school librarians

School Library Service (SLS) part of the public library service which supports school libraries and teachers

school librarian [ˈskuːl laɪˈbreəriən] *noun* specially qualified librarian employed to run the resource centre or library in a school

school of librarianship [ˈskuːl əv laɪˈbreəriənʃɪp] *noun* department in an institute of higher education which trains librarians and information specialists

science [ˈsaɪəns] *noun* knowledge which can be tested and proved usually according to natural laws; **science fiction** = fiction books based on imaginative ideas about the future on this and other planets

SCONUL = STANDING CONFERENCE ON NATIONAL AND UNIVERSITY LIBRARIES

SCOOP = STANDING COMMITTEE ON OFFICIAL PUBLICATIONS

scope [skəʊp] *noun* area covered by an activity or piece of work

SCOPE = SYSTEMATIC COMPUTERIZED PROCESSING IN CATALOGUING

Scottish Vocational Qualification [ˈskɒtɪʃ vəˈkeɪʃnl kwɒlɪfɪˈkeɪʃn] *noun* work related qualification gained in Scotland after a period of post school training

score [skɔː] *noun* printed version of a musical work

scrapbook [ˈskræpbʊk] *noun* book of large blank pages into which cuttings, pictures, photographs, etc., can be stuck

scratch pad [ˈskrætʃ ˈpæd] *noun* area of computer memory used for temporary storage of data

screen [skri:n] **1** *noun* flat surface capable of displaying pictures and words such as on a computer monitor or a television screen; **screen editor** = software which enables text to be edited on screen **2** *verb* to investigate or check people or things for a specific defect or danger; *the information was screened to check that it was completely accurate*

screenful ['skri:nful] *noun* one complete frame of information displayed on a computer monitor

script [skrɪpt] *noun* **(a)** written text of a play or film **(b)** handwriting which is made to look like printing

scroll [skrəʊl] **1** *noun* roll of paper or parchment containing writing **2** *verb* to move text up or down a computer screen one line at a time; **to scroll downwards** = to move down the text on screen towards the end of a document; **to scroll upwards** = to move up the text on screen towards the beginning of a document

seal [si:l] *verb* to close something so that it is airtight and cannot be opened easily; *once an envelope is sealed it should only be opened by the addressee*

search [sɜːtʃ] *verb* to look through a document in order to find a specific item or word; **search and replace** = facility on a word-processor which allows the user to find a word, words or string of characters and change them; **search for** = to go and look for something very thoroughly; **search skills** = ability to search efficiently through a database, references or library for specific information; **search strategy** = plan for searching a database for information using specific keywords in order to maximize the use of computer time; **search term** = word or phrase input into a database to find the relevant records

search engine ['sɜːtʃ 'endʒɪn] *noun* **(a)** software that carries out a search of a database when a user asks it to find information; **(b)** (on the Internet) web site

that allows contains a database of millions of other web sites and allows a user to search for sites that contain particular information

seasonal analysis ['si:znl ə'næləsɪs] *noun* method of analysing data which takes into account the seasonal variations throughout the year

seating plan ['si:tɪŋ plæn] *noun* diagram showing where people should sit at a formal function such as a dinner

second ['sekənd] **1** *noun* **(a)** thing which is counted as number two; **second best** = considered to be slightly inferior, not the best of its kind; **second class** = not so valuable or important as the first class,; *second class postage in the UK is cheaper but takes longer to be delivered;* **second language** = language which you speak quite fluently and use for work but is not your mother tongue **(b)** sixtieth part of a minute **2** *verb* to support a person or proposal

secondary ['sekəndri] *adjective* second in importance; **secondary education** = period of schooling between primary school and further or higher education, usually from about 11 to 16 or 18 years of age; **secondary entry** = catalogue entry which is not the main entry; *see also* ADDED ENTRY **secondary school** = school which provides education after primary school; **secondary sources** = sources of information which have been quoted or reprinted from an original source

secondhand [sekənd'hænd] *adjective* not new, something which has been previously owned by someone else

secondment [sɪ'kɒndmənt] *noun* limited period of time working at something away from one's normal duties

secretary ['sekrətri] *noun* person whose job is to keep records, write letters and organize an office

section [sekʃn] *noun* one part of a whole that has been divided up into smaller parts

sector ['sektə] *noun* division of a group or area which is also part of a larger one

secure system [sɪ'kjuə 'sɪstəm] *noun* system that cannot be accessed without the permission of the owner

security [sɪ'kjuərɪti] *noun* measures taken to make a place or person safe from attack or danger; **security barrier** = device which prevents users leaving a library with materials which have not been checked out; **security device** = something which ensures the safety of something; *a password is a security device which protects computer files;* **security system** = system of alarms and guards which protects an organization from burglars

see [siː] *verb* indexing command referring the user to a different entry; **see also** = indexing command referring the user to additional entries for comparison or added information

seek [siːk] *verb* to look hard for something or someone; **seek to do something** = to attempt to do something; (NOTE: **seeks - sought - has sought)**

segment ['segmənt] *noun* one part of the total which can be treated separately

select [sɪ'lekt] *verb* to find and choose specific information or data; **select committee** = government committee chosen to do a particular task in a limited time

selection [sɪ'lekʃn] *noun* range of products and services available and chosen

selective [sɪ'lektɪv] *adjective* choosing what to do, say or buy with great care

selector [sɪ'lektə] *noun* person who chooses other people or things for specific jobs

self- [self] *prefix* combines with nouns or past participles to form new nouns or adjectives which describe activities done alone; *self-educated;* **self-carboning paper** = paper which will produce a copy of anything written on it on paper placed underneath it, without the need for carbon paper; **self-financing** = not dependent on any outside source of funds; **self-help** = provision of support through informal groups of people with similar experiences

sell [sel] *verb* to offer something to another person in exchange for money; **to sell off** = to sell something because you need the money; **to sell out** = to sell all the goods in stock so that none are left

selling rights ['selɪŋ 'raɪts] *noun* legal right to sell specific goods or services

semantic relationship [sɪ'mæntɪk rɪ'leɪʃnʃɪp] *noun* all types of relations between words

semantics [sɪ'mæntɪks] *plural noun* branch of linguistics which deals with the meanings of words

semester [sə'mestə] *noun* division of the academic year in colleges and universities

semi- ['semi] *prefix* combines with nouns and adjectives to form words which describe something which is only in a part state; **semi-colon** = punctuation sign (;) used to join rather than separate two parts of a sentence, as in 'the safe which had been broken into was on one side of the room; the other safe appeared to be intact'

semi-structured ['semi 'strʌktʃəd] *adjective* partly controlled by a structure and partly free; **semi-structured interview** = interview which is conducted partly with pre-written questions and partly gives the opportunity to talk freely; **semi-structured questionnaire** = set of questions some of which are closed and some of which require open answers

seminar ['semɪnɑː] *noun* meeting of a group of people called together to discuss a particular topic

semiotics [semi'ɒtıks] *plural noun* science of signs

send [send] *verb* to arrange or cause something to be transported from one place to another either physically as by post or electronically as in e-mail

sense [sens] **1** *noun* possible meaning of words or phrases **2** *verb* to become aware of something either personally or with a machine

senseless ['senslɔs] *adjective* something which has no apparent meaning

sensible ['sensəbl] *adjective* able to think and behave in a logical and common sense manner

sensitivity [sensə'tıvıti] *noun* ability of a person or a machine to be aware of other people's feelings or physical conditions; **sensitivities** = subjects that are likely to cause argument so must be approached very carefully

sensitive ['sensətıv] *adjective* strongly able to be aware of feelings; **sensitive subject** = topic which is liable to cause strong feelings when discussed

sentence ['sentəns] *noun* group of words containing a subject and a verb

separate ['sepəreıt] *verb* to cause two things to be apart and unconnected

separator ['sepəreıtə] *noun* piece of card or plastic which keeps things apart; *the file had different colour separators for each division*

sequence ['si:kwəns] *noun* arrangement which follows a consecutive order

sequential [sı'kwenʃl] *adjective* when things follow each other in a pre-arranged order; **sequential access** = when information can only be accessed in a given order

sequel ['si:kwəl] *noun* book or film, etc. which continues the storyline with the same characters as a previous one

serial ['si:riəl] **1** *noun* **(a)** journal or magazine which is published at regular intervals; **serial processing** = organization of journals so that they can be retrieved easily **(b)** story published in regular instalments **2** *adjective* referring to a series; **serial number** = number given to an item which identifies it by its position in a sequence

serial line internet protocol (SLIP) communications protocol that allows a computer to connect to the internet using a modem and telephone link instead of a permanenet network connection

serials department ['si:riəlz dı'pa:tmənt] *noun* section of a library with responsibility for organizing the journals and periodicals purchased by the organization

series ['si:ri:z] *noun* group of related items ordered in a sequence, such as the volumes in a set of books

series authority file ['si:ri:z ɔ:'θɒrıti 'faıl] *noun* list of series headings used in a catalogue with the references made to them from other forms

serif ['serıf] *noun* small decorative line added to letters in certain fonts; *see also* SANS SERIF

server ['sɜ:və] *noun* computer with a large storage capacity which provides a function to a network of terminals

service ['sɜ:vıs] **1** *noun* work which supports another person or organization's activities; **service point** = places in a library or information centre at which the public is served **2** *verb* to clean, adjust and repair a machine so that it keeps running; **service agreement** *or* **service contract** = arrangement with the suppliers of a machine that they will maintain it regularly and repair it if it goes wrong

session ['seʃn] *noun* one meeting of an official group undertaking a specific activity; **academic session** = school or university year, or one complete part of a year, such as a term or semester

set [set] **1** *noun* group of related items **2** *verb* to decide the price, time or level of an item or activity; **to set out** = to state conditions or facts in a clear organized way; **to set up** = to make the necessary preparations for a machine or an activity to start

setting ['setɪŋ] *noun* **(a)** time and place where the action of a book or film happens **(b)** position of the controls on a machine; *there are two settings: fast and slow*

shade [ʃeɪd] **1** *noun* variation in colour or black & white texture of printing produced by adding black **2** *verb* to colour in a certain section of a drawing by adding a darker colour or a textured pattern

shadow ['ʃædəʊ] *verb* to follow someone very closely throughout their working day in order to study what they do

share [ʃeə] **1** *noun* one of the parts into which the capital of a company is divided, which can be bought by investors **2** *verb* to own or use something together with someone else; **shared resources** = working materials which are used by several group, for example schools or companies

sheaf [ʃiːf] *noun* bundle of long or thin things; *he was carrying a sheaf of papers*

sheet [ʃiːt] *noun* large flat piece of material or paper; **sheet feed** = device which feeds single sheets of paper into a printer one at a time

shelf [ʃelf] *noun* horizontal piece of wood or metal attached to a wall, or in a bookcase or cupboard; **shelf label** = written notice attached to a library shelf which indicates the classification of the books stored there; **shelf life** = period of time that an item such as a

library book is likely to last before it needs replacing; **shelf list card** = card which lists the items held on a particular shelf; **shelf mark** = classification or call number of a book; **shelf number** = number allocated to a shelf to assist the retrieval of books; (NOTE: plural is **shelves**)

shift [ʃɪft] *noun* period of time spent at work at any time during a 24-hour period; *librarians often have to work an afternoon and evening shift*

shift key ['ʃɪft 'kiː] *noun* key on a keyboard which raises a letter to a capital or combines with other command keys for word processing and computing functions

ship [ʃɪp] *verb* to transport goods by sea

shipment ['ʃɪpmənt] *noun* quantity of goods, usually of the same kind, sent together to a destination by any form of transport, not just by sea; *the shipment of library equipment has just arrived at the airport*

shoot [ʃuːt] *verb* to use a camera to take photographs or make a film

short [ʃɔːt] *adjective* having only a few words or pages

short-handed *or* **short-staffed** ['ʃɔːt 'hændɪd *or* 'stɑːft] *adjective* without enough people to do the work required

short list ['ʃʊt 'lɪst] **1** *noun* small group chosen from a larger group, from which the final choice is made; *five titles were on the short list for the Booker Prize* **2** *verb* to choose a few names of people or titles of books, etc., from a longer list as a first step towards deciding on a person for a job or the winner of a competition

short loan collection ['ʃɔːt ləʊn kə'lekʃn] *noun* books and materials in a library which are in heavy demand so can only be borrowed for a very limited time, such as 24 hours

short run ['ʃɔːt 'rʌn] *noun* print run of only a small number of copies

short term ['ʃɔːt 'tɜːm] *adjective* only relevant to the near future; *see also* PLANNING

shorten ['ʃɔːtn] *verb* to reduce the length of something

shorthand ['ʃɔːthænd] *noun* system of signs and symbols which enables spoken words to be written down very quickly; *see also* TYPIST

shot [ʃɒt] *noun* photograph or still frame from a film

show [ʃəʊ] **1** *verb* to take something to someone and enable them to see it **2** *noun* **show of hands** = method of counting votes by counting the number of raised hands

shred [ʃred] *verb* to cut something into long thin strips

shredder ['ʃredə] *noun* machine that cuts paper into very small pieces, usually long thin strips, used to destroy confidential documents

shut down ['ʃʌt 'daʊn] *verb* **(a)** to close a factory, shop or organization permanently or temporarily **(b)** to close down a computer or engine temporarily

side [saɪd] *noun* one surface of something flat like a tape or piece of paper; *it is possible to record on both sides of this tape*

side with *or* **side against** ['saɪd wɪθ *or* ə'genst] *verb* to support or oppose someone in an argument

side by side ['saɪd baɪ 'saɪd] *adjective* next to each other

sign [saɪn] **1** *noun* piece of wood, plastic or metal with words or pictures on it giving information **2** *verb* to write your signature on a document; **to sign for** = to put your signature on an official document to say that you have received something; **to sign in** =

write your name on a list to say that you have arrived; **to sign on** = to agree to a contract

signed edition [saɪnd ɪ'dɪʃn] *noun* copy of a book autographed by the author

signal ['sɪgnəl] *noun* means of sending a message over a distance by physical or electronic methods

signature ['sɪgnətʃə] *noun* **(a)** way of writing your name which is special to you and can be recognized as yours by other people **(b)** special authentication code, such as a password, which a user gives prior to accessing a system or prior to the execution of a task (to prove his identity) **(c)** a sentence or paragraph used to end email messages and comments posted on the internet. Normally a signature should be short - no more than four lines - and might include a short advertisement for your ;services and your email address

signatory ['sɪgnətri] *noun* person who has the legal right to sign an official document

significance [sɪg'nɪfɪkəns] *noun* importance or special meaning or value of something

significant [sɪg'nɪfɪkənt] *adjective* of particular importance

Silver Platter Information ['sɪlvə 'plætə] organization set up specifically to provide information by using CD-ROM technology with micro computers

similar ['sɪmɪlə] *adjective* having features which are almost the same as something else

simple mail transfer protocol (SMTP) standard method of sending electronic mail messages over the internet *see also* POP3

simplify ['sɪmplɪfaɪ] *verb* to make something less complex

simulate ['sɪmjʊleɪt] *verb* to copy actions, feelings or objects to produce something that looks similar or acts in the same way

simultaneous [siml'teiniəs] *adjective* happening at the same time

sine loco ['saini 'lɒkəʊ] *Latin phrase* used in catalogue entries to signify no place of publication; (NOTE: Latin abbreviation is **s.l.**)

sine nomine ['saini 'nɒminei] *Latin phrase* used in catalogue entries to signify no known publisher; (NOTE: Latin abbreviation is **s.n**)

single ['siŋgl] **1** *noun* only one; *he asked for a single ticket as he only wanted to travel one way and not come back* **2** *verb* to single **out** = to select one person or thing from a group

single user ['siŋgl 'juːzə] *adjective* which can only be used by one person

singular ['siŋgjʊlə] *adjective* **(a)** grammatical term meaning that there is only one of a kind, opposite of plural **(b)** describes something that is unusual or eccentric

SIS = STRATEGIC INFORMATION SERVICES

site [sait] *noun* place where something is based; **site engineer** = engineer who is allocated to a particular site to maintain the equipment and machines; **site licence** = official permit to an institution and its staff to use particular software; *see also* WEBSITE

situation [sitjʊ'eiʃn] *noun* job; **situations vacant column** = list of job advertisements printed in a newspaper

size [saiz] **1** *noun* **(a)** physical dimensions of something, which tell how big or small it is; the size of a book is usually indicated by its height and width **(b)** mixture of gelatine, alum and formaldehyde used to coat paper surfaces **2** *verb* to calculate the size of something; **to size up** = to study a person or situation and assess the best way of dealing with it

skeleton service ['skelitən 'sɜːvis] *noun* service run by the minimum number of

people possible; **skeleton key** = key which will open many different locks; **skeleton staff** = smallest number of staff able to do the work

skill [skil] *noun* special ability, knowledge or training that enables you to do things well; **skilled staff** = people who work with special knowledge in a particular job

skip [skip] *verb* **(a)** to miss something out **(b)** to decide deliberately not to do something or go somewhere

s.l. = SINE LOCO

SLA = SCHOOL LIBRARY ASSOCIATION

slang [slæŋ] *noun* words and expressions which are very informal and likely to change in meaning every so often

slash [slæʃ] *noun* oblique stroke used in typing (/); (NOTE: in printing called **solidus**)

slashed zero ['slæʃt 'ziːrəʊ] *noun* printed sign which puts an oblique stroke through zero (Ø) to distinguish it from the letter O

sleeve [sliːv] *noun* **(a)** envelope type cover for disks often with information or pictures on it **(b)** book jacket

slew [sluː] *noun* rapid uncontrolled movement of paper in a printer when it is not connected to the feeder

slide [slaid] *noun* **(a)** picture on positive transparent photographic film mounted in a frame; **slide carousel** = container which allows slides to be fed into a projector; **slide mount** = frame around a slide which makes it easier to handle and store; **slide projector** = device that shines light through photographic slides in order to project them on to a screen; **slide storage** = system of storage slides which keeps them clean, safe and easily retrieved; **slide tape package** = synchronized programme of slides and audio tape; **slide viewer** = small portable box which enables slides to be viewed against a light source **(b)**

individual computer screen which can be produced as output in different ;formats

SLIP = SERIAL LINE INTERNET PROTOCOL

slip pages or **slip proofs** ['slɪp 'peɪdʒɪz or 'pruːfs] *plural noun* draft copies of text for printing which are printed on separate sheets of paper

slip-up ['slɪpʌp] *noun* small, unintentional mistake

slow motion ['sləʊ 'məʊʃn] *noun* playing back a film or video at a slower speed than when it was recorded

SLS = SCHOOL LIBRARY SERVICE

small [smɔːl] *adjective* not very large; **small ad** = short advertisement in a newspaper or magazine, usually advertising personal sales or wants; **small caps** = printing style which uses capital letters which are the same size as lower case letters

smart card ['smaːt 'kaːd] *noun* plastic card with an electronic strip which can be read to identify the user on such things as credit cards

SMTP = SIMPLE MAIL TRANSFER PROTOCOL

s.n. = SINE NOMINE

snap decision ['snæp dɪ'sɪʒn] *noun* decision taken quickly without much thought

snapshot ['snæpʃɒt] *noun* personal photograph taken quickly

social skills ['səʊʃl 'skɪlz] *plural noun* ability to communicate with other people at all levels of society

social trend ['səʊʃl 'trend] *noun* direction of changes in the way people in society behave

socket ['sɒkɪt] *noun* device with holes for a plug which connects a machine to the electricity supply

soft copy ['sɒft 'kɒpi] *noun* text on screen as opposed to hard copy printed on to paper

software ['sɒftweə] *noun* computer programs which instruct the hardware what to do; **software costs** = amount of money needed to buy software; **software development** = process of writing programs to implement an original idea; **software documentation** = instruction manuals which explain how to install and use computer programs; **software engineer** = person who can write computer programs to fit specific applications; **software installation** = process of putting a program onto a computer so that it can be used; **software licence** = contract between the producer and the purchaser of software about the use and copying of the program; **software maintenance** = modifications to a program to keep it up to date; **software package** = complete set of instruction manuals and installation disks which enable a program to be used; **software piracy** = illegal copying of software; **software producer** = publisher of computer programs for sale

solicit [sə'lɪsɪt] *verb* to ask for help, advice or money

solidus ['sɒlɪdəs] *noun (printing)* oblique stroke (/)

solution [sə'luːʃn] *noun* answer to a problem

solve [sɒlv] *verb* to find the answer to a problem or difficulty

sophisticated [sə'fɪstɪkeɪtɪd] *adjective* complex and technically advanced

sort [sɔːt] *verb* to put things in to a certain order; *the data can be sorted by name or number*

sort code ['sɔːt 'kəʊd] *noun* combination of numbers which identifies the user

sorting office ['sɔːtɪŋ 'ɒfɪs] *noun* part of a post office where items which have been posted are sorted according to their delivery addresses

sound [saʊnd] **1** *noun* noise that can be heard; **sound effects** = sounds produced artificially to make a play or film seem more realistic; **sound track** = track on the edge of a film on which the speech and music is recorded and synchronized with the pictures **2** *adjective* in good condition, strong and reliable

soundproof ['saʊndpruːf] *adjective* which does not allow sound to pass in or out

source [sɔːs] *noun* place where something originally comes from; **primary source** = original document from which information is extracted; **secondary source** = reference which has already been quoted in another document; **source language** = original language of a text which is being translated into another language; **source term** = first word looked up in an index search from which the searcher is directed to other terms

space [speɪs] **1** *noun* gap or empty place intended for the storage of data; **space bar** = long bar at the bottom of a key board that inserts a space in the text when it is pressed **2** *verb* to arrange things with regular gaps in between them; **to space out** = to organize a series of things or events so that there are gaps or periods of time in between them

spacing ['speɪsɪŋ] *noun* way in which gaps are inserted; *the spacing of words on that line is rather uneven*

span [spæn] *noun* period of time; **attention span** = length of time that a person is able to give undivided attention to something; **span of concentration** = period of time for which a person is able to concentrate on doing something; *the average span of concentration on one activity for children is said to be only 15 minutes*

spare [speə] *adjective* extra to requirements and available for use

spare part [speə 'pɑːt] *noun* component for a machine that can be bought separately to replace one that is broken or worn out

spatial ['speɪʃl] *adjective* relating to space and shapes; **spatial ability** = ability of a person to visualize the relationships between shapes

speaker ['spiːkə] *noun* someone who makes a speech; *see also* LOUDSPEAKER

special ['speʃl] *adjective* different from the normal or ordinary; **special library** = library which is stocked to provide information in a particular area of study; *Research & Development departments of large firms often have their own special libraries;* **special librarian** = qualified librarian employed in a special library; **special offers** = product or service that is offered in place of normal ones and often at a reduced price

specialize ['speʃlaɪz] *verb* to study something in great depth so that you become an expert in that field

specialist ['speʃlɪst] *noun* expert in one particular area of knowledge or skill

specify ['spesɪfaɪ] *verb* to state in detail what is required

specifications [spesɪfɪ'keɪʃnz] *plural noun* detailed instructions about work to be done or products to be supplied

specified amount ['spesɪfaɪd ə'maʊnt] *noun* certain amount according to instructions, *they were asked to deliver only the specified amount and no more*

specific entry [spə'sɪfɪk 'entri] *noun* catalogue entry under the actual subject rather than a broader term

specimen ['spesɪmən] *noun* **(a)** small example of something which gives an idea of what the whole thing will look like **(b)** one example of a species, such as a butterfly, which shows what they all look like; **specimen storage** = system of organizing the storing of physical objects so that they can be studied; *specimens that were on show were stored in controlled conditions in the museum;* **specimen pages** = printed pages produced by the printer for the publisher to show the proposed type style

spectrum ['spektrəm] *noun* range of attributes or colours

speech recognition ['spi:tʃ rekəg'nɪʃn] *noun* ability of a machine to recognize the patterns of individual human voices, sometimes used in security systems

speech synthesizer ['spi:tʃ 'sɪnθəsaɪzə] *noun* machine which takes information from a computer in electronic form and makes it recognizable as spoken words; *the blind student needed a speech synthesizer attached to his computer so that he could hear the written words*

speed [spi:d] *noun* measure of quickness of movement or reaction time; *to photograph moving objects you need a very high speed film*

spellcheck facility ['speltʃek fə'sɪləti] *noun* software facility on a word processing program which enables the user to check spellings against an inbuilt dictionary

spelling error ['spelɪŋ 'erə] *noun* mistake in spelling a word

spend [spend] *verb* to exchange money for goods or time on activities

spike [spaɪk] *noun* sharp piece of metal, which when mounted on a base can be used for temporary storage of papers needing attention

spine [spaɪn] *noun* edge of a book which is all that can be seen when a book is upright on a shelf; **spine label** = label put on the spine of a book to indicate its library location; **spine number** = call or class number put on the spine of a library book; **spine title** = name of the book written down its spine

spiral binding ['spaɪrəl 'baɪndɪŋ] *noun* type of binding for collections of papers which uses a coiled wire inserted into specially punched holes

splice [splaɪs] *verb* to join two pieces of magnetic tape or film together; **splicing tape** = non-magnetic, transparent tape used to join two pieces of tape together

split catalogue ['splɪt 'kætəlɒg] *noun* in which the entries are divided by category and give separate alphabetical lists for title, author, subject, etc.

split site school *or* **college** *or* **university** ['splɪt 'saɪt] *noun* school, college or university with buildings separated on different sites

sponsor ['spɒnsə] **1** *noun* person or organization that pays all or part of the expenses for an event or period of study **2** *verb* to pay to support an activity or person

spool [spu:l] **1** *noun* round object on to which tape or film can be wound **2** *verb* to transfer data from a disc to a tape

spreadsheet ['spredʃi:t] *noun* computer program which allows the calculation of numbers in both columns and rows

sprocket ['sprɒkɪt] *noun* tooth on the edge of a wheel to pick up what passes over it; **sprocket holes** = series of holes at the edge of paper which control its feed through a printer

stable ['steɪbl] *adjective* steady and unmoving

stability [stə'bɪləti] *noun* state of being unchanging and likely to continue

stack [stæk] *noun* **(a)** pile of things one on top of another; *a stack of order forms* **(b)** large and ordered collection of books kept in another area for reference

staff [stɑ:f] **1** *collective noun* people who work for a company or organization; **staff levels** = number of people who are employed to work for a company or organization; *they were criticized for having inadequate staff levels;* **staff profile** = records which show details of staff qualifications and work experience **2** *verb* to provide the staff for a company or organization

staffroom ['stɑːfruːm] *noun* common room where staff can meet informally; **staffroom library** = collection of books on work related subjects kept in the staffroom for use by members of staff

stage [steɪdʒ] *noun* step in a process

stamp [stæmp] **1** *noun* something which marks another object to show that it has been processed; **postage stamp** = small official piece of sticky paper which is stuck to a letter or parcel to show that you have paid for it to be delivered; **rubber stamp** = small block or rubber metal or wood, which is used in combination with ink to make a mark on something to show that it is official or to show ownership; **stamp of approval** = mark of approval given either verbally or by a physical mark **2** *verb* to use a rubber stamp to mark something; *the books are stamped with the date for return*

stand-alone ['stændələʊn] *noun* computer that can be used by itself without the help of larger networks

standard ['stændəd] **1** *noun* acceptable level by which others can be judged **2** *adjective* normal or usual; *they received the standard letter of reply just like everyone else;* **standard author** = author of literary merit who is part of the literature of a country; **standard book number (SBN)** = older form of the International Standard Book Number; *see* **ISBN standard deviation** = statistical term to show how far things are different from the normal; **standard edition** = usually a better quality edition of a book, sometimes including notes; **standard format** = most commonly used format for such things as documents, used many times without any change to the text;

standard serial number (SSN) = older form of the International Standard Serial Number; *see* **ISSN**

standardize ['stændədaɪz] *verb* to make sure that everything conforms to the same standard

standby ['stændbaɪ] *noun* something that is kept ready for use in case of need

standing committee ['stændɪŋ kə'mɪtiː] *noun* permanently established administrative body which supports the work of a large organization; **Standing Committee on Official Publications (SCOOP)** = organization which provides a current awareness service to members; **Standing Conference on National and University Libraries (SCONUL)** = advisory committee on special areas of concern such as buildings, staffing or specific subjects

standing order ['stændɪŋ 'ɔːdə] *noun* (i) regular order for each edition of a serial or annual publication; (ii) an instruction to your bank to pay a fixed regular amount of money to a named person or organization

staple ['steɪpl] **1** *noun* small bent piece of metal which is forced into papers to hold them together **2** *verb* to use a stapler to join papers together using a staple

stapler ['steɪplə] *noun* device which forces staples through papers or other materials to hold them together

start [stɑːt] **1** *noun* beginning **2** *verb* to create something from the beginning; **starting point** = place from where you begin

state [steɪt] **1** *noun* **(a)** country or nation **(b)** government of a country **(c)** condition of something; **state-of-the-art** = as technically advanced as possible **2** *adjective* describes government-run organizations; *state schools*

statement ['steɪtmənt] *noun* formal or official account of events

static ['stætɪk] *adjective* unmoving and unchanging

station ['steɪʃn] *noun* point in a network at which work can be input to the main system; **work station** = desk with a computer, and keyboard and sometimes a printer; **radio station** *or* **TV station** = place from where a particular broadcasting company transmits its radio or television programmes

stationary ['steɪʃnri] *adjective* not moving

stationery ['steɪʃnri] *noun* paper equipment in an office, such as envelopes, writing paper, etc.; **personalized stationery** = letter paper or cards printed with your address and sometimes your name

statistics [stə'tɪstɪks] *plural noun* facts presented in the form of figures

status ['steɪtəs] *noun* position in society or in a work schedule; **status line** = line at the top of a computer screen which gives details of the file currently being worked on

STATUS *noun* information retrieval package which works on the free text principle; **STATUS/IQ** = software system for use with STATUS which understands natural English and can rank its findings in the order of perceived usefulness to the user

statute ['stætjuːt] *noun* regulation or law

statutory instrument ['stætjuːtri 'ɪnstrəmənt] *noun* law or legal requirement

stave [steɪv] *noun* set of five lines on which music is written

STD *see* SUBSCRIBER TRUNK DIALLING

steering committee ['stiːrɪŋ kə'mɪtiː] *noun* group of people in charge of stages of a project which decides the priorities and order of work

stem [stem] *verb* to search a database by inputting only the stem of a word with indicators, such as * or % or ? signs before

and after: *friend* would find befriend, friend and friendship

stencil ['stensəl] *noun* template of shapes or letters which can be used to produce a design or written information

step [step] *noun* one of a series of stages used to accomplish a task

stereophonic [steriə'fɒnɪk] *adjective* where sound signals are directed through two speakers at once to give depth to the sound (NOTE: informal is: **stereo**)

still [stɪl] **1** *noun* one single frame from a video or film **2** *adverb* continuing to exist or function; *they are still working from that office in the town centre*

stock [stɒk] *noun* total amount of items available for use or sale; **stock availability** = whether an item is on the premises and ready for use or sale; **stock control** = process of keeping records of how much stock is bought and sold; **stock selection** = process of choosing items to hold on the premises

stockroom ['stɒkrum] *noun* room where items that are not immediately needed are stored

stocktaking ['stɒkteɪkɪŋ] *noun* process of checking the amount of available stock against records

stop list ['stɒp 'lɪst] *noun* list of words which cannot be used in a system

stop word ['stɒp 'wɜːd] *noun* word which is not significant for an index or library file so is not included, for example, the word 'the'

storage ['stɔːrɪdʒ] *noun* **(a)** process of placing or keeping goods in a store; **storage facilities** = room or space in which to store items; **storage system** = system for organizing items in store so that they can be retrieved **(b)** place for storing things **(c)** money charged for keeping goods in a store

store [stɔː] 1 *noun* place where items can be kept until needed 2 *verb* to place items into safe keeping

story ['stɔːri] *noun* narrative tale

storyboard ['stɔːribɔːd] *noun* planning document used by producers of broadcast programmes

strategic planning [strə'tiːdʒɪk 'plænɪŋ] *noun* policy planning for future developments within a company or organization

strategy ['strætədʒi] *noun* plan which sets out the methods of achieving your goals

string [strɪŋ] *noun* **(a)** indexing term for a series of characters **(b)** indexing term to describe the lists of terms compiled by an indexer with details of how they relate to each other

strip [strɪp] *noun* long narrow piece of material or space; **magnetic strip** = plastic strip with electronic data, fixed to a plastic card which can be read by a machine; *a library card often has a magnetic strip with details of its owner to prevent it being used by anyone else*

stripe [straɪp] *noun* **(a)** line of different colour from the background **(b)** thin magnetic strip on the side of a film opposite to the sound track to control its speed on playback

structure ['strʌktʃə] 1 *noun* underlying plan which gives form to a system or activity 2 *verb* to organize or construct something according to an efficient or logical system

structured indexing language ['strʌktʃəd 'ɪndeksɪŋ 'læŋgwɪdʒ] *noun* use of words in specific order to construct index headings, as in 'libraries, special' instead of 'special libraries'

study ['stʌdi] *verb* to learn about something by spending time reading about it and listening to experts

STUMPERS-L *acronym* Internet bulletin board which lists difficult questions asked of librarians to see if any other librarians can help with the answers

style [staɪl] *noun* way in which a particular writer or editor uses words, sentences and layout to produce a recognizable publication

stylus ['staɪləs] *noun* **(a)** small pointed object which is used in computer graphics to direct the cursor **(b)** small needle used to convert signals on an audio record to electrical signals which can be recognized by the human ear

sub- [sʌb] *prefix* combines with nouns to make other nouns with the meaning of less important; **sub-contract** = to pay someone else to do part of a job for you; **sub-editor** = person who corrects and checks articles in a newspaper before they are printed; **sub-heading** = subsidiary heading which divides text into shorter sections; **sub-section** = small part of a larger section; **sub-series** = series of publications with titles dependent on a previous series

subject ['sʌbdʒɪkt] *noun* idea for study, discussion or treatment; **subject entry** *or* **heading** = index or catalogue heading which indicates the main subject of a document; **subject index** = list of subjects covered by a library with the class numbers to indicate where materials can be found

submission date [sʌb'mɪʃn 'deɪt] *noun* last date by which an assignment, proposal or application can be sent to someone

subscribe to [sʌb'skraɪb 'tʊ] *verb* to pay money in order to receive copies of a regular publication or to gain access to a service

Subscriber Trunk Dialling (STD)

[sʌb'skraɪbə 'trʌŋk 'daɪəlɪŋ] system of automatic telephone connection all over the world which is then charged to your personal telephone account

subscription [sʌbˈskrɪpʃn] *noun* money paid to become a member of an organization or in order to receive regular publications

subscript letter *or* **number** [ˈsʌbskrɪpt] *noun* very small letter or number which is printed slightly below the line level of normal print, such as 'CO₂'

subset [ˈsʌbset] *noun* smaller part of a large division of data

substantiate [sʌbˈstænʃieɪt] *verb* to supply evidence to prove that something is true

substitute [ˈsʌbstɪtjuːt] *verb* to put or use something in the place of something else

subtitle [ˈsʌbtaɪtl] *noun* **(a)** secondary title of a book **(b)** words written at the bottom of a television or cinema screen to enable the spoken words to be read

succeed [sɔkˈsiːd] *verb* **(a)** to follow a person and take over their job **(b)** to gain the intended result

successive [sɔkˈsesɪv] *adjective* following one after the other

sufficient [sɔˈfɪʃənt] *adjective* as much as is needed

suffix [ˈsʌfɪks] *noun* word or group of letters added to the end of a word which changes the grammar and meaning

suggestions book [sɔˈdʒestʃnz ˈbʊk] *noun* book in which the users of a service can write their ideas for how to improve the service

summarize [ˈsʌməraɪz] *verb* to give a brief description of the main points

summary [ˈsʌmri] *noun* short version of something giving only the main points

Sunday supplement [ˈsʌndi ˈsʌplɪmənt] *noun* magazine which comes with a Sunday newspaper

super- [ˈsuːpə] *prefix* combines with adjectives to form new adjectives which suggest that it is of very high quality

superimpose [suːpəɪmˈpəʊz] *verb* to place something on top of something else

superior number [suːpiːəriə ˈnʌmbə] *noun* superscript number often used to indicate a footnote

Super Janet [suːpə ˈdʒænɪt] *noun* updated version of the Joint Academic NETwork system of information transfer within the UK

superscript [ˈsuːpəskrɪpt] *noun* small character printed at a higher level than the normal line of writing, for instance, sup

supersede [suːpəˈsiːd] *verb* to replace something which is old and out of date

supervise [ˈsuːpəvaɪz] *verb* to make sure that a person is working efficiently or a task is done properly

supervision [suːpəˈvɪʒn] *noun* keeping watch over another person or activity

supervisor [ˈsuːpəvaɪzə] *noun* person who has the responsibility for supervising other people or machinery

supplementary [sʌplɪˈmentri] *adjective* added to something else to improve it, update it or make it satisfactory

supply [sɔˈplaɪ] *verb* to provide, give or sell something to someone

supplier [sɔˈplaɪə] *noun* person or company which provides goods, services or equipment

support [sɔˈpɔːt] *verb* to provide help, advice or finance to ensure that someone or something else can work

suppress [sɔˈpres] *verb* to prevent something from being known or done

surf [sɜːf] *verb* to browse through a database; *surfing the internet*

surge [sɜːdʒ] *noun* sudden increase in something such as sales or electrical power

surname ['sɜːneɪm] *noun* family name that is shared by all members of the family

survey [sə'veɪ] *noun* detailed investigation often involving people's opinions; **survey population** = selected sample for an investigation

sustain [sə'steɪn] *verb* to keep or maintain something for a length of time

SVQ = SCOTTISH VOCATIONAL QUALIFICATION

swap [swɒp] *verb* to exchange information, giving one item and receiving another in its place; **swapping information** = process of exchanging data or facts

switch [swɪtʃ] **1** *noun* small device which controls the working of an electrical machine or equipment **2** *verb* **to switch off** = (i) to isolate a machine or equipment from a source of electrical power; (ii) (informal) to stop listening; **to switch on** = to connect a machine or equipment to a source of electrical power; **to switch over** = to change to another machine

switchboard ['swɪtʃbɔːd] *noun* central control unit for a telephone system within an organization from which calls can be redirected to extension lines; **switchboard operator** = person who receives calls and redirects them

symbol ['sɪmbəl] *noun* shape, icon or picture which represents something else

symbolic [sɪm'bɒlɪk] *adjective* which either acts as a symbol or uses symbols; *symbolic language uses words to represent items rather than just describing them*

symposium [sɪm'pəʊziəm] *noun* conference of experts to discuss particular topics; (NOTE: plural is **symposia)**

syndetic [sɪn'detɪk] *adjective* connected by cross-references; **syndetic catalogue** *or* **syndetic index** = dictionary catalogue or index using a system of cross-referencing

synecdoche [sɪ'nekdəkiː] *noun* figure of speech which uses one species for the whole genus such as 'pennies' for money in general:; *I will have to save my pennies in order to buy the set of encyclopaedias*

synonym ['sɪnənɪm] *noun* word of phrase which has almost the same meaning as another word or phrase

synopsis [sɪ'nɒpsɪs] *noun* summary of a longer text; (NOTE: plural is **synopses)**

syntax ['sɪntæks] *noun* term in linguistics to describe the grammatical structure of a language

synthesize ['sɪntəsaɪz] *verb* to make an artificial combination from a variety of small components; *the computer is now able to synthesize sounds and make them seem like a human voice*

synthesis ['sɪnθəsaɪz] *noun* artificial combination of ideas and styles

synthesizer ['sɪnθəsaɪzə] *noun* machine which combines electrical sounds to make them recognizable as speech or music

system ['sɪstəm] *noun* set of rules or plans which are used to accomplish a task; **operating system** = basic software which controls the functions of the hardware; **system analysis** = method of finding out how a system works; **system analyst** = person who works at finding out the strong and weak points in a system; **system design** = deciding on the most appropriate system to provide the solution to a problem; **system diagnosis** = process of finding faults in a system; **system software** = programs which make applications work on the hardware

Systematic Computerized Processing in Cataloguing (SCOPE) system used in university libraries for the systematic control of periodicals

systematic sampling [sɪstəˈmætɪk ˈsɑːmplɪŋ] *noun* use of a regular order of choice for the selection of a sample; *they chose to use the method of systematic sampling and interview every tenth person from the list of names*

Tt

tab [tæb] *short for* TABULATE

tab key ['tæb 'kiː] *noun* one of the keys on a typewriter or computer keyboard which enables work to be tabulated

table ['teɪbl] *noun* list of data arranged in rows and columns printed or on a computer screen

tabloid ['tæblɔɪd] *noun* small size newspaper with a less serious approach to the news than the broadsheets

tabulate ['tæbjʊleɪt] *verb* to arrange work on a word processor using the tab key to move from one column or row to the next

tact [tækt] *noun* ability to deal with people or a situation without upsetting anyone

tactic ['tæktɪk] *noun* method of achieving what you want

tactical planning ['tæktɪkl 'plænɪŋ] *noun* discussion and decisions about future tactics

tactile ['tæktaɪl] *adjective* using the sense of touch; **tactile feedback** = information discovered by the sense of touch

tag [tæg] *noun* character or symbol attached to a record to aid retrieval

tail end ['teɪl 'end] *noun* final entry or activity

tail off ['teɪl 'ɒf] *verb* to become less in amount or value until it finally stops or disappears completely

take ['teɪk] *verb* to move something physically from one place to another; **to take a message** = to listen to information in order to pass it on to someone else; **to take a photograph** = to use a camera to create a picture of something; **to take into account** = to consider certain aspects before making a decision

take out ['teɪk 'aʊt] *verb* **(b)** to arrange; *they made arrangements to take out a mortgage to buy the house* **(b)** to borrow a book from a library

talking book *or* **talking newspaper** ['tɔːkɪŋ 'bʊk *or* 'njuːzpeɪpə] *noun* tape or cassette recording of a book or newspaper usually for the use of blind people

talks [tɔːks] *plural noun* **(a)** formal discussions **(b)** informal lectures

tally ['tæli] **1** *noun* informal cumulative record of amounts collected **2** *verb* to agree with another conclusion or total; *the figures in the accounts did not tally with the office records*

tape [teɪp] *noun* narrow strip of plastic, coated with magnetic material on which to record sound or pictures; **audio tape** = tape which is used to record and play back sounds for listening to; **video tape** = magnetic tape which can be used to record pictures and to play them back on a television set; **tape recorder** = machine which is used to record and play back sounds on audio cassettes or reel to reel tape

target ['tɑːgɪt] **1** *noun* result or goal which is the aim of work done; **target audience** = group of people at which specific products, services or written or spoken information is aimed; **target date** = date by which a task must be done; **target language** = in translation, the language of the final version; **target market** = type of customer who is thought likely to buy specific goods or services **2** *verb* to aim to have an effect on a specially chosen group

tariff ['tærɪf] *noun* charge made for goods or services

task [tɑːsk] *noun* job which has to be done; **task identity** = code which indicates which is the job to be done

teacher ['tiːtʃə] *noun* person whose job is to organize the learning of others

teacher librarian ['tiːtʃə laɪ'breəriən] *noun* person who is dually qualified both as a teacher and a school librarian

team teaching ['tiːm 'tiːtʃɪŋ] *noun* two or more teachers working together to teach a group of students

teamwork ['tiːmwɜːk] *noun* group of people working well together

technical ['teknɪkl] *adjective* **technical author** = person who writes specialized instructions and manuals on technical subjects; **technical information centre** = organization which acquires, processes and distributes technical information; **technical manual** = book which gives instructions about how to work a machine; **technical support** = system by which the users of machines are helped by people who understand how they work

technician [tek'nɪʃn] *noun* person who specializes in working with and maintaining machines or scientific equipment

technique [tek'niːk] *noun* particular skill or ability which can be learned

technology [tek'nɒlədʒi] *noun* application of scientific knowledge to practical purposes; *see also* INFORMATION TECHNOLOGY

teething troubles ['tiːðɪŋ 'trʌblz] *plural noun* small difficulties which occur at the start of a project

tele- ['teli] *prefix* meaning across a distance; **tele-communications** = science of using electronic equipment to send messages over a distance; **tele-conferencing** = several people using a telephone network to speak to each other at the same time; **tele-cottage** = house where a person both lives and works; *she used her home as a tele-cottage by running her information services from there;* **tele-message** = message sent by telephone but delivered as a card; **tele-ordering** = using the telephone to order goods which are then delivered to your address; **tele-sales** = process of telephoning people without warning to try to sell them things; **tele-shopping** = using the telephone to do your shopping which is then delivered to you

telegram ['telɪgræm] *noun* message sent by telegraphy and then printed on to paper and delivered

telegraphy [te'legrəfi] *noun* means of sending telegrams using radio or electric signals

telephone ['telɪfəʊn] **1** *noun* instrument which can be used to talk to someone over a long distance, by means of dialling a series of numbers; **telephone call** = conversation with someone on the telephone; **telephone directory** *or* **telephone book** = book containing an alphabetical list of names, addresses and telephone numbers of people in a given city, town or area; **telephone**

extension = extra telephone linked to the main line into the building; **telephone exchange** = building where telephone lines can be connected when a call is made; **telephone number** = unique number which identifies a telephone line; **telephone operator** = person who works in a telephone exchange, connecting calls and answering problems; **telephone subscriber** = person who pays money to a telephone company in order to be able to connect a telephone to the national network; **telephone switchboard** = central point in a private telephone network where all the lines meet and can be connected **2** *verb* to make contact with someone at a distance by using a telephone

teletext ['telɪtekst] *noun* system of transmitting written text using a television signal

television (TV) [telɪ'vɪʒn] *noun* **(a)** system of transmitting pictures and sound over a distance so that they can be received and seen on a television set **(b)** machine for receiving broadcast television programmes

teleworker ['telɪwɜːkə] *noun* someone who works from home by means of computers, modem, phone and fax machines

telex ['teleks] *noun* system of sending international messages using telephone lines, the text is typed on one machine and immediately printed out at the receiving end

Telnet remote login program; electronic gateway to the Internet worldwide

template ['templeɪt] *noun* thin sheet of metal or plastic with cut-out shapes which enable exactly the same shape to be reproduced many times

temporary ['tempri] *adjective* which does not last a long time; **temporary storage** = short-term, not permanent place to keep things

temporarily ['temprərəli] *adverb* only for a short time

tender ['tendə] **1** *noun* formal offer to supply goods or services at a stated price **2** *verb* to make a formal offer to do something; *he tendered his resignation;* **to put work out to tender** = to ask for companies to state their price for doing a certain job

term [tɜːm] *noun* **(a)** set or limited period of time; *the term of office for the chairperson is one year* **(b)** one of the three divisions of the academic year; *the year starts in October with the autumn term* **(c)** word used in the terminology of indexing; **broad term** = wide subject heading which is broken down into narrow terms; **compound term** = name which consists of two words, as in 'primary schools' and could be indexed with a 'see also' reference (as in: 'schools, see also primary schools'); **lead term** = term chosen by the indexer to head the entry; **narrow term** = specific and detailed word under a wider subject heading; **permitted term** = terms which are used according to certain indexing conventions and must follow specific order rules; **preferred term** = word chosen by the indexer to head all synonyms which are known as 'non-preferred' terms

terminal ['tɜːmɪnəl] *noun* processor with screen and keyboard used to access a central computer system; **terminal user interface** = hardware and software used by a person at a terminal to enable contact with the central computer

terminate ['tɜːmɪneɪt] *verb* **(a)** to stop completely **(b)** to end something

terminology [tɜːmɪ'nɒlədʒi] *noun* set of specialized words and phrases belonging to a specific subject

terms [tɜːmz] *plural noun* **(a)** headings, words and phrases used in a classification scheme **(b)** conditions agreed between people for a sale or job

tertiary ['tɜːʃri] *adjective* third in order or stage of development; *universities are the tertiary stage of education after primary and secondary schools*

test [test] **1** *noun* trial of someone or something to see if they are suitable for a certain task **2** *verb* to test someone's knowledge as in an examination

test pattern ['test 'pætən] *noun* design which uses different textures and colours on a television screen to see if all the components are adjusted properly

text [tekst] *noun* main part of a written document; **text editing** = work done on a word processor to change, add, delete or move words, phrases or paragraphs; **text retrieval** = facility on a word processor which allows the user to find the text of documents to be edited or worked with; **text to table** = facility on a word processor which allows the user to convert text into table form

textbook ['teksbʊk] *noun* academic book on a particular subject used for study

textual analysis ['tekstʃuəl ə'næləsıs] *noun* investigation into the techniques used in a particular style of writing

thematic catalogue [θiː'mætık 'kætəlɒg] *noun* musical catalogue containing the main themes of a composer's works, usually arranged in chronological order

thermal ['θɜːməl] *adjective* using, producing or caused by heat; **thermal imaging** = technique which uses a TV camera sensitive to heat rather than light to produce pictures; **thermal paper** = paper which is chemically coated so that it can be used with a thermal printer; **thermal printer** = printing machine which uses heat sensitive paper

thesaurus [θɪ'sɔːrəs] *noun* type of dictionary which groups synonyms together; **computer-based thesaurus** = dictionary installed as a word processing facility which checks the spelling in written text and suggests alternatives for misspelt words

thesis ['θiːsıs] *noun* piece of extended writing explaining the objectives,

methodology and findings of a research project

third party ['θɜːd 'pɑːti] *noun* person who becomes involved in a situation but is not one of the main parties

Thomson's Local Directory ['tɒmsənz 'ləʊkl daɪ'reltri] *noun* private publication in most areas of the UK giving local information such as business telephone numbers, post codes and maps

thorough ['θʌrə] *adjective* very careful and complete

thread [θred] *noun* idea or theme which connects the different parts of a story together

three-dimensional (3D) ['θriː daɪ'menʃənəl] *adjective* having width, breadth and depth and so appearing solid

thriller ['θrɪlə] *noun* novel telling of crime and criminals in an adventurous way

throughput ['θruːpʊt] *noun* amount of information processed in a given period of time

tier ['tiːə] *noun* one of a number of levels; *there were five tiers of shelves*

tilde ['tɪldə] *noun* pronunciation symbol (ñ) written over certain letters in Spanish & Portuguese

tilt [tɪlt] *verb* to alter the angle of something so that it is not vertical; **tilt & swivel** = used to describe something, such as a computer monitor, mounted on a pivot so that the angle and direction can be changed

time lag ['taɪm 'læg] *noun* period of waiting between two related events; *there is sometimes a time lag between speakers who are interviewed on television from another country*

time out ['taɪm 'aʊt] *noun* time taken away from normal activities

time slot ['taɪm 'slɒt] *noun* period of time allocated to a specific activity

timer ['taɪmə] *noun* device which can be set or preset to measure the time taken to do an activity

timescale ['taɪmskeɪl] *noun* length of time taken up by a particular activity; *their timescale for writing the book was six months*

timesharing ['taɪmʃeərɪŋ] *noun* arrangement by which several people can be online to a computer at the same time

timetable ['taɪmteɪbl] *noun* schedule of times and activities such as school lessons or bus and train services

title ['taɪtl] *noun* (a) the name given to a book, play or TV programme; **title catalogue** *or* **title index** = alphabetical list of book titles; **title page** = page at the beginning of a book which states the title and publication information; **title-a-line catalogue** = catalogue in which the entries occupy only one line of type each (b) the word used to indicate the status of a person, such as Mr., Mrs., Dr., Rev., etc.

titlonym ['taɪtlɒnɪm] *noun* quality or status used as a title when the name of the author is unknown such as 'a doctor';

COMMENT: documents with titlonyms are catalogued as anonymous

token ['təʊkən] *noun* small piece of metal used instead of money to work a machine; **book token** *or* **gift token** = method of giving money as a present, but which must be spent on the type of goods or in the shop which provides it; **token effort** = minimum amount of effort required so as to be seen to be trying to do something; **token woman, token black** = woman or black person who is employed to comply with certain regulations about equal opportunities and not because he/she is really needed

tokenism ['təʊkənɪzm] *noun* practice of employing certain types of people in order to be seen to be avoiding discrimination

tone [təʊn] *noun* sound which can be changed to indicate different meanings; *his tone of voice indicated that he was very happy;* **dialling tone** = sound made by a telephone line when it is available for use; **engaged tone** = sound made by a telephone when the line is in use

toner ['təʊnə] *noun* dry ink powder put into a photocopier to develop the image on the copy

tool [tuːl] *noun* anything which is used to help do a specific task; *advertisements are marketing tools;* **teaching tool** = any document or audio visual material that can be used for teaching

top down structure ['tɒp 'daʊn 'strʌktʃə] *noun* policies which are decided by people in authority rather than the people who actually do the work

top left ['tɒp 'left] *adjective* used to describe the part of a sheet of paper or picture which is at the top and on the left

top-level ['tɒplevl] *adjective* used to describe things that are discussed or decided by the people with the most power in a country, company or organization

top management ['tɒp 'mænɪdʒmənt] *noun* most senior members of a management hierarchy

top-secret [tɒp'siːkrət] *adjective* used to describe anything which has a restricted circulation to the people at the top level

topic ['tɒpɪk] *noun* subject of a document or for discussion

topography [tə'pɒgrəfi] *noun* science of mapping the physical characteristics of a land area

topographical information

[tɒpə'græfɪkl ɪnfə'meɪʃn] *noun* description of the physical features of a country, such as mountain ranges and lakes

touch pad ['tʌtʃ 'pæd] *noun* flat surface which is sensitive to touch and can be used to control a cursor on screen or on/off switches

touch screen ['tʌtʃ 'skriːn] *noun* computer display screen which is sensitive to touch and will react when touched according to pre-programmed information

toy library ['tɔɪ 'laɪbri] *see* LIBRARY

trace [treɪs] *verb* **(a)** to find someone or something after a prolonged search **(b)** to copy something by drawing on transparent paper

tracing ['treɪsɪŋ] *noun* copy that is made by drawing on transparent paper placed over the original

track [træk] *noun* concentric ring on a computer disc or tape which is used to store data in separate sections

tract [trækt] *noun* short article dealing with a religious or moral subject

tractor feed ['træktə 'fiːd] *noun* method of controlling paper feed by the use of holes on the edge of the paper and sprockets on the printer

trade [treɪd] *noun* activity of buying, selling or exchanging goods or services; **trade catalogue** = book containing details of the goods manufactured or sold by a firm; **trade directory** = book containing alphabetical lists and information about companies and organizations involved in trade in a particular area; **trade mark** = name, sign or symbol printed on something to show who it is made by; **trade name** = name under which a product is sold; *some drugs are marketed under several different trade names;* **trade union** = organization of workers usually in specific or related trades or professions, formed to represent their concerns especially about working conditions and pay; **trade union information group** = support group for librarians working to provide information to the trade union movement

trade-off ['treɪdɒf] *noun* compromise between two opposite points of view

trail [treɪl] *noun* path followed by someone or something; **audit trail** = record of all interactions with a system kept to assess the level of use

train [treɪn] *verb* to teach someone the skills for a specific job

trainee [treɪ'niː] *noun* person who is learning how to perform specific tasks

trainer ['treɪnə] *noun* person who instructs others

training ['treɪnɪŋ] *noun* activity of teaching someone specific skills; **training consultant** = person who advises other trainers; **training costs** = money needed by a company to pay for training its employees; **training manual** = instruction book which explains how to train someone in a specific skill; **training materials** = teaching materials used for training; **training package** = pack of teaching materials to help trainers to run courses; **training programme** = schedule designed to teach specific skills within a given time

trans- [trænz] *prefix* used to form words with the meaning of moving across time or space

transaction [trænz'ækʃn] *noun* one action which involves the exchange of goods or information; **transaction processing** = way in which a computer deals with instructions given by the user; **transaction data** = information about the data being processed

transcribe [træn'skraɪb] *verb* **(a)** to produce a written version of spoken words; *his speech was transcribed so that it could* *be printed* (b) to write a written text in the alphabet of another language

transcript ['trænskrɪpt] *noun* written form of something which was spoken

transfer 1 [træns'fɜː] *verb* to move something to another location 2 ['trænsfə] *noun* **periodic transfer** = regular movement of records or data at specific time intervals; *periodic transfer of records was done monthly;* **transfer of records** *or* **transfer of materials** = moving a record or material to another system or physical storage location

transform [trænz'fɔːm] *verb* to change completely

transistor [træn'zɪstə] *noun* small electrical device which controls amplification in a machine such as a radio or television

translate [trænz'leɪt] *verb* (a) to change information from one language or format to another (b) to convert ideas into action

translator [trænz'leɪtə] *noun* (a) person who converts text and spoken words from one language to another (b) laptop computer which translates words into other languages

transmit [trænz'mɪt] *verb* to send out information from one device to another by radio waves, cable or wire links

transmission [trænz'mɪʃn] *noun* programme broadcast on television or radio

transmitter [trænz'mɪtə] *noun* equipment used for broadcasting radio or television signals

transparency [trænz'pærənsi] *noun* transparent positive film which can be projected on to a screen by using a light source

transparent [trænz'pærənt] *adjective* easily seen through, recognized or understood

transport 1 ['trænspɔːt] *noun* means of moving goods and people from one place to another 2 [træn'spɔːt] *verb* to carry something or someone from one place to another

treatment ['triːtmənt] *noun* way of writing about something or someone

tree structure ['triː 'strʌktʃə] *noun* way of writing down the connections between items in an indexing string, using a system of branches rather than linear format

trend [trend] *noun* general movement in the way something is developing; **trend analysis** = investigation of the direction and strength of the movement in a development

trial ['traɪəl] *noun* test of someone or something to see if they are suitable for a certain situation; **trial and error** = trying out different ways of doing things until the best way is found

trim [trɪm] *verb* to cut off a small portion of something around the edge

troubleshooter ['trʌblʃuːtə] *noun* person who works at solving problems which occur in companies, organizations, systems or computer programs

true [truː] *adjective* based on provable facts

truncation [trʌŋ'keɪʃn] *noun* shortening of a search term by adding a symbol, such as % or *or* to match all the forms with the same stem; so LIBR% will find library, librarian, librarianship

trunk call ['trʌŋk 'kɔːl] *noun* long distance telephone call

trust [trʌst] *noun* financial arrangement where a company keeps and invests money for someone; **trust directory** = book with an alphabetical list of trust companies

TS = TYPESCRIPT

Turbogopher Macintosh version of the gopher system for accessing the Internet

tune in ['tjuːn 'ɪn] *verb* to adjust a radio receiver until the signal is at its strongest and clearest

turn on ['tɜːn 'ɒn] *verb* to connect the power supply to a machine; **to turn off** = to disconnect the power supply from a machine

turnaround time ['tɜːnəraʊnd 'taɪm] *noun* time taken to complete a job from beginning to end; *the turnaround time for photocopying a document is three hours;* **turnaround document** = document used to record the details of a job and the time taken to complete it

turnkey system ['tɜːnkiː 'sɪstəm] *noun* complete system which is ready for use; the customer has only to switch it on (i.e. turn the key)

turnover ['tɜːnəʊvə] *noun* **(a)** the rate at which people leave a company and are replaced **(b)** the amount of money taken for goods or services sold during a given period of time

turtle ['tɜːtl] *noun* computer peripheral, like a large mouse, used to draw graphics on a VDU; *floor turtles are used in primary schools as teaching aids*

tutor ['tjuːtə] *noun* teacher who is responsible for individuals or small groups, used especially at higher levels of education

TV station ['tiː viː 'steɪʃn] *noun* place from where television programmes are transmitted

two-dimensional ['tuː daɪ'menʃənl] *adjective* having only length and breadth and so looking flat

two-part stationery ['tuː 'pɑːt 'steɪʃnri] *noun* paper documents with two joined pages which provide a top copy and a carbon copy; *two-part invoices*

two-way radio ['tuː 'weɪ 'reɪdiəʊ] *noun* radio transmitter and receiver in a single handset which allows two-way communication with another user

Tymnet local cost call provider of access to the Internet

type [taɪp] **1** *noun* metal characters used for printing **2** *verb* to write using a typewriter

typeface ['taɪpfeɪs] *noun* size and style of printing used measured in 'points' which refer to the height of the characters

typescript (TS) ['taɪpskrɪpt] *noun* typewritten copy of a manuscript

typeset ['taɪpset] *verb* to set text in type ready to be printed

typesetter ['taɪpsetə] *noun* person or company which does the typesetting

typist ['taɪpɪst] *noun* person whose job is to type up documents using a typewriter or a word processor; **copy typist** = person who types from handwritten copy, not from dictation; **shorthand typist** = person who takes down dictation in shorthand and then transcribes it into typewritten form

typography [taɪ'pɒɡrəfi] *noun* design and methods used when working with type

typographic error [taɪpə'ɡræfɪk 'erə] *noun* mistake made when typing

Uu

U3A = UNIVERSITY OF THE THIRD AGE (UK) system of distance learning for people over the age of retirement

UCAS = UNIVERSITIES AND COLLEGES ADMISSIONS SERVICE (UK)

UDC = UNIVERSAL DECIMAL CLASSIFICATION

UFC = UNIVERSITIES FUNDING COUNCIL (UK)

UK = UNITED KINGDOM

ultimatum [ˌʌltɪˈmeɪtəm] *noun* warning that unless someone conforms to regulations and instructions he/she will be punished

ultra- [ˈʌltræ] *prefix* used with adjectives to indicate an extreme level; **ultra-fiche** = microfiche pages with images reduced more than ninety times; **ultra-sonic** = sounds that are above the range of human hearing; **ultra-violet (light) (UV)** = light which is just beyond the spectrum visible by the human eye

umlaut [ˈʊmlaʊt] *noun* pronunciation indicator of two dots above a vowel used in German, such as ü

UN = UNITED NATIONS **UN publications catalogue** = book containing bibliographic lists of documents published by the United Nations

unabridged [ˌʌnəˈbrɪdʒd] *adjective* complete and has not been shortened

unadulterated [ˌʌnəˈdʌltəreɪtɪd] *adjective* complete with nothing added to it

unauthorized [ʌnˈɔːθəraɪzd] *adjective* not officially allowed

uncensored [ʌnˈsensəd] *adjective* (publication or broadcast) which has not been viewed by the official government censor and approved for showing to the public

uncertainty avoidance [ʌnˈsɜːtənti əˈvɔɪdəns] *noun* system in which decisions are only made by people in full possession of all the facts

uncharted [ʌnˈtʃɑːtɪd] *adjective* (area of land) which has had no maps made of it

under discussion [ˈʌndə dɪsˈkʌʃn] *adjective* being talked about but still to be decided

under-funded *or* **under-financed** [ˈʌndə ˈfʌndɪd] *adjective* (organization, project, research, etc.) which does not have enough money allocated to it to do its work properly

undercover [ˌʌndəˈkʌvə] *adjective* (work) that is done secretly to obtain information

undergraduate [ˌʌndəˈgrædʒuət] *noun* student at university who is working for a first degree

underline [ˌʌndəˈlaɪn] *verb* to emphasize something either by talking about it strongly or by drawing a line under a written word or phrase

undocumented [ʌnˈdɒkjuˌmentɪd] *adjective* having no official papers to prove existence

UNESCO [juːˈneskəu] = UNITED NATIONS EDUCATIONAL SCIENTIFIC AND CULTURAL ORGANIZATION

unethical [ʌnˈeθɪkl] *adjective* (behaviour) that is considered to be unacceptable according to a particular code of conduct

uneven pages [ʌmˈiːvn ˈpeɪdʒɪz] *plural noun* right-hand pages which bear the odd numbers such as 1, 3, 5, 7, 9

Uniform Resource Locator (URL) [ˈjuːnɪfɔːm rɪˈsɔːs ləˈkeɪtə] electronic address used to give access to files on the Internet

UNIMARC = UNIVERSAL MACHINE READABLE CATALOGUE

union catalogue *or* **union list** [ˈjuːnɪən ˈkætəlɒg or lɪst] *noun* combined bibliographic list of holdings for either institutions or subjects

unique [juːˈniːk] *adjective* used to describe something of which there is only one example in the world

UNISIST = UNITED NATIONS INFORMATION SYSTEM IN SCIENCE AND TECHNOLOGY

unit [ˈjuːnɪt] *noun* small part of a large organization with a specialized purpose; **unit of enquiry** = one item in a complex series of questions

United Kingdom (UK) [juːˈnaɪtɪd ˈkɪŋdəm] consists of England, Scotland, Wales and Northern Ireland

United Nations (UN) [juːˈnaɪtɪd ˈneɪʃnz] international organization to which most countries in the world belong, which works towards peace in the world and solving international problems

United Nations Educational Social and Cultural Organization (UNESCO) international organization through which richer countries can help poorer countries to develop

United Nations Information System in Science and Technology (UNISIST) international database for information about different areas of science and technology

United States of America (USA) [juːˈnaɪtɪd ˈsteɪts] the states which are united to form the country known as America

universal [juːnɪˈvɜːsl] *adjective* widespread, relevant to very large numbers of people; **universal bibliographic control** = system of listing all the publications in the world; **universal decimal classification (UDC)** = system of classifying information by means of decimal numbering which is used worldwide; **Universal Machine Readable Catalogue (UNIMARC)** = computer-generated index according to a specific system, which can be used worldwide

university [juːnɪˈvɜːsɪti] *noun* institution of higher education where students study for degrees and academic research is done; **university facility** = building or equipment provided by a university for the work and leisure of its staff and students; **university library** = library which caters specifically for the staff and students of a particular university; *see also* ACADEMIC LIBRARIES

Universities and Colleges Admissions Service (UCAS)

centrally administered system for admissions to courses in all the universities and colleges of higher education in the UK

Universities Funding Council

(UFC) government body which controls the money allocated to universities in the UK

unjustified [ʌnˈdʒʌstɪfaɪd] *adjective* (text) where the margins are ragged, i.e. with no justification

unprotected [ʌnprəˈtektɪd] *adjective* which can be modified because it has no security barriers

unsigned [ˈʌnsaɪnd] *adjective* (document) which has no signature to make it official

unstructured interview[ʌnˈstrʌktʃəd ˈɪntəvjuː] *noun* interview which is free ranging and not limited by pre-set questions

up cursor key [ʌp ˈkɜːsə ˈkiː] *noun* one of the four direction keys on a computer keyboard

update 1 [ˈʌpdeɪt] *noun* news item which has the latest information **2** [ʌpˈdeɪt] *verb* to change information so that it is up to date and accurate

updateable [ʌpˈdeɪtəbl] *adjective* which cannot be given a date of origin

upgrade [ʌpˈgreɪd] *verb* **(a)** to improve by bringing up to date or adding more modern equipment **(b)** to regrade a job, giving it a higher salary scale

upkeep [ˈʌpkiːp] *noun* action and cost of keeping buildings, equipment and services in good condition

upload [ˈʌpləʊd] *verb* to send a file from your computer to the hard disk of another computer, particularly used to refer to sending files over the internet to another server *compare* DOWNLOAD

upper case [ˈʌpə ˈkeɪs] *adjective* describes large letters such as A, B, C, as opposed to lower case a, b, c

upshot [ˈʌpʃɒt] *noun* final result or outcome

up-to-date [ˈʌptəˈdeɪt] *adjective* (information) which contains the latest known data

URL *acronym* = UNIFORM RESOURCE LOCATOR system used to standardize the way in which WWW addresses are written; for example, the URL of the Peter Collin Publishing Ltd home page is 'http://www.pcp.co.uk'

USA = UNITED STATES OF AMERICA

usage [ˈjuːzɪdʒ] *noun* generally accepted way words are used which may not necessarily be grammatically correct

use 1 [juːs] *noun* **(a)** to have the ability or permission to use something; *they had the use of the library while they were attending the conference* **(b)** in use *or* out of use = being or not being used; **to be of use** = to be useful; *a directory can be of use in many different ways* **2** [juːz] *verb* **(a)** to employ someone or something for a particular purpose **(b)** to consume; *colour televisions use much more electricity than black and white ones*

useful [ˈjuːsfʊl] *adjective* describes people or things which are helpful to others

user [ˈjuːzə] *noun* person who uses something; **end user** = someone who makes use of hardware and software to do work; **expert user** = someone who uses the service very efficiently because they have experience; **frequent user** = someone who makes use of a service very often; **novice user** = inexperienced user; **occasional user** = someone who uses a facility or service only rarely; **reluctant user** = someone who is forced to use a service but does not want to; *some children are reluctant users of the* *school library;* **trial user** = someone who is asked to use a service to see if it works well; **user education** *or* **user training** = process of teaching the users of a service how to make the best use of it; **user-friendly** = language or software which makes interaction with a computer easy; **user group** = group of people who use a service or facility and come together to discuss how it can be improved; **user interface** = hardware or software designed to make it easier for a user to communicate with a machine; **user representative** = person who speaks for other users and who voices their opinions; **user resistance** = feeling that some people have against using a particular facility or service; **user study** = research which investigates how users function and what they need; **user views** = opinions of people who make use of a facility or service

Usenet very large online bulletin board concerned with the news

utility [juːˈtɪlɪti] *noun* service that is provided for everyone, such as water, gas, electricity; **utility program** = computer program which is concerned with routine activities such as searching, copying, replacing files

UV = ULTRA-VIOLET

Vv

vacate [və'keɪt] *verb* to leave a place or a job empty and available for other people

Vacher's Parliamentary Companion ['væʃəz pɑːlə'mentri kəm'pænjən] reference book which gives information about all aspects of the UK parliament including biographical details of Members of Parliament

vade mecum ['vɑːdi 'meɪkəm] *noun* portable reference book

valid ['vælɪd] *adjective* based on logical reasoning, acceptable to others, such as authorities

validate ['vælɪdeɪt] *verb* to prove that something is true, accurate and correct

value ['væljuː] **1** *noun* amount that something is worth either in money or quantity **2** *verb* to estimate how much money something is worth; **value added tax (VAT)** = tax on goods and services purchased which the seller must then pay to the government; **value added network** = network which leases telecommunications links, adds services and markets the improved network

valuable ['væljʊbl] *adjective* (a) worth a lot of money (b) having great importance

valuation [vælju'eɪʃn] *noun* process of calculating how much something is worth

values ['væljuːz] *plural noun* moral principles and beliefs

vandal ['vændəl] *noun* person who deliberately damages property

vandalism ['vændəlɪzm] *noun* act of deliberately damaging property

variable ['veəriəbl] **1** *noun* factor in a situation that can change, or can be measured according to a set of values **2** *adjective* not always the same; *text was typed with variable spacing between the words*

variance ['veəriəns] *noun* amount of difference from the norm

various dates (v.d.) ['veəriəs 'deɪts] series volumes containing several works of different dates

vary ['veəri] *verb* to change the way that something is done

VAT = VALUE ADDED TAX

VCR = VIDEO CASSETTE RECORDER

VDU = VIDEO DISPLAY UNIT

vellum ['veləm] *noun* smooth, fine parchment or paper made from polished calf, sheep or goat skin

vendor ['vendə] *noun* someone who sells things

vending machine ['vendɪŋ mə'ʃiːn] *noun* automatic machine which dispenses goods when money or a special key or card is put in the slot

Venn diagram ['ven 'daɪəgræm] *noun* graphical representation of the relationship between two or more sets of data

verbatim [vɜː'beɪtɪm] **1** *noun* accurate word for word report of a speech or debate **2** *adverb* copying the spoken word exactly in writing; *he copied the speech down verbatim*

verify ['verɪfaɪ] *verb* to check that something is true and accurate

verification [verɪfɪ'keɪʃn] *noun* act of checking that something is true and accurate

vernacular [vɜː'nækjʊlə] *noun* local language

verse [vɜːs] *noun* **(a)** set of lines which forms one part of the pattern of a poem **(b)** group of sentences which forms a numbered division of a book of sacred writings

version ['vɜːʃn] *noun* copy or form of something that is slightly different from the original

verso ['vɜːsəʊ] *noun* left-hand page of a book, usually given an even number

vertical ['vɜːtɪkl] *adjective* forming an angle of 90ͥ to the ground, upright; **vertical scrolling** = act of moving text up or down a computer screen a line at a time

vertical filing ['vɜːtɪkl 'faɪlɪŋ] *noun* system of filing in which the organization of records is from top to bottom rather than horizontal

very high density (VHD) ['veri 'haɪ 'densɪti] computer (magnetic) disks which can be encoded on both sides

very high frequency (VHF) ['veri 'haɪ 'friːkwənsi] range of frequencies between 30MHz and 300MHz used to broadcast television and radio programmes

via ['vaɪə] *preposition* going through a person or place to reach a destination

VIATEL *acronym* Australian videotex service

video ['vɪdiəʊ] **1** *noun* recording on video tape; **video camera** = portable camera for taking videos; *see also* CAMCORDER **video cassette** = container for video recording tape which enables it to be played back by a VCR; **video cassette recorder (VCR)** = machine which will record and playback television pictures; **video conference** = satellite TV link which enables several people to see and talk to each other at the same time; **video conferencing** = holding a meeting between people at a distance using video screens to enable the people taking part to see each other; **video library** = collection of video tapes available for hire; **video nasty** = film released on video which is extremely violent; **video phone** = telephone which has a video screen attached to it so that the callers can see the person they are talking to; **video scanner** = device which enters pictures or diagrams to be input to a computer; **video tape** = magnetic tape which can be used to record pictures and to play them back on a television set **2** *verb* to film something using a video camera

videodisk ['vɪdiəʊdɪsk] *noun* read only optical disc used to store large amounts of data and pictures

videotex ['vɪdiəʊteks] *noun* generic name for systems which display text and simple graphic shapes on a television screen, often used for information displays

Videotext ['vɪdiəʊtekst] *noun* German system in which text can be displayed on a television screen, now becoming synonymous with videotex

view [vjuː] **1** *noun* opinion about something; *I hold the view that every school* *should have a library* 2 *verb* to look at, to watch

viewer ['vju:ə] *noun* (a) apparatus for looking at photographic slides (b) person who looks at something

viewfinder ['vju:faɪndə] *noun* eyepiece in a camera which enables the photographer to see what is to be filmed

Viewdata ['vju:deɪtə] *noun* trademark for a videotext system

virement ['vaɪəmənt] *noun* authorized transfer of money from one budget to another for urgent purposes

virtual ['vɜːtʃuəl] *adjective* having all the characteristics of something but not really being that thing; **virtual library** = electronic stock of information which can be accessed via databases, but is not held in any one place; **virtual reality** = electronic environment created by a computer which appears to be real to the viewer

virus ['vaɪrəs] *noun* infection in a computer system which can damage the software systems and the data

vis-a-vis ['vi:səvi] *preposition* in comparison with

visit ['vɪzɪt] *verb* **to visit a site** = to read an electronic document on the World Wide Web

visitation [vɪzɪ'teɪʃn] *noun* official visit

Visnews commercial library in the UK of pictures and television news coverage

vistafoil ['vɪstəfɔɪl] *noun* trade name for a form of sticky, transparent plastic covering used to laminate books, pictures or workcards

visual ['vɪʒuəl] *adjective* can be seen; **visual aid** = teaching aid which enables the learner to see pictures or real examples of the subject being taught; *slides, photographs, maps, charts, films are all visual aids;* **visual aid sources** = places where visual aids can be obtained; **visual display unit (VDU)** =

device used with a computer and a keyboard to display words and graphics on a screen; **visual education** = process of teaching how to read visual symbols; **visual literacy** = ability to interpret visual signs and symbols

vital record ['vaɪtəl 'rekəd] *noun* record which is currently in use and must be kept easily accessible

VOA = VOICE OF AMERICA

vocabulary [və'kæbjʊləri] *noun* number of words in a particular language or related to a specific subject; *the vocabulary of information handling is very specialized;* **controlled vocabulary** = limited number of words used to make understanding easier for non-native speakers of a language

vocational qualification [və'keɪʃnl kwɒlɪfɪ'keɪʃn] *noun* certificate which states that you have the skills needed to do a particular job; **vocational training** = courses which teach people the skills for specific jobs or professions

voice [vɔɪs] *noun* sound made by human speech organs; **voice-over** = commentary or spoken text accompanying a television programme, advertisement or film by someone who is heard but not seen; **voice recognition** = ability of a computer to recognize certain characteristics of a human voice and respond appropriately; **voice synthesizer** = computer reproduction of sounds similar to the human voice

Voice of America (VOA) ['vɔɪs əv ə'merɪkə] world-wide broadcasting network of American radio

volatile ['vɒlətaɪl] *adjective* liable to change suddenly and unexpectedly; **volatile storage** = memory mechanism in a computer which loses its data when the power supply is switched off

volume ['vɒlju:m] *noun* (a) (i) book especially a large one; (ii) one of a series in a set of books or journals; **volume signature** = number of the volume, such as vol 1 (b) loudness of noise produced by an electric playback machine; **volume control** = device which enables the user to control the loudness of the noise produced

volunteer [vɒlən'tiːə] *noun* someone who works without being paid

vowel ['vauəl] *noun* the five letters, a, e, i, o, u, in the Roman alphabet, at least one of which is required to make a word pronounceable in most western languages

Ww

w. a. f. *abbreviation for* with all faults

wage [weɪdʒ] *noun* money paid to someone, usually weekly, for their work

WAIS = WIDE AREA INFORMATION SERVERS

waive [weɪv] *verb* to decide not to enforce a regulation

waiver ['weɪvə] *noun* permission to do something although it is not in accordance with the regulations

wall planner ['wɔːl 'plænə] *noun* chart with empty spaces marked with the dates for each day of the year so that events can be written in

WAN = WIDE AREA NETWORK

warn [wɔːn] *verb* to advise someone of danger or the inappropriateness of an action

warning ['wɔːnɪŋ] *noun* spoken or written advice about something bad that may happen

warranty ['wɒrənti] *noun* written guarantee given by a company against faulty goods or workmanship

waste [weɪst] *verb* to spend money, time or effort on something that is not important; *waste no time to do something as quickly as possible*

watermark ['wɔːtəmɑːk] *noun* distinctive mark impressed into the fabric of paper when it is made, which can be seen by holding the paper to the light

waterproof ['wɔːtəpruːf] *adjective* not allowing water to pass through; *plastic book jackets are waterproof*

wavelength ['weɪvlenθ] *noun* **(a)** distance between corresponding points on consecutive cycles of light or sound **(b)** size of the radio wave used to broadcast programmes

weather satellite ['weðə 'sætəlaɪt] *noun* satellite which collects meteorological information enabling changes in the weather to be forecast

web [web] *noun see* WORLD WIDE WEB

web browser ['web 'braʊzə] *noun see* BROWSER

webmaster ['webmɑːstə] *noun* person who maintains and manages a web site on the internet

web page ['web 'peɪdʒ]*noun* single file stored on a Web server that contains formatted text, graphics and hypertext links to other pages on the internet; a Web page is created using HTML codes and is viewed with a browser

web site ['web 'saɪt] *noun* location on the internet that contains a collection of linked web pages; to visit a web site, a user needs to enter the address into a web browser - for example, the Peter Collin Publishing web site can be viewed at 'http://www.pcp.co.uk'

weed [wiːd] *verb* to remove old and out dated items; *they need to weed the library stock every few years*

weeding ['wiːdɪŋ] *noun* discarding materials which are out of date or no further use

week [wiːk] *noun* period of seven days

weekly ['wiːkli] **1** *noun* publication which is produced every week **2** *adjective* happening regularly once a week

weight [weɪt] *noun* **(a)** measurement of how heavy something is; **gross weight** = total weight including all packing; **net weight** = weight after the packing has been deducted; **paper weight** = weight of a certain quantity of paper used to describe its quality; *the paper is 80 gsm quality* **(b)** heavy object (often decorative) used to stop papers from falling or being blown away

weighting ['weɪtɪŋ] *noun* sorting things and adding a tariff or bonus according to their importance or position; *the salary carried a London weighting to compensate for having to live in London where the cost of living is more expensive*

what if? simulation ['wɒt 'ɪf sɪmjʊ'leɪʃn] *noun* management technique which is used for forward planning, in which questions are asked to predict what would happen in certain situations

Whitaker's ['wɪtəkəz] publishing house which produces comprehensive lists of Books in Print on CD, microfiche and hard copy

Whitaker's Almanac ['wɪtəkəz 'ɒlmənæk] reference book which gives details of the establishment, procedures and personalities in the UK as well as general knowledge about the rest of the world

white [waɪt] *adjective* colour of milk or snow

white lie ['waɪt 'laɪ] *noun* lie told to avoid hurting someone's feelings

white noise ['waɪt 'nɔɪz] *noun* random noise on a broadcast transmitter which distorts other signals

White Paper ['waɪt 'peɪpə] *noun* government report printed and distributed for debate in parliament

whitewash ['waɪtwɒʃ] *noun* official attempt to hide unpleasant facts

WHO = WORLD HEALTH ORGANIZATION

Who's Who ['huːz 'huː] publication giving biographical details of well known or important people

wholesale ['həʊlseɪl] *adjective* buying and selling goods in bulk to people who then sell them on in smaller quantities as retail goods

Wide Area Network (WAN) ['waɪd 'eərɪə 'netwɜːk] network of terminals with links outside the local area by radio, satellite and cable

Wide Area Information Servers (WAIS) ['waɪd 'eərɪə ɪnfə'meɪʃn 'sɜːvəz] alphabetical list of electronic sources of information

widely ['waɪdli] *adverb* **widely accepted** = acknowledged as true by the majority of people; **widely available** = able to be found, bought or borrowed by a large number of people in many different places

widespread ['waɪdspred] *adjective* available to a large number of people or over a large area

widow ['wɪdəʊ] *noun* last line of a paragraph printed by itself at the top of a page

wild card ['waɪld 'kɑːd] *noun* symbol, such as * or ? which will represent and call up all files when searching data

WIMP [wɪmp] = WINDOWS, ICONS, MOUSE, POINTER description of an integrated software system that is entirely operated using windows, icons and a mouse-controlled pointer

window ['wɪndəʊ] *noun* **(a)** reserved section of a computer screen, with specific information, which can overwrite other sections on screen and can be selected at any time for editing or reference **(b)** opening in an envelope to show the address printed on the enclosed document

Windows™ ['wɪndəʊz] trademark of a computer system developed by Microsoft, using icons, mouse and windows devised for use with software to make it more user-friendly than the purely keyboard based systems

wipe [waɪp] *verb* to remove all information from a disk

WIPO = WORLD INTELLECTUAL PROPERTY ORGANIZATION

wire ['waɪə] *noun US* telegram

Wisden ['wɪzdən] reference book with details of everything related to the game of cricket, such as players grounds, test matches, records, etc.

withdraw [wɪθ'drɔː] *verb* to remove; *they were told to withdraw some of the old books from the library*

withstand [wɪθ'stænd] *verb* to remain unharmed by events or actions; *library books must be able to withstand constant usage*

word processor ['wɜːd 'prəʊsesə] *noun* computer which will run a word processing

program, usually used to create text; **word-processing package** = software on a program disk with an instruction manual, which enables word-processing to be carried out

words per minute [wɜːdz pɜː 'mɪnɪt] *see* WPM

work [wɜːk] *noun* **(a)** published document **(b)** tasks involved in a job; **casual work** = jobs done by people employed for a short time; **work experience** = situation in which you try out a job to see whether you are suited to it; **work standards** = quality of work required by the management; **work station** = desk with a computer, keyboard and sometimes a printer; **work study** = system of measuring the amount of work possible in certain conditions and during a certain time period

workaholic [wɜːkə'hɒlɪk] *noun* person who cannot stop working to do other things

workbook ['wɜːkbʊk] *noun* textbook with exercises and spaces for the answers to be written in

workflow ['wɜːkfləʊ] *noun* way that work is passed from one part of a production system to another

workforce ['wɜːkfɔːs] *noun* all the people who work for a particular company or organization

working day ['wɜːkɪŋ 'deɪ] *noun* period of time spent working for money; *the standard working day is eight hours long*

working capital ['wɜːkɪŋ 'kæpɪtəl] *noun* money that is available immediately and not tied up in investments, property or equipment

working conditions ['wɜːkɪŋ kən'dɪʃnz] *plural noun* environment in which a job is done

working hours ['wɜːkɪŋ 'aəz] *plural noun* period when most people are at work usually between 9.0 or 9.30 am and 5.0 or 5.30 pm

working party ['wɜːkɪŋ 'pɑːti] *noun* temporary group formed to investigate a particular situation

working population ['wɜːkɪŋ pɒpjʊ'leɪʃn] *noun* people who have jobs

workload ['wɜːkləʊd] *noun* amount of work to be done in a stated time by a certain person or group

workplace ['wɜːkpleɪs] *noun* place at which work is mainly done

worksheet ['wɜːkʃiːt] *noun* teaching aid prepared to give information and reinforce learning with exercises

world [wɜːld] *noun* planet earth; **world atlas** = reference book containing maps of all the countries in the world and articles about them; **world book** = reference book which contains information about all the countries in the world; **World Health Organization (WHO)** = international organization which works to improve health especially in poorer countries; **World Intellectual Property Organization (WIPO)** = international organization which provides guidelines and supports work for international copyright controls; **world index** = reference book of abstracts of articles about all the countries of the world

World Wide Web (WWW) ['wɜːld 'waɪd 'web] hypertext representation of the Internet; a collection of the millions of Web sites and Web pages that together form the part of the internet that is most often seen by users (although the internet also includes electronic mail, Usenet and newsgroups); each Web site is a collection of Web pages; each Web page contains text, graphics and links to other Web sites. Each page is created using the HTML language and is viewed by a user with a Web browser. To navigate between Web pages and Web sites is called surfing; this requires a computer with a link to the internet (normally using a modem) and a Web browser to view the Web pages stored on the remote Web servers

worldwide [wɜːld'waɪd] *adjective* happening throughout the world; *the recession appears to be worldwide*

worthwhile [wɜːθ'waɪl] *adjective* enjoyable and useful so worth time, money and effort spent on it

WPM = WORDS PER MINUTE measurement of the speed of a typist

wraparound ['ræpəraʊnd] *noun* system in word-processing where the writer does not have to put in line endings; the end of each line is automatically marked by the program

write [raɪt] *verb* to use pen, pencil typewriter or electronic machines to produce letters, numbers and symbols on paper so that other people can read them

write protect [raɪt prə'tekt] *verb* to make it impossible to write on or erase anything from a disk

write protect tab [raɪt prə'tekt 'tæb] *noun* small piece of material which covers the write socket on a disk

write-off ['raɪtɒf] *noun* something that is so badly damaged that it cannot be repaired

writer ['raɪtə] *noun* person whose job it is to write books or articles for money

written confirmation ['rɪtən kɒnfə'meɪʃn] *noun* written statement of something that has been said

wrong number ['rɒŋ 'nʌmbə] *noun* telephone connection to a number other than that which was wanted

Wuarchive large electronic archive with pictures

WYSIWYG = WHAT YOU SEE IS WHAT YOU GET system in which the text and graphics on the screen are exactly the same as what will be printed out

Xx

x [eks] *noun* indeterminate symbol used when the name of a person, place or amount is to be kept secret; *he paid £x each to ten people*

x-axis ['eks 'æksɪs] *noun* horizontal axis of a graph

x-rated ['eks 'reɪtɪd] *adjective* used to describe a category in the British film censorship system to indicate a film with scenes of sex and violence only suitable for adult viewing

x-y co-ordinates ['eks 'waɪ kəʊ'ɔːdɪnəts] *plural noun* horizontal and vertical axes of a graph

Xerox ['ziːrɒks] **1** *noun* trademark for a type of photocopier **2** *verb* to photocopy a paper or document

Yy

-**y** *suffix* added to nouns to form adjectives of quality, such as 'wordy'

-**year-old** *suffix* added to numbers to indicate the age of a person or thing; *a ten-year-old file*

y [waɪ] used to represent an unknown quantity; *let y be the number of years since insurance was taken out*

y-axis [ˈwaɪ ˈæksɪs] *noun* vertical axis of a graph

yardstick [ˈjɑːdstɪk] *noun* standard by which other comparable things can be judged

yearbook [ˈjɜːbʊk] *noun* book published once a year with details and information about a particular organization or profession; *the education yearbook*

yearly [ˈjɜːli] *adjective* happening once a year or every year

Yellow Pages [ˈjeləʊ ˈpeɪdʒɪz] telephone directory printed on yellow paper, which is organized alphabetically according to the trade or business of the subscribers

yellow press [ˈjeləʊ ˈpres] *noun* popular name for tabloid sensational newspapers

young adult book [ˈjʌŋ ˈædʌlt ˈbʊk] *noun* book written for adults but considered suitable for adolescents

Zz

zero ['ziːrəʊ] **1** *noun* **(a)** the number 0 **(b)** nothing **2** *verb* **to zero in on** = to give full attention to a problem

zero-based budgeting ['ziːrəʊbeɪst 'bʌdʒɪtɪŋ] *noun* financial policy taking zero as the starting point, without any prior assumptions; *they were working to zero-based budgeting so were not able to take out any loans to get started*

zip code ['zɪp 'kəʊd] *noun* numbers in a USA address indicating the postal area; *see also* POSTCODE

zone [zəʊn] *noun* region or area with particular characteristics; *the enterprise zone had a lot of new small businesses;* **zone library** *see* LIBRARY

Zoo compressing archive program for transfer of electronic files

zoom [zuːm] *verb* to enlarge an area of text on a computer screen so that it is easier to work on

SUPPLEMENT

Five Laws of Library Science

(*S.R. Ranganathan*)

1. Books are for use
2. Every reader his book
3. Every book its reader
4. Save the time of the reader
5. A library is a growing organism

Five Predicables

A series of logical terms and notions, first explained by Porphyry, using his Tree of Porphyry, in his treatise on Aristotle's Topics, and forming the basis of the science of classification. This can be illustrated by classifying the bird the Golden Eagle

class	Bird
order	Falconiform (falcon-like birds)
family	Falconidae (falcon family)
genus	Eagle (scientific group)
species	**golden** (specific characteristics)

Information Skills

Eight questions to ask when finding and using information.

> What information do I need?
> Where can I go to find it?
> How do I locate the relevant sources?
> Which ones shall I select to use?
> How shall I use them?
> How shall I keep records of what I have used?
> How do I check/evaluate what I have found?
> How do I present my findings?

(With acknowledgements to Ann Irving's 'Nine Steps' in Study & Information Skills across the Curriculum, *Heinemann Educational Books (1985))*

Major classification schemes

BC   Bliss Bibliographic classification

Bibliographic Classification devised by Henry Bliss and published in two editions between 1940 and 1976. Thought to be most useful for special collections

CC   (Ranganathan) Colon Classification

Mainly of interest for detailed classification of facet analysis. Widely used in India, but not seen as appropriate for Western libraries

DC   Dewey Decimal Classification

Numerically based scheme, widely used in all types of libraries in the English speaking world. Also used by the British National Bibliography (BNB) and by BNBmarc and LCMARC

LC   Library of Congress Classification

Classification by discipline with letter and number notation. Different schedules are maintained and updated by individual specialists and cataloguers, which causes some uneveness of coverge. Mainly used in the Library of Congress and reflects this to some extent by certain emphases.

UDC   Universal Decimal Classification

Enables detailed indexing of documents, not so useful for shelf arrangement. So, particularly useful for special libraries. Follows the overall outline of the Dewey classification and is essentially enumerative

There are also many locally constructed special classification systems such as for fiction, maps, music, pictures, etc.

Paris Principles

(Cataloguing)

The twelve principles on which an author/title entry should be based. So named at the International Conference on Cataloguing Principles (ICCP) in Paris 1961 which was organised by IFLA. It was intended to serve as a basis for international standardisation in cataloguing. The principles apply to the choice and form of headings and entry words in catalogues of printed books (and other library materials having similar characteristics) in which entries under authors' names, or the titles of works, are combined in one alphabetical sequence. The subjects are:

> Functions of the catalogue
> Structure of the catalogue
> Kinds of entry
> Use of multiple entries
> Function of different kinds of entry
> Choice of uniform heading
> Single personal author
> Entry under corporate bodies
> Multiple authorship
> Works entered under title
> Entry word for personal names

Many other cataloguing codes now use these principles as their common basis; one of the most commonly used is AACR 2.

Reference marks

The order for giving more than one reference on a page is:

1st ref	=	*	(asterisk)
2nd ref	=	†	(dagger)
3rd ref	=	‡	(double dagger)

For subsequent references on the same page these signs can printed twice (**) or three (***) times

Section mark	=	§
Parallel mark	=	‖
Paragraph mark	=	¶

Proof correction marks

Mark in Text	Meaning	Mark in Margin
/	delete	
/	delete and close up	
------	do not change	
⋏	insert	⋏
/	substitute	new word
◯	wrong fount	⊗
word	italic	⊔⊔
word	bold	∿∿
word	caps	≡
word	small caps	=
◯	replace caps by lower case	≢
◯	replace italic by light	
⋏	insert full stop	⊙
⋏	insert semi-colon	;
⋏	insert comma	,
⌐	start new paragraph	⌐
∽	run on (i.e. no paragraph)	∽
⊏	indent	⊏
⊩⊏	full out	
⊏	take over to next line	⊏
⊐	take back to preceding line	⊐
↑	raise	
↓	lower	
⌢	close up	⌢
Y	insert space	Y
⇑	reduce space	⇑

Proof correction marks

A HISTORY OF PRINTING

The development of typesetting and printing came about in Europe in the later Middle ages. As a newly literate middle class arose, so the previous methods of dissemination of literature proved quite incapable of satisfying the demand for large amounts of reading material. Hitherto, manuscripts had been copied in monasteries for wealthy patrons, and even if a dictating pool system was adopted, where ONE person read the text and several others copied it down, production was slow and expensive, and output very small.

Wood blocks were also used, first for making small pictures that could be reproduced cheaply, then for making whole pages of text. This system had the disadvantage of inflexibility, and required skilled wood carvers. It was only when Gutenberg saw that thousands

of identical pieces of metal type could be cast from a single matrix (each piece representing a letter of alphabet), and that pieces of type slotted together to form words could be fitted into pages and used for printing large numbers of identical copies of the same text, that modern typesetting and printing was born. From his invention the enormous expansion of the printed word proceeded.

Book Prizes & Awards

Some of the more important literary prizes and awards.

Arthur C. Clarke Award Given for the best British science fiction novel.

Aurora Award Highest Canadian award for science fiction and fantasy books

Australian Children's Book Awards Awards for children's literature made by the Children's Book Council of Australia

Bargate (Verity) Award An annual UK award for a new and unperformed play

Benjamin Franklin Award Award which recognizes excellence in independent publishing, sponsored by the Publishers Marketing Association of America

Besterman Medal Awarded annually by the Library Association for an outstanding bibliography or guide to the literature first published in the United Kingdom during the preceding year

Booker Prize for Fiction An annual prize of £20,000 for a novel written in English by a citizen of Great Britain, The Irish Republic or South Africa. Sponsored by Booker McConnell plc

Caldecott Book Awards Presented by the American Library Association (ALA), these awards are the most prestigious in children's literature

The Canada Council for the Arts: Governor General's Literary Awards Annual literary awards made by the Canada Council

Carnegie Medal An award made by the British Library Association to the writer of an outstanding book for children. The book must be written in English and have been published in the United Kingdom during the year preceding the presentation of the award.

Children's Book Award An award founded in 1980 and given to authors of fiction for children under the age of 14 by the Federation of Children's Book Groups

Cholmondeley Awards Annual awards made by the Society of Authors (q.v.) for the encouragement of poets

Commonwealth Writers' Prizes Annual awards sponsored by the Commonwealth Foundation, for works of fiction in a number of categories

Cookson (Catherine) Fiction Prize Annual award for an unpublished novel of at least 70,000 words

Cooper (Duff) Memorial Prize An annual UK award for a literary work of biography, history, politics, or poetry in English or French

Crime Writers' Association (CWA) A UK organisation responsible for several annual literary awards: *Cartier Diamond Dagger Award* (outstanding title), *John Creasey Memorial Dagger* (best crime novel by an unpublished author), *Gold and Silver Dagger Awards for Fiction* (best crime novels published in the UK)

Dillons First Fiction Award An annual prize for the best first-time novelist in English

Earthworm Children's Book Award An annual UK award of Friends of the Earth Trust to promote environmental awareness in children's literature

Edgar Allan Poe Awards Presented by The Mystery Writers of America for the best in mystery, fiction, and non-fiction

Elgin (Mary) Award An annual UK award made by Hodder & Stoughton Ltd to encourage new writers of fiction

Emil Award An award organised by the Book Trust and given annually for the children's book 'in which text and illustration are both excellent and perfectly harmonious'; now combined with the Maschler (Kurt) Award (q.v.)

Book Prizes & Awards

Ewart-Biggs (Christopher) Memorial Prize A biennial prize for a work in English or French that contributes to peace and understanding in Ireland, or to co-operation between members of the European community

Faber (Geoffrey) Memorial Prize An award in alternate years for a volume of verse, and a volume of prose fiction of the best literary merit by young Commonwealth or UK authors

Farmer (Prudence) Poetry Prize An annual UK award made for the best poem published in the *New Statesman* magazine

Fawcett Society Book Prize An annual award (alternate years for fiction and non-fiction) for a book that has contributed to the understanding of women's position in society. All submitted work is placed in the Fawcett Library

Fletcher (Sir Banister) Award An annual UK prize of the Authors Club for the best book on architecture of the arts

Florio (John) Prize A biennial prize for the best translation into English

Greenaway (Kate) Medal An award, made by the British Library Association annually with the intention of recognising the importance of illustrations in children's books, to the artist who in the opinion of the Library Association has produced the most distinguished work in the illustration of children's books during the year preceding the award. The work must have been originally published in the United Kingdom. A list of books awarded the medal is published in the Library Association Year book

Gregynog Prize Biennial awards to Welsh publishers for high standards in book production, for adult books, and for children's books

Guardian Children's Fiction Prize An annual prize instituted in 1967 by the *Guardian* Newspaper for an outstanding work of fiction for children written by a British or Commonwealth author

Guardian Fiction Prize An annual award made by the *Guardian* Newspaper for a work of fiction published by a British or Commonwealth writer

Hawthornden Prize An annual award by the Hawthornden Trust for a work of imaginative literature by a young British author

Higham (David) Prize for Fiction Administered by the Book Trust, and awarded for a first novel or book of short stories by a UK or Commonwealth author

Holtby (Winifred) Memorial Prize An annual award of the Royal Society of Literature for the best regional work of fiction or non-fiction by a UK, Irish or Commonwealth author

Jones (Mary Vaughan) Award Awards by the Welsh National Centre for Children's Literature for various categories of Welsh and English children's literature

Kent (Sir Peter) Conservation Book Prize An annual award administered by the Book Trust for a book on environmental issues published in the UK

King (Coretta Scott) Awards Annual awards, established 1970, given for the most outstanding text, and most imaginative illustrations by a black author and illustrator for children's books. Presented by the American Library Association

King (Martin Luther) Memorial Prize An annual UK award for a literary work reflecting the ideals of Dr King, published in the UK

McColvin Medal Awarded annually by the Library Association for an outstanding reference book first published in the United Kingdom during the preceding year

Book Prizes & Awards

McLeod (Enid) Prize An annual award of the Franco-British Society for a book contributing to Franco-British understanding

Macmillan Silver Pen Award An annual award for an outstanding UK novel; sponsored by Macmillan, and administered by the English Centre of PEN International

McVitie's Prize An annual award for a literary work in any form by a Scottish resident; submission in English, Scots or Gaelic.

Maschler (Kurt)/Emil Award Annual UK award for 'a work of imagination in the children's field in which text and illustration are of excellence and so presented that each enhances yet balances the other'

Mind Book of the Year/Allen Lane Award An annual award administered by the UK charity MIND for a book which furthers public understanding of mental illness

Mother Goose Award An award given to the most exciting newcomer to British Children's book illustration

National Medal for Literature An award made annually to a living American author for the whole corpus of his or her work

NCR Book Award An award of £30,000 sponsored by the computer manufacturers NCR for a new work of non-fiction. First awarded 1988

New Writers' Award An annual award for the best unpublished romantic novel, given by the Romantic Novelists Association (UK)

Noma Award A prize awarded by the Japanese publishing firm Kodansha to African writers whose work is published in Africa, to encourage the African publishing industry.

Poetry Society of America Awards Several awards and medals awarded annually by the Poetry Society of America, including the Frost Medal, the Shelley Memorial Award, and William Carlos Williams Award

RITA Awards Awarded by the Romance Writers of America for excellence in the romantic genre

Runciman Award An annual prize offered by the Anglo-Hellenic League and administered by the Book Trust, for a literary work about Greece

Scott Moncrieff Prize An annual UK award of the Translator's Association for the best translation published of a French twentieth century work

Smarties Book Prize An award organised by the Book Trust, and given for children's books in three age categories

Smith (W.H.) Annual Literary Award A cash award which has been offered by W.H. Smith & Son Ltd annually since 1959. The Award is made to the Commonwealth author whose book (originally written in English and published in the United Kingdom within the previous 24 months ending on 31 December) makes, in the opinion of the judges, the most outstanding contribution to literature

Stanford (Winifred Mary) Prize A biennial award offered by Hodder & Stoughton for a UK-published book inspired by the Christian faith

Thomas (Dylan) Award Offered by the Poetry Society (UK) in alternate years for poetry and short stories

Times Educational Supplement Book Awards Two annual awards for authors of the best information books for children published in the UK or Commonwealth. One award is for a book for children up to the age of nine, the other for a book for children aged 10 - 16

Trask (Betty) Awards Annual awards administered by the Society of Authors for young Commonwealth authors of romantic fiction

Book Prizes & Awards

Whitbread Literary Awards Annual prizes awarded to authors living in the UK or Eire for books published in those countries; five categories - novel, first novel, biography, children's novel, poetry - are selected, of which one is further declared *Whitbread Book of the Year.* Administered by the Booksellers Association of Great Britain and Ireland.

Whitfield Prize An annual award made by the Royal Historical Society for the best UK-published work on English or Welsh history by a young author

BASIC REFERENCE TITLES IN PRINT OR ON CD-ROM

General
Encyclopaedias
Quick facts (Chambers)
Guinness Book of Records
Shell Book of Firsts
World of Winners (Gale Research)
McGraw Hill Encyclopaedia of Science & Technology
Directories of British Associations and Associations in Ireland
Whitaker's Almanack
National Trust Handbook
Chambers World Gazeteer
Titles & Forms of Address: a guide to correct use (Black)
Welford's Guides to Reference Material (Library Association)
Books in Print (Whitaker, Bowker)
British National Bibliography
HMSO catalogue

Travel/Communications
Road Atlases and Street Maps
Phone directories: residential and business
Yellow pages
Rail, Bus and Airline Timetables
Accommodation Guides
Postcode Directories (Thomsons)

Media
Benn's Media Guide (Benn Business Information Services)
Blue Book of British Broadcasting (Tellex Monitors)

Business
Company directories:
  Kompass UK & EU
  Kelly's business directory
  Sell's Product's and Services
  Local Directories from Chambers of Commerce
Bankers Almanac
Stock Exchange Official Yearbook
British Trade Union Directory

Education
Education Yearbook (Longman)
UCAS Handbook
World of Learning (Europa)
Independent Schools Yearbook (A&C Black)
International Course Guides
Careers Guides

Law & Public Services
Halsbury's Statutes (Butterworth)
European Communities Legislation (Butterworth)
Municipal Yearbook and Public Services Directory
Housing Yearbook (Longman)
Social Services Yearbook (Longman)
Charities Digest (Family Welfare Association)
Directory of Grant Making Trusts (Charities Aid Foundation)
Legal Aid Handbook (Sweet & Maxwell)

Language & Literature
Dictionaries of Synonyms, Antonyms, Acronyms, Abbreviations, Jargon, Slang, Phrases, Rhymes, Proverbs, Quotations, Thesauri, etc.
Foreign Language Dictionaries
Specialist Dictionaries by Subject
Penguin Companion to Literature (Longman)
Index to Poetry (Columbia U.P.)
Cambridge Guide to Literature in English (CUP)

Medicine
British Pharmacopoeia (HMSO)
Black's Medical Dictionary (A&C Black)
Hospitals and Health Services Yearbook (ISHM)
A-Z of Disability
Health & Safety Directory (Croner)

Interests
Oxford Companion to Art (OUP)
Stamps of the World (Stanley Gibbons)
Groves Dictionary of Music

BASIC REFERENCE TITLES IN PRINT OR ON CD-ROM

Wisden Cricketer's Almanac (John Wisden)
International Authors and Writers Who's
Who (International Biographical Centre)
Writers and Artists Yearbook (A&C Black)
Guinness International Who's Who of
Sport (Guinness)
Chronology of the Ancient World (Barrie
& Jenkins)
Chronology of the Modern World (Barrie
& Jenkins)
Chronology of the Expanding World
(Cresset)

People

Dictionary of National Biography
Dod's Parliamentary Companion
Vacher's Parliamentary Companion
Who's Who UK, USA etc (A&C Black)
International Who's Who (Europa)

Statistics

Guide to Official Statistics (HMSO)
UN Directory of International Statistics
Index to International Statistics
(Congessional Information Service)
Continent based Guides eg. Statistics Asia
and Australsia

For further details, please tick the titles of interest and return this form to:
Peter Collin Publishing, 1 Cambridge Road, Teddington, TW11 8DT, UK
fax: +44 181 943 1673   tel: +44 181 943 3386   email: info@pcp.co.uk

Title	ISBN	Send Details
English Dictionaries		
Accounting	0-948549-27-0	❏
Agriculture, 2nd ed	0-948549-78-5	❏
American Business	0-948549-11-4	❏
Automobile Engineering	0-948549-66-1	❏
Banking & Finance	0-948549-12-2	❏
Business, 2nd ed	0-948549-51-3	❏
Computing, 2nd ed	0-948549-44-0	❏
Ecology & Environment, 3ed	0-948549-74-2	❏
Government & Politics, 2ed	0-948549-89-0	❏
Hotel, Tourism, Catering Mg	0-948549-40-8	❏
Human Resource & Personnel, 2ed	0-948549-79-3	❏
Information Technology, 2nd ed	0-948549-88-2	❏
Law, 2nd ed	0-948549-33-5	❏
Library & Information Management	0-948549-68-8	❏
Marketing, 2nd ed	0-948549-73-4	❏
Medicine, 2nd ed	0-948549-36-X	❏
Printing & Publishing, 2nd ed	0-948549-99-8	❏
Science & Technology	0-948549-67-X	❏
Vocabulary Workbooks		
Banking & Finance	0-948549-96-3	❏
Business	0-948549-72-6	❏
Computing	0-948549-58-0	❏
Colloquial English	0-948549-97-1	❏
Hotels, Tourism, Catering	0-948549-75-0	❏
Law	0-948549-62-9	❏
Medicine	0-948549-59-9	❏
Professional/General		
Astronomy	0-948549-43-2	❏
Economics	0-948549-91-2	❏
Multimedia, 2nd ed	1-901659-01-1	❏
PC & the Internet	0-948549-93-9	❏
Bradford Crossword Solver	0-948549-39-4	❏
Bilingual Dictionaries		
French-English/English-French Dictionaries		❏
German-English/English-German Dictionaries		❏
Spanish-English/English-Spanish Dictionaries		❏
Swedish-English/English-Swedish Dictionaries		❏

Name: ....
Address: ....
....
....Postcode:.........................